Wolfgang Funk, Florian Groß, Irmtraud I
The Aesthetics of Authenticity

Cultural

WOLFGANG FUNK, FLORIAN GROSS, IRMTRAUD HUBER (EDS.)

The Aesthetics of Authenticity

Medial Constructions of the Real

[transcript]

**Bibliographic information published
by the Deutsche Nationalbibliothek**
The Deutsche Nationalbibliothek lists this publication in the Deutsche Nationalbibliografie; detailed bibliographic data are available in the Internet at http://dnb.d-nb.de

© **2012 transcript Verlag, Bielefeld**

Cover layout: Kordula Röckenhaus, Bielefeld
Cover illustration: photo by Wolfgang Funk
Proofread & typeset by: Wolfgang Funk, Florian Groß,
    Irmtraud Huber
Printed and bound in Great Britain by
Marston Book Services Ltd, Oxfordshire
ISBN 978-3-8376-1757-3

Table of Contents

Acknowledgments | 7

Exploring the Empty Plinth
The Aesthetics of Authenticity
Wolfgang Funk, Florian Groß, and Irmtraud Huber | 9

FRAGMENTATIONS

Authenticity as an Aesthetic Notion
Normative and Non-Normative Concepts
in Modern and Contemporary Poetics
Susanne Knaller | 25

Found Objects
Narrative (as) Reconstruction in Jennifer Egan's
A Visit from the Goon Squad
Wolfgang Funk | 41

Monolithic Authenticity and Fake News
Stephen Colbert's Megalomania
Seth Hulse | 63

Authentic Bodies
Genome(s) vs. Gender Norms in *Oryx and Crake*,
The Year of the Flood, and *BioShock*
Sven Schmalfuß | 91

CONTESTATIONS

»The Real Thing«
Authenticating Strategies in Hemingway's Fiction
Melanie Eis | 121

Real Lives – Living Wild
Authenticity, Wilderness, and the Postmodern
Robinsonade in James Hawes's *Speak for England*
and Jeanette Winterson's *The Stone Gods*
Francesca Nadja Palitzsch | 141

Monica Ali and the Suspension of Disbelief
Melanie Mettler | 163

PERFORMANCES

Poet and the Roots
Authenticity in the Works of Linton Kwesi Johnson
and Benjamin Zephaniah
David Bousquet | 187

**The Dilettantish Construction of the Extraordinary
and the Authenticity of the Artificial**
Tracing Strategies for Success in German Popular
Entertainment Shows
Antonius Weixler | 207

»Brooklyn Zack is Real«
Irony and Sincere Authenticity in *30 Rock*
Florian Groß | 237

Authentic Simulacra or the Aura of Repetition
Experiencing Authenticity in
Tom McCarthy's *Remainder*
Irmtraud Huber and Sophie Seita | 261

Contributors | 281

Acknowledgments

The majority of the essays collected in this volume were first presented as papers at the conference *The Aesthetics of Authenticity: Representing Self and Other in Literature and Culture*, held on 5 November 2010 at Leibniz University Hanover (LUH). Organizing such a conference was of course quite an adventure for three (relatively) young and inexperienced doctoral students. So we were and still are very grateful to a number of persons and institutions who helped us on the way from the initial planning stages to the final editing of the essays. The conference would not have been possible without the generous financial and conceptual support of the *Graduiertenakademie* of LUH and *Campus Cultur e.V.* The team of the Leibnizhaus and the student helpers, Stefanie John and Nora Michaelis, were always alert and helpful and ensured that the lively discussions took place in an atmosphere both stimulating and convivial. We thank Prof. Dr. Rainer Emig and Dr. Lucia Krämer for their readiness to chair a session and inspire spirited debate. Not least we would like to thank the participants of the conference, in particular the keynote speaker Prof. Dr. Susanne Knaller, whose papers and animated discussion filled the topic of the conference with life and color.

In the process of turning these papers into the essays you now have in front of you, we relied very heavily on the help of David Schönthal of University of Berne. Thank you, David, not only for your meticulous editing work but also for bearing with our, sometimes quite divergent, whims and fancies. For the final editing, we are equally grateful to Felix Brinker at LUH, who did a fantastic job at straightening out any formal inconsistencies. Any remaining errors are of course the editors' responsibility.

Finally, we would like to thank the Graduiertenakademie of LUH, and in particular Dr. Till Manning, for generously financing the printing of this book.

Exploring the Empty Plinth

The Aesthetics of Authenticity

WOLFGANG FUNK, FLORIAN GROSS, AND IRMTRAUD HUBER

Let us set our scene with a passage from the beginning of Mark Z. Danielewski's novel *House of Leaves*:

> While enthusiasts and detractors will continue to empty entire dictionaries attempting to describe or deride it, ›authenticity‹ still remains the word most likely to stir a debate. In fact, this leading obsession – to validate or invalidate the reels and tapes – invariably brings up a collateral and more general concern: whether or not, with the advent of digital technology, image has forsaken its once unimpeachable hold on the truth. (3)

This quote introduces a fake scientific report about an imaginary documentary film, presented as a real manuscript by a questionable editor, and all of that in form of a novel that itself is, of course, by definition fictional. Working with photographs, footnotes, scientific references both real and fake, as well as analyzing minutely the filmic qualities of its imaginary object of study, Danielewski's complex text insistently employs and exposes both cinematic and literary (or academic) constructions of authenticity. In its complex and fragmented structure the novel interweaves different narrative voices and levels that constantly comment on one another and continually question, dissect, and reassemble each other's claims to authenticity while simultaneously asserting their own dubiously authentic status. Acknowledging the appeal of and a pervasive desire for authenticity, the novel enters into a complex exploration of the means by which authenticity is created and maintained, not only in the cinematic medium but in aesthetic objects in general.

After all, it is not only the image that has lost its hold on the truth nowadays. Baudrillard, Derrida, and many others have tried for the longest time to convince us that reality, as the essential reference point for ontological, epistemological, and ethical existence, has forever been consigned beyond the pale of human representation; the only essence that postmodern thinking seems to accept is the fundamental gap between reality and its symbolic representation in language, images, or ideas. Reality thus is inaccessible, or rather always already mediated. However, even while and precisely because such heavily charged terms as truth, identity, and reality have become highly problematic, the desire for the authentic – as that which (in Danielewski's words) remains when all the dictionaries are exhausted – has increasingly gained momentum. From the ›authentic‹ politician and ›authentic‹ brand handbags to ›authentic‹ food-chains and ›authentic‹ tourist adventures, authenticity today has obviously become a major selling point.[1] In what is only ostensibly a paradox, authenticity is increasingly valued in a society in which new forms of media and new forms of mediation rapidly gain importance and have started to pervade virtually every aspect of life. Promising the genuine and the immediate and by this, at least to some extent, an escape from mediated existence and experience, authenticity itself turns into a quality of mediation and is thus conditioned by what it seems to deny. While definitions of authenticity routinely refer to its immanence and naturalness, its being found not created, recent engagements with authenticity highlight that it is necessarily the result of careful aesthetic construction that depends on the use of identifiable techniques with the aim of achieving certain effects for certain reasons (cf. Lindholm; Mecke). Authentic representation, authentic art, authentic fiction: what might almost

---

1   Random examples that could be mentioned in this context include the fashion label *Esprit*, which advertises its clothes to be »for authentic use« or the organic food chain *Authentic Foods*. An ominous illustration for the inherent volatility of the idea of authenticity is presented by the fate of former German Minister of Defense Karl-Theodor zu Guttenberg, who was hailed as the epitome of an authentic politician (e.g. on the cover of the German magazine *Focus*, 46/10), before being forced to resign for copying large parts of his doctoral thesis.

sound like a series of paradoxes touches the heart of the issues the essays in this collection are concerned with.

Far from being an outdated concept that has been exposed as illusionary and swept away in the tide of postmodernism, authenticity has turned into a prime venue for attempts to gauge the ways in which postmodern insights may be both acknowledged and transcended in contemporary discussions. More than anything else, its protean and paradoxical nature has ensured that the concept continues to play a role and has rendered it consistently resilient to even the most fundamental criticism. The notion of authenticity is a fickle one – on this, at least, there seems to be universal agreement. Ontologically, it hints at genuine origins (of things) and true essences (of selves) while at the same time resisting any attempt to distinctly identify and conceptualize such intimations of ›pure‹ existence. Epistemologically, it can serve as a yardstick both for radical self-searching (γνῶθι σεαυτόν) and for the accuracy or veracity of medial representations. Ethically, it has been categorically rejected as devoid of meaning in our fragmented and fragmentary times (cf. Mecke 114) *and* hailed as a lodestar to lead us out of the postmodern maze of collapsing significations, exhausted identity categories, and contingent value judgments (cf. Taylor; Ferrara). Like few other concepts, authenticity has proven to be a site where postmodern quandaries are played out in all their tearing tensions.

Rather than to empty dictionaries ourselves and to unfurl once more the debate about the term that has been outlined in detail by others (cf. Anton; Guignon; Haselstein, Gross, and Snyder-Körber; Knaller; Lindholm; Richter; Vannini and Williams), our central concern here is with its aesthetic aspects. A focus on the aesthetics of authenticity regards the authentic primarily as an effect of aesthetic objects and aesthetic experience. Consequently, the main interest lies in an analysis of the means by which authenticity is brought forth as a perceptible and consciously constructed quality of cultural artifacts. To detractors, it might seem a mere symptom of the pervasive and superficial self-centeredness of our times if we suggest that the theoretical discussion of authenticity should be approached via the question of aesthetics, that the issue has shifted from inquiring into the nature of authenticity as such to analyzing the various strategies which are used to evoke semblances, feelings, or ascriptions of authenticity. But then again, it would be too easy to simply claim that authenticity is nothing but an effect of careful aesthetic construction. Probing the aesthetics of authenticity always also implies questioning its nature before and beyond aesthetic form. Such a reconsideration of authenticity from the perspective of aesthetics seems especially apt to account for such forms of authenticity in contemporary culture which take their status as always already mediated into account and still do not content themselves with this insight, but continue their attempt to (symbolically) break through to the authentic, if not real, referent of representation. Thus, the shift from ontology to aesthetics may initially re-enact the paradoxical postmodern turn away from and towards the self. As the locus of individual world-making, the postmodern subject is simultaneously disinvested of its claim to absolute representation *and* elevated to the ultimate source of meaning.

At the same time, however, the essays collected in this volume also address the question if and how this postmodern predicament can be overcome. For if reality remains fundamentally inaccessible, authenticity can only manifest itself through its representations, and subjective aesthetic analysis becomes the only means by which the gap between the real (whatever that may be) and the symbolic can possibly be approached. Any aesthetic analysis of authenticity, understood in the etymological sense of ›aesthetic‹ as perceiving something with one's senses, is always already constructivist as it foregrounds the individual's sensual response in the establishment of authenticity as a category. And yet, a focus on the strategies that elicit such constructions can point beyond the realm of the purely subjective. After all, the pervasiveness of contemporary discourses of authenticity bears witness to the fact that authenticity is neither merely a matter of empty sales slogans nor easily dismissed as a solipsistic judgment. Profound controversies about literary fakes like the false Aboriginal identity of the Australian author Mudrooroo/Colin Jackson or of Binjamin Wilkomirski's fabricated concentration camp memoir *Fragments: Memories of a Wartime Childhood* spectacularly prove that authenticity is closely and indissolubly tied to questions of art's relationship to reality. Contemporary aesthetic and critical engagements with authenticity are deeply grounded in postmodern challenges to traditional concepts of reality; yet they are infused with ethical considerations and emotional investments that put them seemingly at odds with postmodern positions.

In its multiple facets, which we have only been able to hint at in these introductory words, authenticity thus presents itself as both increasingly significant and teasingly elusive. How can it be located? Is it connected to the subject or to the object, to referentiality, to the strategies of representation, or to the means of perception? Is it stable, a given value, or dynamic, an ongoing process? Is it a means or an end? Is it available to objective judgment or based on subjective evaluation? The essays in this collection can scarcely claim to answer all these questions; nevertheless, by bringing together analyses of a broad variety of different aesthetic and medial objects and their respective aesthetics of authenticity, the essays collectively point towards three central propositions:

1. *Authenticity is fragmented.* Rather than a unified inherent quality, an aesthetic analysis of authenticity reveals it to reside in fragmentation, in the piecing together of disparate elements, an idiosyncratic collage which can serve to construct the authentic beyond and in spite of essentialism – and yet may very well lay claim to essential truths.
2. *Authenticity is contested.* Not only a highly debated term in academic discourses, authenticity is also always implicated in power structures, ideological constructions, and the politics of signification. Arising from the encounter between Self and Other it becomes the site of ongoing power struggles and endless (re)negotiations of values and meanings that circumscribe the individual's role in and relationship to society.
3. *Authenticity is performative.* As an aesthetic construct, authenticity is deeply implicated in the process of communication that is realized in the interplay between production, aesthetic object, context, and reception. Authenticity, in this regard, becomes a matter of form and style in which the authentic is realized as a performative *effect.*

Being thus fragmented, contested, and performative, authenticity is constantly negotiated and infinitely (re)created and (re)discovered, always open to revision and reinvention – and yet constantly alludes to a realm beyond the profane and ephemeral. If authenticity as a concept is to carry any meaningful weight, the process of its aesthetic (re)construction must therefore endeavor to be both subjective and collective, personal and communal; it is an attempt to understand and transcend the purely symbolic and thus to penetrate the space in-between experience and representation, being and time, Self and Other. Sometimes even, tentatively, it might amount to an exploration of the possibility to construct essence out of emptiness.

Constructing essence out of emptiness could also figure as an implicit motto of Antony Gormley's *One and Other*. The cover of this volume displays a photograph of this project, which, in conclusion to these brief introductory remarks, may serve as a paradigmatic illustration of the central aesthetic issues informing this collection of essays. Gormley's project provides an object lesson on how to evoke and creatively engage with the kind of authentic, in-between spaces we have been suggesting here in the context of a work of art. Between July and October 2009, Gormley turned the famously empty Fourth Plinth on London's Trafalgar Square into an open performance stage, which gave (randomly) selected members of the public the chance to exhibit themselves in whatever way they chose for the duration of an hour each.[2] Gormley's project imbues the empty space of the vacant plinth with aesthetic and artistic potential, thereby conjuring presence(s) out of nothingness. By renouncing interpretative authority over content and form of the individual performances and by foregrounding the essential, structural emptiness of the space in which this aesthetic construction is realized, *One and Other* enables, indeed foregrounds, artistic reflexivity and medial self-awareness. This is not all, however. The artwork – contrived and staged as it certainly is – meets many of the criteria traditionally assigned to the authentic: it can be traced to genuine origins (both Gormley and the ›plinthers‹ are identifiable entities); it consists in the exhibition of individual selves; the medium through which the artwork is displayed is the human body (corporeality has often been seen as the one phenomenon that can escape symbolic representation); and it reaches out to ›ordinary‹ people, evoking the ›authentic‹ everyday and the guilelessness of the amateur, thereby avoiding the alleged inauthenticity of the professional. The aesthetic significance of the project as a whole, it might be argued, derives from

---

2 Pictures of all 2,400 ›performances,‹ which included impersonations of Lord Nelson and Godzilla, interactive experiments, readings, and, unsurprisingly, various displays of nudity, can be accessed via the project's archived website (cf. Gormley).

the interplay between author (Gormley), context (setting), content (performances), and audience, an interplay that ultimately questions the very categories to which its individual components are allocated. In the process of bringing about the work of art, the traditional onto-logical and epistemological hierarchies between these roles are inter-twined, tangled beyond recognition, and it is in this enigmatic space of confused categories, in this oscillation between stable positions that the issue of authentic representation is negotiated and acted out.

The essays collected in this volume all partake of this negotiation. They employ various forms of aesthetic analyses to trace strategies of how and why notions of authenticity emerge in different medial for-mats, from literary dystopias to news satire, from TV programs to computer games. In itself serving as a kind of empty plinth to be filled by collective endeavor, this book brings together widely different per-spectives, voices, and arguments. As varied as the media under con-sideration are, as numerous are the aesthetic strategies employed and as multifarious the forms in which authenticity becomes manifest: it pervades not only the aesthetic object itself, but governs the discourses about such objects, both academic and popular; it finds expression both in form and in content; it is intractably fused with issues of iden-tity formation, knowledge, and power.

The essays in the first part of this collection foreground authentici-ty as a patchwork product of disparate and fragmented elements, not only on the level of representation but also with respect to identity construction and corporeal integrity. Susanne Knaller's contribution opens up the intricacies of authenticity's various uses and meanings by juxtaposing normative and non-normative conceptions of the term. Normative usages set the work of art apart in its singularity as an aes-thetic object, while a non-normative approach understands authenticity as a dialectic process that evolves in time and space. Pointing to paral-lels in the work of contemporary photographer Wolfgang Tillmans and modernist novelist Nathalie Sarraute, Knaller shows how an aesthetic practice of dissociation and fragmentation serves to turn authenticity into a promise of connections between self and others, external and internal realities. As Sartre has argued in his preface to Sarraute's novel *Portrait d'un Inconnu* (1948), authenticity is here paradoxically established through inauthenticity, in a balance between the singular and the common that establishes a *lieu commun*, a shared space. Knal-ler suggests that the categories of authenticity and inauthenticity make it possible to reconsider Sarraute's modernist aesthetics as a new kind of realism beyond questions of referentiality, as authenticity is established in dynamic processes of ever new mises en scène.

In his analysis of Jennifer Egan's *A Visit from the Goon Squad*, Wolfgang Funk argues that the novel synthesizes literary realism and metafiction to arrive at the level of authentic narrative. This authentic narrative is based on a conscious conflation of story and plot, as well as the novel's explicit foregrounding of plotting; furthermore, it depends on Egan's relinquishment of authorial control over the fragmented text in favor of stimulating its readers to (re)create story and plot from the novel's *récit*. Beyond the formal dimension, Funk also traces the novel's engagement with authenticity on the story level. Similar to the aspects of plot reconstruction, the characters' various approaches to authenticity converge on a postmodern note, where authenticity has to be conceptualized as a fleeting aesthetic effect of (literary) reconstruction. In the novel's particular aesthetics, however, this postmodern note is the point from which an approach to authenticity becomes possible that transcends purely postmodern aesthetics of authenticity.

Seth Hulse's contribution traces authenticity in the fake news comedy show *The Colbert Report with Stephen Colbert*. Reading the television show's foregrounding of the constructedness of news alongside *The Colbert Report*'s own construction of Stephen Colbert's identity, Hulse argues that we need to understand the show's aesthetics along the lines of parody rather than satire. It is in the paradoxical relation between Colbert's assertion of a stable identity and the simultaneous conflation of various identities in the same person(a) that authenticity in the form of an authorless object arises. Focusing on *The Colbert Report*'s representation of the controversy around the nomination of Sonia Sotomayor to the U.S. Supreme Court, Hulse analyzes Colbert's pluralistic patchwork self as an indicator of the need to read the program as essentially urging its audience to partake in Colbert's decentering of stable identities and thus dismantle singularizing attempts at constructing authenticity.

Shifting the focus from identity construction to bodily integrity, Sven Schmalfuß investigates the corporeal aspects of authenticity. Taking Donna Haraway's notion of the cyborg as a starting point, he poses the question if and how an authentic body can be depicted and defined in an age in which the human body is inscribed with ever stricter rules and norms, while at the same time its borders are being dissolved as corporeal functions are being outsourced to all kinds of technical devices. Focusing on the genre of science fiction in order to question the possible utopian/dystopian implication of this informatics of domination, Schmalfuß analyzes Margaret Atwood's novels *Oryx and Crake* and *The Year of the Flood* as well as Irrational Games's franchise *BioShock*. He reads the novels, with their disturbing images of genetic engineering gone awry, as a profound treatise on the biological and ethical dimension of existence, which – according to Helmuth Plessner – is rooted in the paradoxical state of both having a body and being a body (cf. 37). Schmalfuß then connects the theoretical questions raised by Atwood with a more practical analysis of the ethical and aesthetic dimension involved in playing a game such as *BioShock*, where users, in their ambiguous role as both player and avatar, not only serve as obvious examples for cyborgs but are also faced with complex moral dilemmas. These are often acted out in an indistinct space between ethical and aesthetic concerns, an interspace in which the authenticity of human bodies has to be negotiated.

While the articles in the first section show that authenticity can arise from fragmentation and is thus always essentially at variance with itself, the contributions in the next part foreground authenticity as an effect of an always contested and contestable negotiation between Self and Other. Addressing the masculinity anxiety prevalent in the work of Ernest Hemingway, Melanie Eis shows how primitivist discourse serves Hemingway's protagonists to reaffirm the authenticity of their own masculinity. By drawing attention to the role of racializing and primitivizing discursive moves, Eis points to an aspect of this important literary figure that, in her opinion, has not been sufficiently addressed in the prolific scholarly discourse. Hemingway's protagonists frequently draw upon the primitive, be it represented by Africa, by Native American, or by rural Spain, in order to address and repress the anxieties besetting their own heterosexual, white masculinity in a modernized world. In Eis's reading, authenticity therefore becomes a derivative quality that draws strength from the exploitation of a nostalgic alterity in which the Other provides both the source of authenticity and its antithetical confirmation.

In Francesca Nadja Palitzsch's contribution, images of humankind in the wild become a foil on which the issue of authenticity is negotiated. Both texts she uses in her analysis, James Hawes's *Speak for*

England and Jeanette Winterson's *The Stone Gods*, juxtapose places of primeval wilderness, where individuals are forced to come to terms with their own status *sub specie aeternitatis*, with dystopian images of present or near-future societies, where authentic existence is all but annihilated by the spectacle and simulations produced by and in the name of consumer capitalism. While Hawes uses the topic of national identity, i.e. the question what it really means to be English, to mirror his protagonist's quest for an experience of authenticity, in Winterson this pursuit is enacted as a search for genuine emotions in the face of universal destruction. Palitzsch identifies both texts as postmodern Robin-sonades, in which any kind of identity, personal as well as national, can only ever be fragmented, the result of the multiple narrative selves fashioned by the protagonists. The quest for authenticity thus becomes a search for the moral of their personal narratives.

Moving from the level of the aesthetic text to the field of the literary marketplace, Melanie Mettler's contribution addresses problems arising from the increasing marketability of authenticity, especially for authors writing in a postcolonial or minority context. Using the controversy about Monika Ali's first novel *Brick Lane* as a case study, Mettler goes on to consider both the marketing strategies and reviewers' reactions to Ali's first and subsequent novels in order to expose the pervasiveness of an often unacknowledged demand for authenticity, be it on the level of text, author, or reader. Ali's attempts to escape from authenticizing and exoticizing ascriptions by resisting reader expectations serve as a thoughtful reminder of the ways in which different guises of authenticity continually tend to inform assessments of literary value.

As both fragmented and contested, authenticity insistently reveals itself to be the product of a continual performative process between production, representation, and reception, a dynamics which is emphasized in the contributions of the third part of this collection. That authenticity is a predominately Western concept, which has to be rethought significantly in other cultural contexts, comes to the foreground in David Bousquet's contribution. Presenting the case of dub poetry, Bousquet argues that in the context of Creole culture authenticity cannot be reduced to stable ascriptions or traced back to single origins. Closely related to the musical and cultural practice of sound systems, dub poetry thrives on sampling, borrowing, and the remix. Dub poetry establishes itself as authentic, Bousquet suggests, not so much in its text, but in the moment of its performance, as a dynamic process of interaction and authentication involving all participants alike.

Focusing on a very different kind of musical performance, Antonius Weixler argues that the German folk music television shows in the *Fest der Volksmusik* series generate authenticity through their blatantly amateurish and artificial aesthetics. With the help of Luhmann's system theory and an extensive historical analysis of the dilettante in relation to authenticity, Weixler argues that the shows' nexus of popular culture, dilettantism, and artificiality provides their target audience with a means of identification. This identification, in turn, is the ground upon which the audience is able to ascribe authenticity to the program as well as its creators and performers. For Weixler, it is the shows' strategy of creating exceptionality through dilettantish means that makes the mundane extraordinary and the artificial authentic.

If dilettantism puts emphasis on artlessness as an aesthetic strategy to construct authenticity, recent television also takes the opposite path by employing exaggerated self-consciousness. While the increasing prevalence of a postmodern metareferential and ironic stance in television has come under criticism for being ultimately at the service of commodification, Florian Groß demonstrates how irony itself can be ironically inflected in a meta-ironic aesthetics, thereby attempting to construct an authenticity that could be called ›sincere.‹ Discussing excessive metareferentiality in the recent television series *30 Rock*, Groß delineates the ways in which the series ironically reflects on its own conventionalized aesthetics of visual authenticity and then comments in turn on this very ironic reflection. In the tension between a fake authentic discourse, its exposure, and the ironic comment on this exposure, *30 Rock* thus simultaneously uses and moves beyond the postmodern, establishing a kind of paradoxical third-order authenticity that attempts to situate itself as both within and at a critical distance to the dictates of capitalist consumer culture.

Finally, in Irmtraud Huber and Sophie Seita's contribution, authenticity is presented to be the ultimate and ultimately unattainable goal in a post-Baudrillardian world of interminable repetition and inevitable simulation. In their in-depth analysis of Tom McCarthy's novel *Remainder*, the authors introduce a new category of authenticity, which they call authenticity of experience, and which accounts for the observation that any claim to such authenticity can only be grounded in radical subjectivity. In the case of the novel's protagonist, this subjectivity manifests itself in ever more meticulous re-enactments of everyday scenes, a compulsion to repeat which reveals the quest for authenticity to be rooted in a radical and nihilistic aestheticism. Huber and Seita consequently argue for a strong connection between authenticity and the notions of trauma and death, as the incessant reconstruction is based on a sense of profound loss and can only be resolved with the annihilation of the individual. The termination of subjectivity signifies both the realization of authenticity and its dialectical sublation.

In keeping with the general argument proposed in this introduction, it goes without saying that the essays in this collection themselves can only offer views of the concept that are fragmented, contested (or contestable), and performative in that they engage in a continually ongoing dialogue about a category that has become one of the guiding values of our times. Considering authenticity's protean nature, its aesthetic analysis, it seems, can only be usefully employed if it is itself understood in Derridean terms as ›performative,‹ as a cautious transformation rather than a confident apprehension of the very thing it explores (cf. Derrida 51). In other words, if aesthetic analysis is willing to engage with the contingency of existence. If authenticity, as the essays in this collection suggest, can only be grasped as fragmented, contested, and performative, the aesthetic pursuit of authenticity can never come to a positive conclusion; its aesthetic strategies eventually can never be determined once and for all. This insight, however, should not stop us from ascending and exploring the empty pedestal of authenticity.

WORKS CITED

Anton, Corey. *Selfhood and Authenticity*. Albany, NY: State U of New York P, 2001.

Danielewski, Mark Z. *House of Leaves*. New York, NY: Pantheon Books, 2000.

Derrida, Jacques. *Spectres of Marx: The State of the Debt, the Work of Mourning, and the New International*. Trans. Peggy Kamuf. New York, NY: Routledge, 1994.

Ferrara, Alessandro. »Authenticity without a True Self.« *Authenticity in Culture, Self, and Society*. Ed. Phillip Vannini and Patrick Williams. Farnham: Ashgate, 2009. 21-35.

»Mut zum Ich!: Wie Authentizität erfolgreich macht.« *Focus* 15 Nov. 2010.

Gormley, Antony. »One and Other.« *UK Web Archive*. n.d. Web. 23 Feb. 2010. http://www.webarchive.org.uk/wayback/archive/20100 223121732/http://www.oneandother.co.uk/

Guignon, Charles. *On Being Authentic*. London: Routledge, 2004.

Haselstein, Ulla, Andrew Gross, and MaryAnn Snyder-Körber, eds. *The Pathos of Authenticity: American Passions of the Real*. Heidelberg: Winter, 2010.

Knaller, Susanne. *Ein Wort aus der Fremde: Geschichte und Theorie des Begriffs Authentizität*. Heidelberg: Winter, 2007.

Lindholm, Charles. *Culture and Authenticity*. Malden, MA: Blackwell, 2008.

Mecke, Jochen. »Der Prozess der Authentizität: Strukturen, Paradoxien und Funktion einer zentralen Kategorie moderner Literatur.« *Authentizität: Diskussion eines ästhetischen Begriffs*. Ed. Susanne Knaller and Harro Müller. Munich: Fink, 2006. 82-114.

Plessner, Helmuth. *Lachen und Weinen: Eine Untersuchung nach den Grenzen menschlichen Verhaltens*. Arnhem: Van Loghum Slaterus, 1941.

Richter, Virginia. »Authenticity: Why We Still Need It Although It Doesn't Exist.« *Transcultural English Studies: Theories, Fictions, Realities*. Ed. Frank Schulze-Engler and Sissy Helff. Amsterdam: Rodopi, 2009. 59-74.

Taylor, Charles. *A Secular Age*. Cambridge, MA: Belknap Press, 2007.

Vannini, Phillip, and J. Patrick Williams, eds. *Authenticity in Culture, Self, and Society*. Burlington, VT: Ashgate, 2009.

Wilkomirski, Binjamin. *Fragments: Memories of a Wartime Childhood*. Trans. Carol Brown Janeway. New York, NY: Schocken Books, 1996.

Fragmentations

Authenticity as an Aesthetic Notion

Normative and Non-Normative Concepts in Modern and Contemporary Poetics

Susanne Knaller

I.

The current meanings of ›authentic‹/›authenticity‹ – as genuine, truthful, immediate, undisguised, unadulterated, certified, guaranteed, binding – can be conceived of in terms of an interplay between two developments: on the one hand, ›authentic‹ and ›authenticity‹ are taken as synonymous with terms from philosophy and aesthetics of the 18th and 19th centuries (*sincerity*, *naïvité*, *truth*). On the other, the shades of meaning for ›authentic‹ and ›authenticity‹ are drawn from metaphors or abstractions originating in juridical, philological, and theological discourses (authorized, in reference to an author, certified) (cf. Knaller, »Genealogie« 25).

In the field of modern artistic authenticity, the referential and empirical components of meaning that have determined the concept from the beginning (certification via origin, author, or belongingness) are perpetuated in terms of aesthetic value. An artistic object can be authenticated when it is not adulterated, when it can be ascribed to a specific style of a period, a specific technique, or/and when it properly adheres to certain qualitative criteria, or/and is the result of a specific capacity of certification of a specific medium. Beyond that, artistic authenticity is often connected to an unadulterated will to art and a truthful creation based on artistic, subjective, or moral integrity. Subsequently, the recursive certificatory relationship between artist/author (creator) and work can lead beyond the demonstrability of a determinate origin to become a normative criterion which presupposes an artistic subject upon whom the task of (artistic) self-realization and originality is incumbent. To take an example for this normative approach from music: »The most important legacy of the historical performance movement may be those performances that attain authenticity in the deepest sense: that of conviction, self-knowledge, spontaneity, and emotional honesty« (Sherman 169). Authenticity is, moreover, employed as an ontological concept to determine the difference between art and non-art. Concepts such as ›original‹ and ›truthful‹ are then connected with the meanings of authenticity that have remained valid into the 20th century (authorship, adherence to tradition, genuineness) in order to procure a ›universal‹ validity for the artwork and the artist against the background of elusive generalities, reproductive media, and shifting or eradicated medial boundaries between art and non-art. This often remains the case up to today:

Thereby the notion of authenticity is in a very broad and basic sense understood to be the defining criterion of an art that is authentic and unadulterated in the fact that it differs from non-art. [...] The formula ›authenticity of the aesthetic‹ here rather refers to the aesthetic validity claim itself. (Ostermann 11; my translation)[1]

At the bottom of this normativity thus lies the differential relationship, constitutive of a modern concept of art, between authenticity and inauthenticity. The constructedness of the same is recognized by Umberto Eco, who notes that every conception of authentic art as something irreproducible and singular is legitimized through »authorial authenticity« (»autenticità autoriale« 168; my translation) and presupposes an abstract and conceptual notion of truth. The actual problem thus lies not in determining the falsity of the falsified object, but rather the authenticity of the authentic object – »But if we thought that *authenticity* means *truth*, then it is good to remember that this truth, like all those

---

1   »Der Begriff der Authentizität wird dabei in einem sehr weiten und grundlegenden Sinne als das entscheidende Kriterium einer Kunst verstanden, die darin echt und unverfälscht ist, dass sie sich von Nichtkunst unterscheidet. [...] Die Formel ›Authentizität des Ästhetischen‹ meint hier vielmehr den ästhetischen Geltungsanspruch selbst.«

which comfort us, is still largely conjectural« (Eco 191; emphasis in the original; my translation).[2]

Theodor W. Adorno was the first to describe consistently how the notion of authenticity, as an aesthetic concept of validity and value, mediates between the empirical, form, and transcendence. Authenticity is mobilized just as much against the discussions of *Existenzphilosophen* like Jaspers and Heidegger, with their concepts of truthfulness (*Wahrhaftigkeit*), genuineness (*Echtheit*), and authenticity (*Eigentlichkeit*) (cf. Müller 57), as it is against a genuine poetics of mimesis: »With advancing enlightenment, only authentic works of art have been able to avoid the mere imitation of what already is« (Horkheimer and Adorno, *Dialectic* 13).[3] For Adorno, authenticity is also not simply some subjective category of expression: »No artwork, not even the most subjective, can completely merge with the subject that constitutes it and its content« (Adorno, *Ohne* 167; my translation).[4] Consequently, Adorno is confronted with the basic paradoxical structure of the aesthetic concept and inscribes authenticity as a driving aesthetic force, as a conciliatory concept in a subversive and utopian truth constellation. In his essay »Words from Abroad« Adorno maintains:

It is supposed to be the characteristic of works that gives them an objectively binding quality, a quality that extends beyond the contingency of mere subjective expression, the quality of being socially grounded. If I had said simply ›Autorität‹ [authority], using a foreign word that has at least been adopted into German, I would have indicated the force such works exercise but not the justification of that force by a truth that ultimately refers back to the social process. (197-98)[5]

---

2   »Ma se ritenevamo che *autenticità* volesse dire *verità*, è bene ricordare che anche questa verità, come tutte quelle che ci confortano, è sempre ampiamente congetturale.«

3   »Mit fortschreitender Aufklärung haben es nur die authentischen Kunstwerke vermocht, der bloßen Imitation dessen, was ohnehin schon ist, sich zu entziehen« (Horkheimer and Adorno, *Dialektik* 24).

4   »Kein Kunstwerk, auch das subjektivste nicht, geht auf in dem Subjekt, das es und seinen Gehalt konstituiert.«

5   »Es soll der Charakter von Werken sein, der ihnen ein objektiv Verpflichtendes, über die Zufälligkeit des bloß subjektiven Ausdrucks Hinausreichendes, zugleich auch gesellschaftlich Verbürgtes verleiht. Hätte ich

Authenticity thus remains a category of singularity (*Singularitätskategorie*) at odds with all attempts to subsume it under a teleologically construed, universal concept. Therein also lies the attraction of authenticity in modernity: the authentic is the outcome of a time- and place-specific process of certification, which must be continually re-established without guarantee, and for which one can specify, at best, only weak, formal, and transcendental requirements (cf. Knaller, »Genealogie« 32).

II.

This capability of authenticity – to function, on the one hand, as a modern category of certification and validity, and on the other, to shape a recursive subject-object dynamic that assumes both an individual perspective and an objectifying process of authentication – points to the difficulty of fixing universally valid concepts in times of a broken relationship between subjects, objects, and language. The strength of authenticity thus lies in its possible application as both a normative and a non-normative, critical concept. Authenticity is normative, for example, when the concept as a category of singularity makes the claims of subjective impressions explainable and describable.

In this case, the concept of authenticity retains its validity even when the traditional implications of the artist as someone constituted by craftsmanship and creativity no longer form any basis for art. In spite of the delegation of manufacturing work from the artist to professionals and industry, the demand for the work and the author to be original is upheld. Minimalist artists who have worked with industrial materials rejected the replications of their work that were put together for an exhibition at the Guggenheim Museum at the beginning of the 1990s with the following argument:

---

einfach ›Autorität‹ gesagt, also ein wenigstens eingebürgertes Fremdwort, so wäre dadurch zwar die Gewalt bezeichnet worden, die solche Werke ausüben, nicht aber das Moment von deren Berechtigung kraft einer Wahrheit, die schließlich auf den gesellschaftlichen Prozeß zurückverweist« (Adorno, »Wörter« 127).

[T]hat neither the objects themselves nor the plans were sufficient to create replicas equal in value to the originals, because chance can unexpectedly change the appearance during production, so that the materiality of the individual work has significance and the necessary authenticity can therefore be attributed only by the artist. (Tietjen 43; my translation)[6]

A non-normative concept of authenticity would be a space- and time-bound concept that constructively reflects both mediality and formation. A quotation from Wolfgang Tillmans clarifies this point. In art photography in particular, different aspects of authenticity can be found coming into contact with one another: the attribution of objectivity and facticity (and therefore of what I have called referential authenticity), as well as the attribution of subjective composition and individual, artistic expression (subject authenticity) are fusing into and constituting an aesthetic concept (aesthetic or artistic authenticity) (cf. Knaller, *Wort* 21-24):

The authentic is always a question of standpoint, a question of how prepared one is to accept something as authentic – there the brain is really quite flexible. It will probably always penetrate further into our common awareness that this has very little to do with a fixed unit of measurement but rather with a construct. For me, my pictures are authentic in that they ›authentically‹ reproduce my fiction of the moment; for the viewer, it can only ever be just a suggestion for how they might also view what is depicted. An interesting picture for the role of photography is, for me, ›Michael Bergin & Fan.‹[7] [...] The whole situa-

---

6   »[D]ass weder die Objekte selbst noch die Pläne ausreichten, um den Originalen gleichwertige Repliken herzustellen, da bei der Produktion der Zufall das Erscheinungsbild unvorhergesehen verändern könne, damit die Materialität des einzelnen Werkes Bedeutung habe und sich die notwendige Authentizität deshalb allein vom Künstler zuschreiben lasse.«

7   The photo shows the famous underwear model for *Calvin Klein*, Michael Bergin, with a young female fan wearing a *Calvin Klein* T-shirt while holding a red signal street flag. This picture is a perfect example of Tillmans's ability to relate symbols with a straightforward materiality of things and their pure shape. In this way, genre (here portrait and street photography – the couple stands next to a construction site – meet in the streets) becomes a media-reflexive quotation as well as a space where things fall into place.

tion and both of the people in it draw their identity from photographically mediated identities. This is a good example that a traditional concept of authenticity is no longer applicable, since an understanding of photography is determined by the image itself. (258-59; my translation)[8]

This simultaneity of subjective perception and documentation, effects of immediacy, and references to images and media technologies, works to undermine the predominance of referential authenticity of objects and photography itself. Authenticity becomes only more applicable as a polemical antithesis. Again Tillmans:

The desire of the public for ›authentic‹ pictures is in fact undermined by these photographers [like Nan Goldin, Larry Clark] and by myself as well. I believe that none of us wants to be explicitly documentary [...]. I believe that we share very little common terrain, but that we do share a common understanding of the mediated nature of all photography. I find, once one has internalized this understanding, that the issue of authenticity becomes annoying and superfluous. This issue, at least in how it is discussed, has not interested me at all since I began as a photographer. What does interest me is how to photograph people and things, so that what I see in them still appears in the image afterwards, just as I felt it at the time. (260; my translation)[9]

---

8 »Authentisch ist immer eine Frage des Standpunktes, eine Frage, wie sehr man bereit ist, etwas als authentisch anzunehmen, da ist das Hirn ja sehr flexibel. Es wird wahrscheinlich immer mehr ins allgemeine Bewußtsein vordringen, daß es sich hierbei nicht um eine fixe Größe handelt, sondern um ein Konstrukt. Für mich sind meine Bilder authentisch, da sie ›authentisch‹ meine Fiktion dieses Moments wiedergeben, für den Betrachter können es immer nur Vorschläge sein, das Dargestellte auch so zu sehen. Ein interessantes Bild zur Rolle von Fotografie ist für mich ›Michael Bergin & Fan.‹ [...] Diese ganze Situation und beide Personen in ihr ziehen ihre Identität aus fotografisch vermittelten Identitäten. Das ist ein gutes Beispiel, daß ein traditioneller Authentizitätsbegriff nicht mehr anwendbar ist, da das Wissen um Fotografie das Bild selbst bestimmt.«

9 »Der Wunsch des Publikums nach ›authentischen‹ Bildern wird eigentlich unterlaufen von diesen Fotografen und auch von mir. Ich glaube, keiner von uns will explizit dokumentieren [...]. Ich glaube, wir teilen wenig gemeinsames Terrain, aber trotzdem haben wir ein Verständnis gemeinsam für die vermittelte Natur aller Fotografie. Ich finde, wenn man dieses Be-

What Tillmans is stressing against the attribution of a straight referential authenticity in photography, is a subject authenticity which considers the complex of the artistic process, medial dynamics, and the receptive perception of things and images. One could read this sort of perceptive realism (or mimesis) as a contemporary example of the doxa of artistic subjectivity in modernism (valid also for art photography since the 19th century) (cf. Solomon-Godeau 86-103). One could also reach back to Rudolf Arnheim, who in his later days was approaching a more realist conception of art and photography, but is still stating, in the tradition of modernist subjectivity, that in art and photography two sorts of authenticity are necessarily overlapping: »They [the figurative arts] are authentic to the extent that they do justice to the facts of reality, and they are authentic in quite another sense by expressing the qualities of human experience by any means suitable to that purpose« (537). For photography as for painting it would be necessary to be ›legible‹ through its authentic form »by creating convincing images« (539). But Tillmans's concept goes further than this when he considers the always present- and image-forming self-reflexivity, as well as the medial process as a basis for photographer and viewer. Subject authenticity in this case is not authorial in the sense of Eco's »autenticità autoriale« but a perceptive phenomenon.[10]

This denial of the normative component of referential authenticity alongside the simultaneous demonstration of its medial dependence and functioning can also be found in a novel that appeared nearly half a century before Tillmans's work: Nathalie Sarraute's *Portrait d'un Inconnu* (1948).

---

wußtsein verinnerlicht hat, ist das Thema Authentizität nervig und überflüssig. Es hat mich zumindest, so wie es diskutiert wird, noch keinen Tag, seit ich fotografiere, interessiert. Mich hat interessiert, wie ich Menschen und Dinge so fotografieren kann, daß das, was ich an und in ihnen sehe, hinterher auf dem Bild immer noch so aussieht, wie ich es empfunden hatte.«

10 For the development and specifics of photography in the 1990s, cf. Holschbach; Knaller, *Wort*.

III.

Already the title of Nathalie Sarraute's innovative novel refers to several unknown persons and their conflictual representation: the man portrayed on a panel painting that the narrator repeatedly sees and the figures he observes, an old man and his daughter, whom he presents in momentary shots of miniscule events and conversational fragments (cf. Knaller, »Porträt« 134-36). Momentarily created connections, such as relations between portrait figures and the persons portrayed, are lost in traces, intervals, and the remains of speech and gestures. The latter flow over the ever-wandering gaze of the narrator and his restless, random pursuit of both subjects in momentary dramas that seem to evoke what their conventional behavior as to speech conceals: »secret, undisclosed, barely conscious movements« (»mouvements secrets, inavoués, à peine conscients« n.p.; my translation). In these images, a reality appears that cannot referentially be traced back either to its supposedly objective surface or to a subjectively established authenticity. Sarraute organizes a perennial emergence and disappearance of things (»objects«) within their sometimes menacing relationships to the perceiver. »[T]he very edge of reality, sharp, accurate« (»[L]e bord même, tranchant, précis, de la réalité« 120; my translation) lies in a piece of soap that the old man inspects in the middle of the night in order to discover if his daughter is stealing from him.

He has reached the end. He has groped into the very depths. There is no need to seek further. [...] He feels a weariness, a nausea; his brain seems hardened, empty; only the small ball rolls tirelessly on. He makes an effort to give it an impulse that will make it jump out of the groove; he tries to push it into another direction: the book that he has just read, which he promised himself to think thoroughly about, this new remarkable theory of evolution, this interesting little booklet ... but no, there is nothing to be done about it, the ball stays in its groove: the cut bar of soap, inflexible reality grips him within its rigid walls. [...] His awakening is peaceful. The bar of soap on the shelf above the sink gleams softly in the morning sun, like the glistening beach sand after a stormy night. Nothing remains of the obsessions, the torments of the night. [...] There is no longer any link between us. No more signs from him to me. No other look of complicity. I could try to follow him, parade up and down in front of him to catch his attention, reestablish contact – he would watch me distractedly without seeing me. (122-24; my translation)[11]

The image, only visible for a short time, vanishes back again into the endless talk of everyday life: »Nothing in common now, not the least connection between him and the grotesque form of the night« (127; my translation).[12]

Jean-Paul Sartre deployed the concepts of ›inauthenticity‹ and ›authenticity‹ for these speech and visual constellations. In his preface dated 1947, he categorized the dialogues and monologues of observer and observed as »Gerede« (»ramblings,« in the Heideggerian sense), and thereby as a mark of »everyman,« the inauthentic that, up to that point, would have been excluded from the novel because it could be dissimulated by the subjective, the individual – the authentic. Authenticity as being other than the »ramblings« thus admittedly remains a phantom of the universal »everyman.« In other words, the fact that both inauthenticity and authenticity remain in equal balance between singularity and generality allows for the fixing of that place of social and cultural agreement that Sartre called »commonplace,« a place where each individual as well as the others are found (together): »The

---

11   »Il est arrivé tout au bout. Il a sondé jusqu'au fond. Il n'y a pas à chercher plus loin. [...] Il sent une fatigue, un écœurement, son cerveau est comme durci, vidé, seule la petite boule, inlassablement, court toujours. Il fait un effort pour lui donner une impulsion qui la fasse bondir hors du sillon, il cherche à la pousser dans une autre direction: le livre qu'il vient de lire, auquel il s'était promis pourtant de bien réfléchir, cette nouvelle théorie si curieuse sur l'évolution, ce petit bouquin si intéressant ... mais non, il n'y a rien à faire, elle est maintenue solidement: la barre de savon coupée, l'inflexible réalité l'enserre entre ses parois rigides. [...] Le réveil est paisible. La barre de savon, posée sur la planche au-dessus de l'évier, luit doucement au soleil matinal, comme le sable moiré de la plage après une nuit d'orage. Rien ne subsiste des obsessions, des tourments de la nuit. [...] Il n'y a plus de lien entre nous. Plus de signes de lui à moi. Aucun regard de connivence. Je pourrais essayer de le suivre, passer et repasser devant lui pour attirer son attention, rétablir un contact – il me regarderait distraitement sans me voir.«

12   »Rien de commun maintenant, pas le moindre lien entre lui et la forme grotesque de la nuit.«

commonplace belongs to everybody and to me« (10; my translation).[13]
In this configuration of subjectivity and universality, the authentic itself becomes a commonplace, promising a harmony between internal
and external realities, between the self and others – »*Authenticity*, the
genuine relationship to others, to oneself, to death, is suggested everywhere but invisible. One has an inkling of it because one flees it«
(12; emphasis in the original; my translation).[14]

Experimental structures like that offered by Sarraute's novel an-
nounce a turning point: the logical-causal narration of stories, rational
chronology, and the classification of characters, the spatial organization of the action, and the referentiality of speech are no longer incontestable factors. Chronology, typology, and speech are not necessarily
assembled illusionistically, coherently, or causally in the act of reception. Representation comes along with self-reference and retraces its
steps back to a poetics that is outlined by the form of self-reflection. In
this, it is a new form of realism. Unlike in the traditional realistic novels of the 19th century and, later on, the 20th (albeit already recognizable in radical naturalistic texts such as those by Zola, Holz, and
Flaubert), speech here does not serve as a medium for securing references or a platform for mediating objects, perceptions, and descriptions in the same manner that verbality itself does not lay claim to any
mono-medial legitimacy, but should rather be understood against the
backdrop of visualization strategies and visual possibilities. Sarraute
fashions dramatic moments as images that only yield rudimentarily to
a story. That these hold moments of sleuthing interest (what are the
subjects doing, what could their motives be?) arises from the dissection of their verbal behavior and gestures, in which the narrator admittedly no longer holds the orchestrating scalpel. A multi-perspective
media complex of plural discourse ›opens up‹ reality, thereby simultaneously displaying the discursive concepts that reality and its portrayal
render possible. In the case of the reality presented here, subjectivity,
morals, art, and – as may be added – science (»les specialists«) guarantee the conditions of success for representation as well as communication, as even Sartre can affirm. Subjective reflection, moral
valuation, and art-referential dialogues and monologues, metaphors

---

13 »Le lieu commun est à tout le monde et il m'appartient.«

14 »L'*Authenticité*, vrai rapport avec les autres, avec soi-même, avec la mort,
est partout suggérée mais invisible. On la present parce qu'on la fuit.«

and symbols thicken, above all, in order to dissolve back immediately into the idle talk, prattle, and tediousness of the *lieu commun*. In this process from climax to degeneration, objects are presented as threatening and hence incapable of being referenced, verbalized, or governed on a stable basis.

IV.

Nathalie Sarraute does not spell out any specific and explicit concept of authenticity.[15] However, her poetics of a new realism precedes an art that, since the 1960s, has been advancing and persistently revising the art-concepts developed by the avant-garde movements at the beginning of the 20th century. Against the abstract and conceptual character of these art forms many times emphasized, I would call attention to the realist claim, the realist project within abstraction that was just as radical as that established and pursued for literature (cf. Pany, »Visualität«; »Realismus«). Further developing the avant-garde approaches, realistic forms since the 1960s are marked by the inclination towards ordinary objects and rituals of daily life, their materiality, the use of media long denied or discussed as non-artistic, such as photog-

---

15 At this point I would like to stress an important distinction to be made: the difference between observations of (poetical and critical) discourses on the one side and categorical groundings on the other, between the observation of theories and poetics where authenticity/authentic is explicitly a categorical, self-descriptive notion, and the groundings of critical and general notions of authenticity/authentic. This amounts to the distinction between a perspective of observation of categories and of participation (in categorization). Observation and participation can only be related to each other without a strict homogenization. In the worst case the disregard of this differentiation leads to observations and contestations that could also be formulated without the help of an authenticity discourse. In less problematic cases we are confronted with an approach that sees authenticity in too many places, if not everywhere. Closely connected to this non-differentiating approach is the often notable negligence regarding specific linguistic particularities. *Authenticité* in French, for instance, has another tradition and discursive possibility than in German. In all the mentioned approaches the non-differentiation leads to categorical errors.

raphy and later video and similar techniques, and genres such as silk-screen printing, television formats, documentary forms, etc. Precisely the concept of authenticity in inauthenticity that Sartre claimed for Sarraute may be employed in this regard as a key concept for artistic and theoretical concerns, which transcends the traditional realistic poetics of referentiality. Admittedly – and here I would like to deviate from Sartre's expression – authenticity is not only fleeting (»insaisissable« Sartre 12-13) since it is only conceivable in the context of and within a dialectic process with inauthenticity or as a perennial moment of longing (i.e. a utopia), but rather, due to its ever-significant paradoxical configuration, authenticity is explicitly put to use poetologically: as authenticity in the paradoxical field of tension surrounding autology and certification. Jonathan Culler describes this as a basic dilemma: »that to be experienced as authentic it must be marked as authentic, but when it is marked as authentic it is mediated, a sign of itself, and hence not authentic in the sense of unspoiled« (139). It is precisely this paradoxical character of the concept of authenticity that makes the new realisms possible, where the moment of mise en scène, of setting into form, is as present as the moment of situating it into subjective perspective and the moment of objective certification.[16] Objects are only authentic where appointed to be so by the legitimized party. Subjects are authentic if they can be certified as authors and originators of themselves or of objects; but the certifying and legitimizing authorities are historically variable and replaceable. Authenticity always presumes a dynamics of subject and object; it persists in ever-renovated mises en scène.

Through the example of Chris Marker's documentary essay on Japan, »Sans Soleil,« Michael Wetzel is likewise able to refer to this productive double-bind of authenticity. This is not about »an authentic other world or somewhere« (Sartre's »fleetingness,« an authenticity eluding capture or representation) but rather about »the strength resid-

---

16 At the same time, authenticity with its normative and non-normative aspects could form a criterion for differentiating between traditional realisms devoted to *representation* and newer realist programs in art and literature arising since the 1960s that turn to modalities that fall under the concept of *performativity*. For a further discussion of this, cf. Knaller, »Autobiografie«; »Porträt.« For a general description of the notion of performativity, cf. particularly Wirth.

ing in pictures *as* pictures, if indeed [...] images care about images« (54; emphasis in the original). Chris Marker describes the procedure as follows:

My friend Hayao Yamaneko has found a solution: if the images of the present do not change, to change the images of the past [...]. He showed me the fights of the sixties processed by his synthesizer. Images less dishonest, he says, with the conviction of a fanatic, than the ones you see on television. At least they pass for what they are, images, not the portable and compact form of a reality already become inaccessible. (262; my translation)[17]

Authenticity is thus a concept that does not abandon its paradoxical position between subjective legitimization and objective certification. In its reflexive self-dramatization, it becomes comprehensible as a polemic antithesis as well as a term of value, certification, and legitimization. Assuming that concepts of reality are important interactive acts originating in the physical and cognitive capacities and their organization, authenticity may be understood as positing and self-description, the observation of which can give insights into the rules of development, preservation, and transformation of cultural systems.

WORKS CITED

Adorno, Theodor W. *Ohne Leitbild: Parva Aesthetica*. Frankfurt am Main: Suhrkamp, 1967.

——. »Words from Abroad.« *Notes to Literature, Volume One*. Trans. Shierry Weber Nicholson. Ed. Rolf Tiedemann. New York, NY: Columbia UP, 1991. 185-99.

——. »Wörter aus der Fremde.« *Noten zur Literatur 2*. Frankfurt am Main: Suhrkamp, 1961. 110-30.

---

17 »Mon copain Hayao Yamaneko a trouvé une solution: si les images du présent ne changent pas, changer les images du passé [...]. Il m'a montré les bagarres des Sixties traitées par son synthétiseur. Des images moins menteuses, dit-il avec la conviction des fanatiques, que celles que tu vois à la télévision. Au moins elles se donnent par ce qu'elles sont, des images, pas la forme transportable et compacte d'une réalité déjà inaccessible.«

Arnheim, Rudolf. »The Two Authenticities of the Photographic Media.« *The Journal of Aesthetics and Art Criticism*. 51.4 (1993): 537-40.

Culler, Jonathan. »Semiotics of Tourism.« *American Journal of Semiotics* 1.1/2 (1981): 127-40.

Eco, Umberto. *I Limiti dell'Interpretazione*. Milan: Bombiani, 1990.

Holschbach, Susanne. »Die Wiederkehr des Wirklichen? Pop(uläre)-Fotografie im Kunstkontext der 90er Jahre.« *Konfigurationen zwischen Kunst und Medien*. Ed. Sigrid Schade and Christoph Tholen. Munich: Fink, 1999. 400-12.

Horkheimer, Max, and Theodor W. Adorno. *Dialectic of Enlightenment: Philosophical Fragments*. Trans. Edmund Jephcott. Ed. Gunzelin Schmid Noerr. Stanford, CA: Stanford UP, 2002.

——. *Dialektik der Aufklärung*. Frankfurt am Main: Fischer, 1969.

Knaller, Susanne. »Autobiografie und Realismus in der Zeitgenössischen Kunst.« Knaller, *Realitätskonstuktionen* 57-75.

——. »Das Porträt und Selbstporträt im Kontext Realistischer Programme der Moderne: Mit Bemerkungen zum Authentizitätsbegriff./Portrait and Self-portrait in the Context of Modern Realist Programs: Remarks on the Concept of Authenticity.« *Social Dogma*. Ed. Thomas Henke. Heidelberg: Kehrer, 2010. 112-47.

——. *Ein Wort aus der Fremde: Geschichte und Theorie des Begriffs Authentizität*. Heidelberg: Winter, 2007.

——. »Genealogie des Ästhetischen Authentizitätsbegriffs.« Knaller and Müller, *Authentizität* 17-35.

——, ed. *Realitätskonstruktionen in der Zeitgenössischen Kultur*. Vienna: Böhlau, 2008.

Knaller, Susanne, and Harro Müller, eds. *Authentizität: Diskussion eines Ästhetischen Begriffs*. Munich: Fink, 2006.

Marker, Chris. »Sans Soleil.« *Traverses* 38.9 (Nov. 1986): 256-66.

Müller, Harro. »Theodor W. Adornos Theorie des Authentischen Kunstwerks: Rekonstruktion und Diskussion des Authentizitätsbegriffs.« Knaller and Müller, *Authentizität* 55-67.

Ostermann, Eberhard. *Die Authentizität des Ästhetischen: Studien zur Ästhetischen Transformation der Rhetorik*. Munich: Fink, 1999.

Pany, Doris. »Realismus und Realitätskonzeptionen in der Russischen Avantgarde: Von den Projektiven Realitätsentwürfen der Vorrevolutionären Periode zur Auseinandersetzung mit dem Materialismus der Sowjet-Zeit.« *Realitätskonzepte in der Moderne: Beiträge zu*

Literatur, Kunst, Philosophie und Wissenschaft. Ed. Susanne Knaller and Harro Müller. Munich: Fink, 2011.

———. »Visualität und Wirklichkeit: Vom Realismus des 19. Jahrhunderts zum Realismus der Avantgarde.« Knaller, *Realitätskonstruktionen* 77-94

Sarraute, Nathalie. *Portrait d'un Inconnu.* 1948. Paris: Gallimard, 2005.

Sartre, Jean-Paul. »Preface.« Sarraute 9-15.

Sherman, Bernard D. »Authenticity in Music.« *Encyclopedia of Aesthetics.* Vol. 1. Ed. Michael Kelly. New York, NY: Oxford UP, 1998. 166-69.

Solomon-Godeau, Abigail. *Photography at the Dock: Essays on Photographic History, Institutions and Practices.* Minneapolis, MN: U of Minnesota P, 1991.

Tietjen, Friedrich. »Das Multiple als Original.« *Kunst ohne Unikat.* Ed. Peter Weibel. Köln: W. König, 1998. 31-43.

Tillmans, Wolfgang. »Authentisch ist immer eine Frage des Standpunkts: Ein Gespräch von Martin Pesch.« *Kunstforum* 133 (1996): 256-69.

Wetzel, Michael. »Artefaktualitäten: Zum Verhältnis von Authentizität und Autorschaft.« Knaller and Müller, *Authentizität* 36-54.

Wirth, Uwe. »Der Performanzbegriff im Spannungsfeld von Illokution, Iteration und Indexikalität.« *Performanz: Zwischen Sprachphilosophie und Kulturwissenschaften.* Ed. Uwe Wirth. Frankfurt am Main: Suhrkamp, 2002. 9-60.

Found Objects

Narrative (as) Reconstruction in Jennifer Egan's

A Visit from the Goon Squad

WOLFGANG FUNK

BACK TO PLOT, BACK TO REALITY?

Plot summaries of novels, as Will Blythe in his review of *A Visit from the Goon Squad* for the *New York Times Sunday Book Review* concedes, are usually considered to be of inferior significance, a necessary evil at best on the road towards profound structural, contextual, or poetic insights. Students of literature are regularly exhorted *only* to recapitulate plot elements if they are relevant for an advanced interpretation, which is more often than not expected to connect aspects of content, form, and context. This development mirrors the academic interest in narrative fiction, which in the course of the 20th century has shifted (very broadly speaking) from the level of the story (what kind of story is narrated?) to the level of discourse (how is the story mediated?) and – in recent decades – even to the level of a contextual meta-discourse (how and under which circumstances can any story be mediated at all?). The concept of the plot, understood as the organizational principle behind the author's presentation of the story, links the different levels of narrative, insofar as it describes the ›raw material‹ of the story in terms of authorial devices such as chronology, causality, consequence, and sequentiality. The analysis of plot must therefore be central not only to interpretations of individual works. Since any identity (group or individual) can always be read as the accumulation of narratives (cf. Eakin), the general significance accorded to the abstract notion of plot must also shed light on how any given society perceives itself.

In terms of literary criticism, the significance of plot has not been the main focus of attention during large parts of the 20th century. In the first part of my article I will provide a very concise historical sketch of the waning reputation of plot, which I read in the context of a transition from realist fiction to certain anti-realist strategies of narration, which gained prominence in the 1960s and 1970s and which have been subsumed under the label ›metafiction.‹ I will then present an analysis of Jennifer Egan's novel *A Visit from the Goon Squad* (2010) as a synthesis of these two seemingly irreconcilable positions, proposing the category of ›authentic narrative‹ to describe her approach to plot and story. Authenticity, I argue, emerges from an explicit foregrounding not only of the constituents of literary communication (as in metafiction), but of the plotting as such, as the author (who is not only etymologically chained to the idea of authenticity) forfeits her implicit authority to structure the representation of the story for an explicit stimulation of the readers to (re)create the story and the plot themselves.

WHICH TRUTH? REALISM IN/AND FICTION

Much has been written on the significance of truth in the context of literature. There seem to be two fundamental and fundamentally opposed lines of thinking, traditionally – and somewhat unduly – traced back all the way to Plato and Aristotle. While the former, or so received wisdom has it, saw literature at best as the bad copy of an already deficient reproduction of an original idea with no claim to any truth whatsoever (book X of *The Republic*), the latter endowed poetic texts with a direct access to a higher form of truth, the approximation of which must be the inherent objective of all faithfully mimetic literary endeavors. During the 19th century, this debate crystallized around the question of R/realism in literature,[1] providing literary critics with

---

1   While ›Realism‹ is used in this article to refer to a (supposedly) distinct genre or period of literary or art history, as in 19th century Realism or Magical Realism, ›realism‹ describes a general attitude, which is founded on the conviction that art has the potential to truthfully reproduce the real world. In this context it is worth noting Wilhelm Worringer's elementary analysis of the relationship between any given society's worldview and its

the still dominant metaphor for describing the tenuous bond between human existence and its mediation/representation in and as an artistic product.[2] Alison Lee defines realism as the »notion that art is a means to truth because the artist has a privileged insight into a common sense of what constitutes ›reality‹« (4) and although the means to convey this privileged insight may have changed in the course of the 19th century (from Dickensian ›Social Realism‹ to the naturalistic offerings of Ibsen or Hauptmann), the general conviction holds that reality is something on which large sections of society find themselves in agreement and which therefore can be truthfully represented in art.

With the arrival of structural and structuralist analysis of language in the beginning of the 20th century, a fresh way of describing the connection of life and letters offered itself. Building on the works of Karl Bühler, Roman Jakobson, and Ferdinand de Saussure, Jan Mukařovský's in-depth exploration of the *Structure, Sign, and Function* of language lays particular emphasis on the aesthetic function of language.[3] This, in his view, sets poetic language (i.e. language use dominated by the aesthetic function) apart from all other uses of language, as

in all ›practical‹ functions, the telos lies outside of the object which is the vehicle of the function, either in the subject whose particular need is to be satisfied or in the surrounding context which is to be changed. In contrast to this, the telos of an object dominated by the aesthetic function lies in the object itself.

---

attitude towards naturalistic/realistic art, which Brian Stonehill paraphrases as follows: »Worringer [...] suggests that naturalistic art expresses a Weltanschauung in which man feels himself to be living in harmony with the cosmos. The arts of classical Greece and of the Renaissance exemplify such naturalism. Non-naturalistic art (Byzantine art, Romanesque sculpture) occurs when the felt relationship between man and the universe is one of disequilibrium and dissonance« (38).

2   For the topicality of the concept of realism, cf. Fluck's analysis of a ›New Realism‹ in contemporary American fiction, which takes as its basis not a common representation of what is real, but »a system of rhetorical strategies in order to claim special authority for one's own interpretation of reality« (67).

3   Mukařovský's most important essays were translated into English and collected in a volume with this title by Burbank and Steiner.

[...] In other words, the difference between the practical and aesthetic functions is that the former is allotelic whereas the latter is autotelic. (Steiner xxii-xxiii)

The products of artistic creation are, in Mukařovský's own words, »not oriented toward a specific external goal but are themselves the goal«; the work of art as a sign is *per definitionem* purposeless, it constitutes its meaning in and through itself alone; it is an »autonomous sign lacking an unequivocal relation to reality« (»Intentionality« 94).[4] However, in order to signify at all, there must be an extrinsic reference point for the work of art and this, Mukařovský claims, is no less than »the total context of social phenomena of the given milieu« (»Art« 88). While everyday, practical language can only signify in a particular set of circumstances, literature – and art in general – always necessarily references the totality of the discursive framework which enables and structures the economy of reference in the first place. Artistic discourse is thus always already metareferential. As this frame of reference, which would later be called ›episteme‹ (Foucault) or ›paradigm‹ (Thomas S. Kuhn), is constantly being reshaped through discourse, the idea of an unchanging aesthetic norm can hardly be maintained. Rather, Mukařovský argues, if there is a regulatory principle which controls artistic creation, it must consist in the ceaseless violation of seemingly normative structures; it »makes felt its activity and hence its existence precisely at the moment when its violation occurs« (»Norm« 54). Art is not only inherently metareferential; it is also necessarily transgressive and subversive with regards to the norms by which it is ostensibly governed. In terms of the truth value of literature, this means that there can indeed be no such thing as a faithful reproduction of real objects, emotions, or events; the truth in literature is never mimetic but always suggestive. Artistic creation can never claim truth in and for itself; it can only ever allude to a notion of truth which is not subject to any specific frame of reference as it *constitutes* this frame of reference itself.

---

4   Steiner argues that »it is precisely this ›zero utility‹ of an object dominated by the aesthetic function which lifts it from the context of everyday life and renders it art« (xxiv).

The second half of the 20th century sees the systematic development and critical reception of a variety of prose fiction which takes this paradoxical and self-reflective precondition of art as its aesthetic point of departure; in turns labeled ›self-conscious novel‹ (Stonehill), ›narcissistic narrative‹ (Hutcheon), ›introverted novel‹ (Fletcher and Bradbury), or most frequently ›metafiction,‹ the defining feature of this kind of narrative is that it »draws attention to its status as an artifact in order to pose questions about the relationship between fiction and reality« (Waugh 2). Reverting to Mukařovský, one could say that the ›meta‹ in metafiction is defined by making explicit the aesthetic function of poetic language. This can be achieved, or at least attempted, by foregrounding/emphasizing the fictiveness of the individual components of any literary communication: among the regular strategies employed in metafiction there is the direct address to the *reader* (John Barth's »Life-Story«), intrusions of the *author* (André Gide's *The Counterfeiters*), explicit reference to the fictiveness of the story/*message* (Italo Calvino's *If on a Winter's Night a Traveller*), a foregrounding of the linguistic system itself/*code* (Walter Abish's *Alphabetical Africa*) or a direct reference to the communicative situation/*channel* (B.S. Johnson's *The Unfortunates*). More often than not, the literariness of these works is further highlighted by disturbing and entangling the supposedly stable hierarchies between various levels of the diegetic set-up of a novel through devices known as narrative metalepsis[5] or *mise en abyme*[6] (as in Julio Cortázar's »Continuity of Parks« or R.C. Phelan's »Something Invented Me«).[7] If this kind of self-disclosing literary creation – disinclined readers and critics might

---

5   The term is, of course, Genette's and describes the transition from one diegetic level to another (cf. *Erzählung* 168-69). For further discussion of the term, cf. also Malina; Wolf, »Metalepsis.«

6   The term, heraldic in origin, was introduced by André Gide into literary criticism. The defining study is Dällenbach.

7   All of these techniques have, of course, been used prior to the 20th century. The scope of this article precludes a more thorough introduction of the various diachronic and synchronic manifestations of metafictional elements. For detailed studies on the narratological and aesthetic implication of this phenomenon, as well as typologies and exemplary readings, cf among others Boyd; Currie; Fludernik; Hutcheon; Imhof; Stonehill; Waugh; Williams; Wolf, *Metareference*.

call it ›navel gazing‹ – can lay claim to any sort of truth, it is certainly not the faithfulness of realistic description or evocation, but rather a truthfulness of/in representation, or more precisely the process of representation. Stonehill even declares that »by virtue of its greater honesty, its manifest awareness of its own limitations, and its peculiar sophisticated humility before life itself, self-depicting fiction can in fact be *more* persuasive than purely naturalistic fiction« (18; emphasis in the original).

The price for the aesthetic honesty/truthfulness which Stonehill and others claim for metafictional narrative seems to be, above all, realist notions of plot and character which have to be sacrificed at the altar of revelatory self-awareness. What I will do in the remainder of this essay is attempt to reintegrate these notions into a mode of truthful/honest literary representation, in which the apparently contradictory positions of realistic fiction and metafiction are synthesized on a higher level, which I call ›authentic narrative.‹ I see this as a possible way out of the impasse described by James Wood, who argues that fiction is currently dominated by what he calls »hysterical realism,« »novels of immense self-consciousness with no selves in them at all, curiously arrested and very ›brilliant‹ books that know a thousand things, but do not know a single human being« (n.p.). Madalena Gonzales describes the predicament of contemporary writers in similar fashion as »the relentless questioning of the medium in which any author worth his postmodern salt must indulge so as to make patent his awareness of the flawed nature of representation« (115).

AUTHENTIC NARRATIVE: META-NARRATION AND THE RECONSTRUCTION OF STORIES IN *A VISIT FROM THE GOON SQUAD*

Reconstructions of Lives and Stories: Authenticity on the Level of the Narration

It would be insincere to preach a revival of plot without practicing the long-disregarded form of the plot summary, so here we go. Egan's novel is made up of thirteen chapters, which depict in a seemingly random order events ranging from the late 1970s to the 2020s. As it transpires, the chapters are held together (if ever so loosely) by their explicit or implicit significance for the lives of Bennie Salazar (a music producer) and Sasha (who at some point worked for him). I will first present short summaries of the chapters in the order in which they appear in the book:

1. »Found Objects« describes Sasha's one-night stand with Alex and reveals her affliction with kleptomania.
2. »The Gold Cure« introduces Bennie as a successful music producer trying to fire up his slagging libido.
3. »Ask me if I Care« shows Bennie with his high school friends Rhea, Jocelyn, Alice, and Scotty in the heyday of punk in the 1970s, where they meet Lou, who seduces Jocelyn and becomes Bennie's mentor.
4. »Safari« portrays Lou's trip to Africa with his children and his student girlfriend Mindy.
5. »You (Plural)« brings us forward to Lou on his deathbed being visited by Rhea and Jocelyn.
6. »X's and O's« describes a meeting between Scotty (who is down on his luck as a musician) and Bennie.
7. »A to B« depicts Bennie's family life in Crandale and introduces his wife Stephanie and her brother Jules Jones.
8. »Selling the General« follows Dolly, Stephanie's boss, on a trip to save the reputation of a genocidal dictator. She is accompanied by her daughter Lulu and fading filmstar Kitty Jackson.
9. »Forty-Minute Lunch« consists of a newspaper article written by Jules Jones, in which he recapitulates his failed rape of Kitty Jackson during an interview.
10. »Out of Body« relates how Rob, Sasha's university pretend-boyfriend, drowns while swimming with Sasha's real boyfriend Drew.
11. »Good-bye, my Love« recounts the attempt of Sasha's uncle Ted to meet her in Naples, where she had ended up after running away from home at 17.
12. »Great Rock and Roll Pauses by Alison Blake« portrays in the form of a slide show the family life of Sasha, who has married Drew, and their children.
13. »Pure Language« describes how Bennie, Alex, and Lulu (Bennie's new assistant) manage a concert of Scotty on the site of the World Trade Center, after which they try to locate Sasha's old apartment.

Throughout the chapters, Egan places hints both to the chronological sequence of these events (e.g. references to 9/11, to Jules's rape of Kitty, or to Sasha's employment with Bennie) and to the interconnections between the various characters, from which the reader must piece together the succession of events, i.e. the life-stories of the characters, which very crudely (and with no claim whatsoever to any kind of completeness) could read something like that:

- After an unsuccessful stint with a punk band in high school, Bennie Salazar meets Lou (chapter 3), a ladies' man without too much empathy towards his children (4,5), who after seducing his friend Jocelyn sets Bennie on his way to becoming a successful producer himself (2). Bennie is married to, later divorced from, Stephanie (7,2), whose brother Jules had tried to rape actress Kitty Jackson (9) during an interview. Some time later, Kitty traveled with Dolly, Stephanie's former employer, and her daughter Lulu to rescue the reputation of General B. (8). At some point, Bennie re-encounters his former high school friend and band-mate Scotty (6) and ends up organizing a concert of him at the Footprint with the help of Alex and Lulu (13).
- Sasha runs away from home and her divorced parents to Naples at the age of 17 (11). Back home, she studies at NYU with Rob, her pretend-boyfriend, who drowns while taking a swim with Drew (10). Later, Sasha is employed as Bennie's assistant, and she has random sex with Alex (1). After re-encountering Drew on Facebook, they get married, start a family, and she becomes an artist (12).

Even if it seems very much like stating Basil Fawlty's famous ›bloody obvious,‹ the plot of any piece of narrative fiction can be described as the way in which the author decides to present the events of the story, the movements in time and space of the central characters, their relationships and encounters, their little dramas and great aspirations, their loves, affairs, divorces, and deaths. The reader's (and the narratologist's) task is to (re)construct both the story (*histoire*, the chronological and causal succession of events) and the plot (*narration*, the arrangement of these events) from the text of the book, which Genette calls *récit* (cf. *Revisited* 13). In the case of *A Visit from the Goon Squad*, however, things are not quite as clear cut. Due to the dazzling complexity of Egan's textual cosmos, the narratological focus is not primarily on the reconstruction of the *histoire*, but also – and essentially so, I would argue – on the reconstruction of the plot (*narration*). That means, before the reader has a chance to establish relations between characters, they first have to determine the temporal and causal correlation between the thirteen chapters which constitute the novel's *récit*. The *récit*, in other words, has to be rearranged by the reader in order to retrace the author's *narration*. The establishment of the novel's plot is possible only on a meta(diegetic) level (let us call it ›meta-narration‹), on which diegetic and extradiegetic aspects merge.[8] To put it more unequivocally, reading the novel in this case means a simultaneous reconstruction of the *histoire* of Bennie and Sasha and the *narration* of Jennifer Egan, thus metaleptically collapsing the conventional narrative levels and introducing a meta-level, on which *histoire, narration*, and *récit* converge and which, so I would like to argue, forms the basis for authentic narrative.

The novel's *narration* itself is extraordinary and designed to destabilize any notion of a monolithic and pervasive author figure. Egan not only effortlessly includes presumably un-literary genres such as a newspaper report (chapter 9) or (quite ingeniously) a PowerPoint slide show (12) into her narrative; she also offers a variety of narrative point of views – from rather traditional authorial narrator figures (2,4,7) to first person narrations (3,5,6), from personal reflection (1,8,11,13) to the rather rare form of second person narration (10).[9] This variety of form is, I would argue, representative of Egan's (authentic) narrative approach, i.e. to present human existence as a ›heap of broken stories‹

---

8 I am using the term ›metadiegetic‹ here not as Genette does to describe any subordinate level of a story-within-a-story (cf. *Erzählung* 163), but to designate an ontologically paradox level, which both partakes of textual and contextual aspects and which constitutes the only possible point of view on which any narrative can truly be said to reflect upon itself. The structural foundation of this level is the existence of tangled hierarchies between the levels of *récit, narration*, and *histoire*. Cf. Funk for a more comprehensive analysis of the phenomenon of tangled hierarchies as a narratological device.

9 All terms, except for second person narration, are taken from Stanzel's dusty but still useful model of narrative situations (cf. 16-17).

without an ordering, authoritative instance to guide the reader through the incongruity of this mortal coil.

At certain points in the novel, Egan employs metaphors which echo her extradiegetic strategy of reconstructing stories from ostensibly accidental pieces of information. In narratological terms, this can be described as a *mise en abyme*, defined by Lucian Dällenbach as »any aspect enclosed within a work that shows a similarity with the work that contains it« (8). Sasha, for example, is subjected to frequent bouts of kleptomania and displays the items she steals in her apartment. Although these things are superficially no more than just »a heap of objects« that was illegible yet clearly not random,« they still »contained years of her life compressed« and represent »the raw, warped core of her life« (15). This idea, that if there is an essence to existence (real or narrative) at all, it can only be accessed/approximated through the opaque assemblage of indiscriminate events and experiences, epitomizes *en miniature* the narratological agenda of Egan's book. Sasha's display of stolen goods, as it were, metaleptically mirrors Egan's display of stories. By the end of her story, Sasha has managed to channel her compulsion to appropriate objects into artistic creativity. In her slide-show diary, Alison, Sasha's daughter, informs us that her mother makes collages from everyday objects »from our house and our lives,« which she glues »onto boards and shellacs them« (265). These objects include a shopping list, flight tickets and several memos reminding someone of picking up shoes or calling grandma. According to Sasha, these objects are »precious because they're casual and meaningless« yet »they tell the whole story if you really look« (265). Again, this can be read as a diegetic commentary on Egan's metadiegetic agenda and Sasha's progress from compulsive kleptomaniac to careful collagist in turn reflects the reader's progress from baffled recipient of plot elements to thoughtful reconstructor of (life-)stories.

It is not only through objects, however, that life-stories are (re)constructed in the book; people more often than not seem to exist mainly as fragments, either in the obscurity of memories or disintegrating into a quantity of assumed identities. Only by relinquishing any claim to a wholeness of personality, it seems, people can actually influence the existence of other human beings; the tiniest shift in rearranging one's memory or identity can have unforeseeable consequences, even for people one has not met yet or has already long forgotten (call it the ›butterfly effect of human interaction‹). Even in the run-up to her sexual tryst with Alex (chapter 1), Sasha experiences an almost epiphanic moment of metaleptic self-awareness: »It jarred Sasha to think of herself as a glint in the hazy memories that Alex would struggle to organize a year or two from now: *Where was that place with the bathtub? Who was that girl?*« (14; emphasis in the original). Both the *histoire* and the *narration* eventually prove her right: in the very last scene of the book, Alex and Bennie try to relocate Sasha's apartment and their respective feelings towards her. While Alex struggles to remember Sasha at all, who has of course long vacated the apartment, the only thing that has stuck in his memory is the bathtub, which has, due to its uniqueness – »A bathtub in the kitchen – she'd had one of those! It was the only one he'd ever seen« (339) – superimposed itself on any other features of Sasha's personality. Definite objects do not seem to help with reconstructing life-stories, as they tend to incorporate and thus eventually annihilate any personal remembrance.

The memory of others is not the only space where lives and life-stories are distorted. As Jules Jones quite adroitly analyzes in his report on the interview-turned-rape with Kitty Jackson (chapter 9), every human being exists in the form of fragmented identity constructions, which can be turned out as befits the occasion:

the waiter's treatment of Kitty is actually a kind of sandwich, with the bottom bread being the bored and slightly effete way he normally acts with customers, the middle being the crazed and abnormal way he feels around this famous nineteen-year-old girl, and the top bread being his attempt to contain and conceal this alien middle layer with some mode of behavior that at least approximates the bottom layer of boredom and effeteness that is the norm. In the same way, Kitty Jackson has some sort of bottom bread that is, presumably ›her,‹ or the way Kitty Jackson once behaved in suburban Des Moines where she grew up, rode a bike, attended proms, earned decent grades and, most intriguingly, jumped horses, thereby winning a substantial number of ribbons and trophies and, at least briefly, entertaining thoughts of becoming a jockey. On top of that is her extraordinary and possibly slightly psychotic reaction to her new-found fame – the middle of the sandwich – and on top of that is her own attempt to approximate layer number one with a simulation of her normal, or former, self. (170-71)

In chapter 11, which recounts Sasha's time in Naples, we find another powerful image for how the gist of existence might be caught in and through innocuous and apparently inconsequential objects: her uncle Ted has at long last managed to descry her whereabouts and finds himself in her apartment wondering about »a crude circle made from a bent coat hanger« which adorns a window (232). Even twenty years on, when he visits Sasha and her family, he still remembers »the jolt of surprise and delight he'd felt when the sun finally dropped into the center of her window and was captured inside her circle of wire« (233); the memory of his trip to Naples, presumably safely folded away in his unconsciousness has been retained in the memory of this apparent piece of junk. This moment of recollection, the interruption of the seemingly stable narrative of self by an absent and accidental object, constitutes, so I would argue, an authentic moment. This occurs when the purposeless contingency of an object, its genuine existence, intrudes upon the apparent consistency and discipline of the narrated identity of the self, when in other words the abyss of our existence and our memories encroaches on our self-image. Authenticity, in this context, can only ever be understood as a transitory phenomenon, traceable only in a flickering instant where the boundaries of absence and presence, object and subject, feeling and knowledge, the physical and the metaphysical, are obscured.

Egan's collage of chronologically and causally disjointed snippets of life can be read as an attempt to re-enact this stratification of individual identity formation on a narrative, metadiegetic level. This re-enactment in turn constitutes, or so I would argue, a pursuit of that elusive thing, authentic being, the ›bottom bread‹ as it were of Jules's metaphorical sandwich.[10] Egan's narrative approach in *A Visit from the Goon Squad* can be read as an attempt to retrace these flickering moments of authenticity, both in the fragmented (re)construction of her characters and plot and more explicitly in various instances on the story level.

---

10 For another example of the paradoxical relationship between re-enactment/repetition and authenticity, cf. Huber and Seita in this volume.

The Warped Core of Life: Authenticity on the Level of the *Histoire*

Sasha's uncle Ted also provides a stunning image for the fact that normal human interaction and communication is enabled by and structured through the codification of essentially uncoded, unstructured, and contingent influences such as emotions, relationships, or circumstances, in other words, how life is only possible when authentic existence is kept in check; his diminishing desire for his wife Beth is emblematized as being folded in half every couple of years, until it »was so small in the end that Ted could slip it inside his desk or a pocket and forget about it, and this gave him a feeling of safety and accomplishment, or having dismantled a perilous apparatus that might have crushed them both« (210). By systematizing what was once »a drowning, helpless feeling,« Ted finds a way to reign in his passion, to conceive of his life in terms of economy and reality rather than the authenticity of »an edgy terror of never being satisfied« (210). Both Jules's rather outlandish metaphor of the bottom bread in everyone's identity sandwich and Sasha's »raw, warped core of her life« (15) are intimations of such an authentic and terrifying *ousias*, of an essential layer of human existence and interaction which is (supposedly) prior to, or at least outside of any level of structural signification and which thus hints at a realm of pure, unmediated, and unmeditated presence, described – or rather circumscribed – variously as *jouissance* or *le sinthome* (Lacan), *le sémiotique* (Kristeva), or *khôra* (Derrida). The notion of authenticity in itself comes furnished with an inbuilt epistemological paradox, i.e. its simultaneous claim to immediacy and mediation,[11] to essence and constructedness.[12]

As I have already discussed in the preceding chapter, Sasha and Jules are trying their level best to come to terms with this paradox: I have already analyzed Sasha's attempts in various forms to distill meaning and stories from apparently insignificant but authentic objects, and Jules's article constitutes (even apart from and above the

---

11 Cf. Zeller's notion of authenticity as »*vermittelte Unmittelbarkeit*« (mediated immediacy).

12 For a more detailed discussion, cf. the introduction and essays collected in Funk and Krämer, where this phenomenon is described as the ›black-box-effect‹ of authenticity.

sandwich metaphor) in many ways an ›anatomy of authenticity,‹ in which he uses every tool in the narrative rulebook to lay open, dissect, and examine (satirically but still accurately) the constructed layers of his own identity as a male celebrity journalist. With the benefit of hindsight, Jules construes the spectacular failure of his attempt to force himself on Kitty, which ends with him being teargased and stabbed in the calf with a Swiss Army knife (cf. 183), as an applied lesson in the difficulty of matching authentic existence with the norms and regulations of real life. Jules, however, is nothing if not a fighter, and it is not surprising that – as soon as he is released from prison – he dedicates himself to chronicling another attempt of blurring the boundaries between existence and representation: Bosco's »Suicide Tour,« which, so the aged guitarist envisions, will explicitly and purposefully feature every insalubrious cliché of rock 'n' roll life on the road, leading up to and including a celebrated death (cf. 128-30), when, we could say, real life and the stereotypes catch up with one another in the finite nothingness of death.

Throughout the book, Egan uses music as a yardstick to gauge the authenticity of human expression. Lincoln's interest in music is confined to songs which include long pauses. Being Sasha's son, he interprets those as miniatures of real life: »The pause makes you think the song will end. And then the song isn't really over, so you're relieved. But then the song *does* actually end, because every song ends, obviously, and THAT. TIME. THE. END. IS. FOR. REAL« (281; emphasis in the original).

Bennie bemoans the inauthenticity of the music business, which even goes so far as to fabricate simulations of authenticity to cater for current tastes, thereby providing a striking example for hyperreality as described by Jean Baudrillard:

He listened for muddiness, the sense of *actual* musicians playing *actual* instruments in an *actual* room. Nowadays this quality (if it existed at all) was usually an effect of analogue signaling rather than bona fide tape – *everything was an effect* in the bloodless constructions Bennie and his peers were churning out. (22; emphases added)

Bennie's resentment towards the inauthentic is not restricted to theoretical lamentation, however; he is fired from his label »after serving his corporate controllers a boardroom lunch of cow pies« in an attempt to visually and olfactorily ram home his assessment of the company's products (312) – a definitely unequivocal and probably authentic gesture. It is also through music that the idea of the authentic stages its ultimate confrontation with the forces of simulation, inauthenticity, and consumer capitalism which govern the dystopian world of Egan's final chapter (which I will turn to in more detail below). After many a struggle and deliberation, Scotty Hausmann gives a concert at the site of the former World Trade Center, which epitomizes both the inherent longing for authentic expression (by an authentic character) and its irreducible insignificance (or rather its insignificability).[13] Scotty performs

> ballads of paranoia and disconnection ripped from the chest of a man you knew just by looking had never had a page or a profile or a handle or a handset, who was part of no one's data, a guy who had lived in the cracks all these years, forgotten and full of rage, in a way that now registered as pure. Untouched. But of course, it's hard to know anymore who was really *at* that first Scotty Hausmann concert – more people claim it than could possibly have fit into the space, capacious and mobbed though it was. Now that Scotty has entered the realm of myth, everyone wants to own him. And maybe they should. Doesn't a myth belong to everyone? (336; emphasis in the original)

Scotty can only come to incorporate/transmit authenticity because he is not part of the symbolic structures that shape this society; he is pure because he has evaded interpellation and is therefore »part of no one's data.« As soon as the authenticity he symbolizes/communicates is performed (both in a musical and a Butlerian sense), however, it immediately becomes part of popular mythology and therefore open to appropriation. Authenticity, it seems, is a singular gift, the magic of which is based on its irreproducibility, its one-off character, its sub-

---

13 The site in question is an apt location for the staging of authentic expression, as it consists of reflecting pools called ›the Footprint,‹ which evoke the memory of 9/11 in the form of incommensurable absence rather than concrete presence: »The weight of what had happened here more than twenty years ago was still faintly present for Alex, as it always was when he came to the Footprint. He perceived it as a sound just out of earshot, the vibration of an old disturbance« (331).

limity. Authenticity is both irreducible and irreproducible. Itself untouched by signification, it can intimate not designate.

Inauthenticity and New Significance: Visions of the Future of Reference

The last chapter of *A Visit from the Goon Squad* not merely connects most of the threads Egan has scattered throughout the preceding narrative (Alex, Bennie, Sasha; Lulu, Bennie; Scotty). It also presents a dystopian setting in a near future (the early 2020s) which Egan sets up as the – in many ways logical and inevitable – consequence of a way of life which has lost the ideal of authentic existence as a guiding metaphor, which it has traded in for a gadget-oriented form of hyperconsumerism. In a frightening, yet not all that implausible, development of current phenomena such as Facebook or iTunes, childhood, traditionally the archetypal embodiment of an authentic rapport with one's own being-in-the-world, has been invaded by all sorts of electronic implements. Most notably among those is a mysterious device called Starfish, which not only comes with a GPS system to help kids learn to walk, but which enables them to make consumer decisions (such as downloading music) as soon as they can point their finger. Accordingly, the advertising industry disparagingly refers to this preverbal target group as »the pointers« (313). By absorbing the (quint)essential gesture of reference within the system of consumer capitalism, reference as a concept in its own right becomes literally pointless.

Egan further accentuates the dangers of this impending demise of conventional forms of (authentic) reference by satirizing two prevalent forms of communication. Lulu, Bennie's current assistant, is described as »a living embodiment of the new ›handset employee‹: paperless, deskless, commuteless, and theoretically omnipresent« (317). She is fluent in a marketing and business idiom, an extreme version of ›Economese,‹ which primarily functions by translating complex concepts into two- or three-letter acronyms, like EA for »ethical ambivalence« (320) or DM for »disingenuous metaphor« (319). The latter quite neatly exemplifies the Newspeak-like ratio behind this new vernacular, as it designates terms such as ›selling out‹ or ›being bought,‹ which according to Lulu »look like descriptions, but they are really judgments« (319). Personal, individual judgments are, of course, regarded with a fair amount of suspicion in a world based on the uncriti-

cal acceptance of marketing ploys and so all DMs are structurally rendered insignificant; they are dismissed as »part of a system we call
atavistic purism. AP implies the existence of an ethically perfect state,
which not only doesn't exist and never existed, but it's usually used to
shore up the prejudices of whoever's making the judgments« (319).
Ethical judgment presupposes individuals with individual configura-
tions of referencing the world (like, for example, children pointing). It
is probably here that we can assume the locus of the authentic, a paradoxical space where authentic existence (authenticity of the subject)
and authentic reference (authenticity of the object) amalgamate: in a
radically individual gesture of referencing and making sense of the
world, individual in that it is both in the etymological sense ›irreducible‹ and un-shareable.[14] The endless possibilities which are theoretically offered by language in this regard are the first victims of an
inauthentic relationship to existence. Consequently, Egan's dystopian
vision includes T'ing, a version of the kind of SMS jargon we already
know as txtspk in our day and age, which has become so ubiquitous
that it is not only used in handset communication, but has also crept
into people's thinking, an occurrence Alex refers to as »brain-T«
(330). Confronted with all the children who make their way to Scotty's concert, he contemplates that »*if thr r children, thr mst b a fUtr,
rt?*« (331). A gadget-centered consumerism, in the form of T'ing, has,
so it would seem, even conquered and therefore disabled utopian
thinking itself.

The major casualties in this brave new world of digitalized referencing, Egan implies, are significance and signification. Humankind
systematically disinvests itself of the tools to make sense of the world
and thus of its own being-in-the-world. What remains is a society
trapped in endless, solipsistic, and inauthentic self-reference, without

---

14 Cf. in this regard Charles Taylor and Alessandro Ferrara's works on the
    ethical implications of authenticity. Taylor sees a will to authenticity as an
    antidote against postmodern fragmentation, relativity, and solipsism and
    infers from it an almost Kantian categorical imperative to responsibility;
    Ferrara, in contrast, argues from the assumption of just this relativity and
    defines authenticity in moral terms as the »courage to stand by one's ethi-
    cal intuitions even in the face of one's contingent inability to work them
    out in the language of abstract reflection« (136).

the means to envision and appeal to an authentic Other and therefore bereft of the ability to know itself. Rebecca, Alex's wife, has gained considerable academic eminence for her investigation of »word casings, a term she'd invented for words that no longer had meaning outside quotation marks« (323). These empty signifiers, »drained of life by their Web usage« (324), pointedly include words – and therefore necessarily concepts – such as ›friend,‹ ›real,‹ ›story,‹ ›search,‹ and ›change‹ (cf. 324), all of which have been erased by a simulated corporeality/corporate reality that has turned thinking human beings into consuming cyborgs.

CONCLUSION

The tone and subject matter of the last chapter of *A Visit from the Goon Squad* is considerably bleaker than in the rest of the novel, which – though being exceedingly tragic at times (Rob's drowning, for example) – can be seen essentially as a playful, though elaborate, exercise in plot reconstruction. It is only through the gravity of the final dystopian vision that these potentially ludic shenanigans are elevated to serious meditations on the reality of life and literature and their implications for human existence. Authenticity, in *A Visit from the Goon Squad*, does not refer to a misty nostalgia for pre-postmodern times, is not an indicator for those prelapsarian days when experience and representation, signifier and signified, were supposedly reconcilable. Authenticity, here, is quintessentially postmodern; it can only be witnessed as an artistic, maybe even artful, effect, an effect of literary reconstruction, both with regards to form and to content. But maybe – and this is a rather substantial maybe – this paradigm of reconstruction has the potential to look beyond the constraints of the postmodern condition; maybe an aesthetics of reconstruction will arise out of the aesthetics of deconstruction. Egan's novel is emblematic, even celebratory, of the irremediable fragmentation of human existence. It deduces, however, from that condition an appeal to the individual, an ethical imperative even, to preserve their unique and genuine, authentic understanding of the greater frame of reference, in which their existence is played out.

If literature can, as Mukařovský implies, at its best function as a recalibration of the human position and self-positioning within a frame of reference too great to be comprehended by individual reflection, and if we understand authenticity as an adumbration of this deficient, yet radically subjective and irreducible experience and interpretation of existence, then Egan's novel offers a profound narrative paradigm in this (hopefully) unending quest for authentic experience.

WORKS CITED

Blythe, Will. »To Their Own Beat.« *The New York Times Sunday Book Review*. 8 July 2010. Web. 13 July 2011. http:// www.nytim es.com/ 2010/07/117books/review/Blythe-t.html/

Boyd, Michael. *The Reflexive Novel: Fiction as Critique*. Lewisburg, PA: Bucknell UP, 1983.

Burbank, John, and Peter Steiner, eds. *Structure, Sign, and Function: Selected Essays by Jan Mukařovský*. New Haven, CT: Yale UP, 1978.

Currie, Mark. *Postmodern Narrative Theory*. Basingstoke: Macmillan, 1998.

Dällenbach, Lucien. *The Mirror in the Text*. Trans. Jeremy Whiteley and Emma Hughes. Cambridge: Polity Press, 1989.

Eakin, Paul John. *How Our Lives Become Stories: Making Selves*. Ithaca, NY: Cornell UP, 1999.

Egan, Jennifer. *A Visit from the Goon Squad*. New York, NY: Anchor Books, 2010.

Ferrara, Alessandro. *Modernity and Authenticity: A Study in the Social and Ethical Thought of Jean-Jacques Rousseau*. Albany, NY: State U of New York P, 1993.

Fletcher, John, and Malcolm Bradbury. »The Introverted Novel.« *Modernism: 1890-1930*. Ed. Malcolm Bradbury and James McFarlane. New Jersey, NJ: Humanity Press, 1978. 394-415.

Fluck, Winfried. »Surface Knowledge and ›Deep‹ Knowledge: The New Realism in American Fiction.« *Neo-Realism in Contemporary American Fiction*. Ed. Kristiaan Versluys. Amsterdam: Rodopi, 1992. 65-85.

Fludernik, Monika. *Towards a ›Natural‹ Narratology*. London: Routledge, 1996.

Funk, Wolfgang. »The Quest for Authenticity: Dave Eggers' *A Heartbreaking Work of Staggering Genius* between Fiction and Reality.« *The Metareferential Turn in Contemporary Arts and Media: Forms, Functions, and Attempts at Explanation.* Ed. Werner Wolf. Amsterdam: Rodopi, 2011. 125-144.

Funk, Wolfgang, and Lucia Krämer, eds. *Fiktionen von Wirklichkeit: Authentizität zwischen Materialität und Konstruktion.* Bielefeld: transcript, 2011.

Genette, Gérard. *Die Erzählung.* Trans. Andreas Knop. Munich: Fink, 1998.

——. *Narrative Discourse Revisited.* Trans. Jane E. Lewin. Ithaca, NY: Cornell UP, 1988.

Gonzales, Madalena. »The Aesthetics of Post-Realism and the Obscenification of Everyday Life: The Novel in the Age of Technology.« *Journal of Narrative Theory* 38.1 (2008): 111-33.

Hutcheon, Linda. *Narcissistic Narrative: The Metafictional Paradox.* New York, NY: Methuen, 1984.

Imhof, Rüdiger. *Contemporary Metafiction: A Poetological Study to Metafiction in English since 1939.* Heidelberg: Winter, 1986.

Lee, Alison. *Realism and Power: Postmodern British Fiction.* London: Routledge, 1990.

Malina, Debra. *Breaking the Frame: Metalepsis and the Construction of the Subject.* Columbus, OH: U of Ohio P, 2002.

Mukařovský, Jan. »The Aesthetic Norm.« Trans. John Burbank and Peter Steiner. Burbank and Steiner 49-56.

——. »Art as a Semiotic Fact.« Trans. Wendy Steiner. Burbank and Steiner 82-88.

——. »Intentionality and Unintentionality in Art.« Trans. John Burbank and Peter Steiner. Burbank and Steiner 89-128.

Stanzel, Franz K. *Typische Formen des Romans.* Göttingen: Vandenhoeck & Ruprecht, 1964.

Steiner, Peter. »Jan Mukařovský's Structural Aesthetics.« Burbank and Steiner ix-xxxix.

Stonehill, Brian. *The Self-Conscious Novel: Artifice in Fiction from Joyce to Pynchon.* Philadelphia, PA: U of Pennsylvania P, 1988.

Taylor, Charles. *The Ethics of Authenticity.* Cambridge, MA: Harvard UP, 1991.

Waugh, Patricia. *Metafiction: The Theory and Practice of Self-Conscious Fiction.* London: Routledge, 1984.

Williams, Jeffrey. *Theory and the Novel: Narrative Reflexivity in the British Tradition.* Cambridge: Cambridge UP, 1998.

Wolf, Werner. »Metalepsis as a Transgeneric and Transmedial Phenomenon: A Case Study of the Possibilities of Exporting Narratological Concepts.« *Narratology Beyond Literary Criticism: Mediality, Disciplinarity*. Ed. Jan Christoph Meister. Berlin: De Gruyter, 2005. 83-107.

——, ed. *Metareference across Media: Theory and Case Studies*. Amsterdam: Rodopi, 2009.

Wood, James. »Tell Me How Does It Feel?« *The Guardian* 6 Oct. 2001. Web. 19 June 2011. http://www.guardian.co.uk/books/2001/oct/06/fiction

Worringer, Wilhelm. *Abstraktion und Einfühlung: Ein Beitrag zur Stilpsychologie*. 1907. Paderborn: Fink, 2007.

Zeller, Christoph. *Ästhetik des Authentischen: Literatur und Kunst um 1970*. Berlin: De Gruyter, 2010.

Monolithic Authenticity and Fake News

Stephen Colbert's Megalomania

SETH HULSE

DESIRING AUTHENTICITY

Authenticity is an idea that lurks behind every claim in every news story, as it is ascribed to medial narratives by sender, receiver, and the dissemination medium itself. Journalists caress authenticity by trying to enhance their stories with images and sounds from historical reality while news consumers try to inform themselves about their historical reality by confronting the claims made by journalists and deciding on what to believe. Although consumer confidence in news media, and television news in particular, has steadily fallen in recent decades, consumers still rely on broadcast television as their primary source of news information (cf. Rosenstiel 17-18). Also, despite having a low amount of trust in media institutions, as detailed in the expansive Pew Research Center report by Rosenstiel, American news consumers continue to long for information that informs their conceptions of society. As Jan Berg persuasively writes in his essay »Techniken der medialen Authentifizierung,« our desire for authenticity can be understood as a longing for the all-powerful, for the wondrous, the holy, and the authorless object (cf. 56, 65). He describes the modes and the depiction techniques of authenticity and posits that authenticity need not only be seen as a relic of undisputable omnipotence, magnificence, and holiness, but that instead one can also understand it as »a specifically modern modus of truth, a mode of compensation, which in the modern world shifts into those positions that have become empty as a result of

Enlightenment and de-deification« (Berg 56; my translation).[1] Most interestingly, Berg highlights an important facet of the authentication process, namely that of self-ascription, of supposed authorlessness. Objects are not only ascribed an authentic status by recipients. Some objects tend to convey a depiction of authenticity that excludes the recipient. In effect, this tendency tries to draw a recipient's attention away from any reference to the required stagedness in acts of depiction (cf. Berg 66). Authentic objects instead tell recipients: We are authentic for we have conferred upon ourselves the status of authenticity, and, moreover, you are not to question our logical fallacy of circular reasoning. Objects that wish to seem more authentic by means of appearing authorless, and therefore somehow outer-worldly or even holy, try to evade inspection.

The Colbert Report with Stephen Colbert (*TCR*) delves into the topic of the authorless object by asking its viewers to scrutinize those cultural narratives that try to evade inspection. Being a fake news comedy show that airs nightly in the U.S. and Canada right after *The Daily Show with Jon Stewart*, *TCR* deals with topics ranging from the constructedness of news to the truth and ethical relativism of news discourse to the construction of identity. With a focus on identity, this paper will analyze the construction« of the Colbert persona and examine how this multifaceted persona is negated if *TCR* is solely interpreted as a satire instead of as a parody or even satiric parody. Through his megalomaniacal character, which is constituted by all of the broadcast news personalities he parodies, he presents an identity with seemingly clear boundaries, unwavering beliefs, and a certainty unbeknownst to most. Yet the theoretical and televisual framework in which the projection of this singular, essentialist, Colbertian identity occurs not only undermines it, but also replaces this singularity of self – Colbert's delusion – with an at times incoherent, disjointed collection of identities belonging to the same person, media persona and parodist Stephen Colbert.

By interpreting the *TCR* as a satiric parody, which would give one an apolitical focus on how and why narratives are used and maintained, and not as a parodic satire, which would focus one politically

---

1   »Authentizität läßt sich aber auch auffassen als eine spezifisch moderne Wahrheitsfigur, eine Kompensationsfigur, die in der Moderne an jene Stelle rückt, welche durch Aufklärung und Entgötterung leer wurde.«

on social mores, one is able to draw conclusions about Colbert's pluralistic self. Yet, therein lies the main problem involving most current interpretations of *TCR*. Despite many available interdisciplinary theories of alterity and constructive identity, media critics for the most part disregard any notion of a pluralistic self when analyzing *TCR*.[2] This, in turn, leads to the common interpretation of *TCR* as news satire, which it is, in a way. However, it can be much more than that. The difference between interpreting something as a parodic satire or a satiric parody might seem nitpicky, but this difference in interpretation is telling of how theories of fragmented identity are failing to find any cultural resonance and impact in U.S.-style communication studies or even within the news media itself.

The labeling of *TCR* as a deadpan satire, where the satirist never breaks character such as Colbert always remaining within his conservative persona, or just plain satire with elements of news parody mirrors a cultural desire not to acknowledge the constructedness of our own identities. Furthermore, any notion of an authentic, singular self hinders us from maintaining and developing other selves and in the case of *TCR*, negating parody as the dominant comedic device in turn negates Colbert's overt presentation of a dialogical self. Satirist Colbert is singularized and purposively utilized for socio-political means, whereas parodist Colbert, in the name of intertextual decoding, demands that the decoder enter into dialogical relations with the presented narratives. However, rather than enter into the narrative collision zone, most opt for the singular path of direct criticism of social mores via satire. I instead will traverse the road of narcissism, narrative chaos, and dialogism, via parody.

COLBERT PERSONA

Stephen Colbert, the persona, who can be described as a right-wing, blow-hard, ignorant-of-the-facts, God-praising, George Bush-loving, and highly narcissistic late night news pundit, has been attributed with being a satirist (cf. Stanley; LaMarre, Landreville, and Beam) or the »Man in the Irony Mask« (Mnookin 1), all the while using elements of parody to make fun of news media (Stanley). The interpretations of

---

2   Cf. Dowd; LaMarre, Landreville, and Beam; Mnookin; Stelter; Stanley.

Colbert's comedic performances always involve the descriptors satire, parody, and irony, though the dominant descriptor depends on the author of the article, as descriptions of Colbert vary not only between firms but also from within publishers such as *The New York Times* (compare Stanley to Stelter) and Schiller. Further compounding problems of interpretation are Colbert's narcissism and his persona's relation to actual news pundits.

While Colbert was interviewed by veteran CNN desk anchor Larry King, King referenced an interview in which he himself was a guest on *TCR* during which Colbert basked in the interview spotlight instead of focusing it on his guest. King gave Colbert a good-natured chastising for having employed poor interviewing techniques that were narcissistic in nature in comparison to King's own journalistic standards (cf. »Episode 3028« and King). King exclaimed that when conducting an interview, a television host should avoid using the words ›I‹ and ›me‹ as much as possible. Colbert, who, unannounced, does interviews in character, informed King that *TCR* is chiefly about Colbert, and furthermore, that if it could have been done, the interview would have centered itself more on Colbert (cf. »Episode 3028«). To add to the narcissistic dismay, Colbert, whose anchor desk takes the shape of a C, has his name displayed in over 14 on-camera set-locations, in case the viewer fails to recognize that *TCR* really is really about him.

In his introduction to *I am America (And So Can You!)* and while referencing his self-evident truths, which brings one back to authorless authenticity, Colbert denies having done actual research for this book project since the only type of research that was needed »was a long hard look in the mirror. For this book is My Story and, as such, it is the American Story« (ix, capitalization in the original). In megalomaniacal style, Colbert never overtly hints at the other media personas present within his own persona, as that would undermine the essentialist, singular identity his conservative character has come to represent. He fittingly concludes his self-absorbed introduction with a quote from Walt Whitman, who »defined the character of this new nation« with lines such as »I celebrate myself, and sing myself, / And what I assume, you shall assume« (Whitman qtd. in Colbert et al. ix). The obvious narcissistic characteristics, such as the aesthetic self-consciousness displayed by the television and author persona of Stephen Colbert, draw overt attention back onto the content creator, promoting a focus on self-reflexivity and identity in Colbert's mediated products.

Referring back to King's concern about journalism standards, Colbert tries to distance *TCR* from direct journalistic responsibility by saying that »it is incumbent upon us [Colbert and Jon Stewart] to be funny, not necessarily to get [the news] exactly right [...] accuracy comes second.« To understand how he distances his nightly, pretaped performance enough so that *TCR*'s remediated content does not seep onto the creative turf of Bill O'Reilly and other news anchors, Colbert explains that he models his persona after a »cult of personality,« which takes on the facets of many night time news anchors all at once. Yet Colbert confuses this creative distance when he escalates his cult of personality to delusional heights by grossly exaggerating his overt, self-serving narcissism and subsumption of other pundit figures to such an extent that the Colbert persona no longer recognizes its own genesis. The predominant characteristic, upon which the Colbert persona dwells, is thus that of megalomania, or of someone who »suffers from delusions of power or importance« (»Megalomania«).

Furthermore, Colbert describes the modern night-time news anchor as someone who is no longer »the voice of God anchor,« but rather an »avenging angel kind of anchor,« and that the Colbert persona can be »broken up into little fiefdoms of different people's shows, but it's all a cult of personality« as is overtly apparent by Colbert's incessant references to his viewers, whom he constantly labels »Nation,« namely his nation (Colbert, »A Conversation«). Moreover, and explaining why Colbert dons a Republican persona, an avenging angel kind of anchor functions better when the anchor has a »monolithic tone and a shamelessness, and one thing that [American Democrats] are not is unified generally in their thought.« In comparison to the Democratic political platform, the stereotypical Republican platform is more superficially uniform and so it is the conservative, less populist-orientated approach to which Colbert adapts his persona in portraying his on-screen person as a Republican-leaning anchor. The television persona of Stephen Colbert therefore draws on conservative news moderators such as Glenn Beck and Bill O'Reilly for his political approach, but he also draws on such aesthetic characteristics as Stone Phillips's »patent head turn« (»Episode 1001«), with which the former *Dateline NBC* anchor reaffirmed his authority when delivering news of a serious nature. Despite *TCR*'s use of news aesthetics and stories

from left-leaning, neutral, and right-leaning anchors, the Colbert persona is most commonly interpreted as a satirical attack against conservative American politics. To change this interpretive outcome, I
will have to show the difference between satire and parody and why
TCR falls under the latter term.

PARODY AND SATIRE

The difference between parody and satire comes down to structure and
function in that the form of parody is always intramural and deals with
aesthetic norms of the conventions being parodied while that of satire
is extramural and deals rather with social and moral norms (cf. Hutcheon 25). Ziva Ben-Porat writes that there are different variants when
one combines satire and parody (cf. 247). She provides clearly distin-
guishable definitions respectively for parody and satire:

Parody = An alleged representation, usually comic, of a literary text or other
artistic object – i.e., a representation of a ›modelled reality,‹ which is itself already a particular representation of an original ›reality.‹ The parodic representations expose the model's conventions and lay bare its devices through the
coexistence of the two codes in the same message.

Satire = A critical representation, always comic and often caricatural, of ›non-
modelled reality,‹ i.e., of the real objects (their reality may be mythical or hy-
pothetical) which the receiver reconstructs as the referents of the message. The
satirized original ›reality‹ may include mores, attitudes, types, social structures, prejudices, and the like. (247-48)

Following Ben-Porat, for *TCR* to be a satire it would be a critical representation of a non-modeled reality, namely of American political
culture. For *TCR* to be a parody it would be a representation of a modeled reality, namely of the American news media system, which itself
provides only representations of an original reality, namely of American society at large. More importantly, Ben-Porat also explores the
relationship between parody and satire. Parody becomes »indirect satirical parody« when it criticizes phenomena outside of the parodied
model (248), which is what one finds in the case of *TCR*. While I argue that *TCR* is primarily a parody, the show does utilize a satire that

is directed against conservative values and politics. In one of his most satirically aggressive pieces, Colbert the comedian was invited to the 2006 White House Correspondents' Dinner as the after-dinner speaker, where the Colbert persona showed up and comedically roasted President George Bush, who was also on stage, sitting just a matter of feet off to Colbert's right. Of the many pointed jokes delivered, the following speech excerpt offers a good example of the comedic tone typically used both in this speech and on the show in general:

I stand by this man. I stand by this man because he stands for things. Not only for things, he stands on things. Things like aircraft carries and rubble and recently flooded city squares. And that sends a strong message: that no matter what happens to America, she will always rebound – with the most powerfully staged photo ops in the world. (Colbert et al. 223)

Although one can see the criticism pointed at Bush's 2003 Mission Accomplished Speech and his visits to Ground Zero after 9/11 and to New Orleans after Hurricane Katrina, Colbert finishes this joke by emphasizing the stagedness of these events and the role of news media. Thus, instead of excoriating conservative politics and mores in greater detail, Colbert's intramural approach focuses the viewer less on the content of the message and more on the form of the message. This makes for humor that at first does mock conservative viewpoints, but in a way that does not greatly disparage self-described conservative viewers.

This approach allows *TCR* to draw on the large left-leaning audience carryover from *The Daily Show* and at the same time does not necessarily repel conservative viewers. As the 2010 Pew Research Center survey shows, and almost identical to its lead-in program, *The Daily Show*, 19% of *TCR*'s viewers identify themselves as conservative, 41% as moderate, and 35% as liberal (cf. Rosenstiel 56). Since criticism of reality's structures is by common definition satire (cf. Ben-Porat 248; Ogborn and Buckroyd 13), it becomes all too easy for critics of *TCR* to classify it as such. In contrast, the term ›indirect‹ in my labeling of *TCR* as an indirect satiric parody merely indicates the »relationship between the parody [*TCR*], the model [American news media system] and the original [American society at large] in terms of the satire involved« and not the degree to which there is conspicuousness or acrimony (Ben-Porat 248). My claim would therefore hold that, although *TCR* uses satire as befitting the Colbert persona and the lead-in audience coming from *The Daily Show*, its main comedic target is not the social and political mores of the Republican party, but rather the process of information dissemination itself. Shortly after the photo op joke, Colbert proceeds to focus the audience even more on the role of news media:

As excited as I am to be here with the President, I am appalled to be surrounded by the liberal media that is destroying America, with the exception of Fox News. Fox News gives you both sides of every story: the President's side and the Vice President's side. Over the last five years [2001-2006] you people were so good – over tax cuts, WMD intelligence, the effect of global warming. We Americans didn't want to know and you had the courtesy not to find out. Those were good times, as far as we knew. (Colbert et al. 224)

Using a common delivery pattern found on the show, Colbert sets up the initial joke with conservative talking points (of there being a liberal bias in the news), then, usually using irony, delivers the satiric element (the liberal talking point that Fox News is not fair and balanced), and then finally either draws the joke into absurdity or makes a generalizing comment that moves beyond the conservative talking points (Fox News and others not having provided adequate representations of reality). Interpretive differences arise when one focuses primarily on the satiric element (Fox's bias) and not also on the end (emphasis on the fallibility of all representations). Placing interpretive focus on an entire joke and not just on select parts will also lead the interpreter to an intertextual analysis.

If the encoded parodied text is successfully decoded by the text's recipient, writes David Kiremidjian, then the receiver will experience an »introverted« form of art that is not only »curious about its own being,« but an art form that is utilizing its form in the name of »self-knowledge« (18). The introspective nature of parodic forms, as described by Hutcheon, Ben-Porat, and Kiremidjian, relies on dialogism between two or more coded discourses. To more fully understand Colbert's joke about Fox News and other destructive liberal news media and thus gain access to the aforementioned dialogism, the recipient should, for example, be familiar with *The New York Times*' pre-Iraq War coverage, which is nicely chronicled in *When the Press Fails* by Bennett, Lawrence, and Livingston. As one can see, the activation of this background text – the secondary coded discourse – requires decoder competence. It is here, in the realm of decoder competence where confusion arises, as is evident in the various news articles and studies describing *TCR*.

Despite the confusion caused by parody's interpretive possibilities – its pragmatic ethos – which can range from scornful ridicule to reverential homage, one characteristic that all forms of parody share is the substitution of elements from the background text(s) into the parodic text. The result is a trans-contextualization, or a parodic text that »stands in an inverse or incongruous relation to the borrowed text« (Hutcheon 36). Furthermore, a parody need not necessarily ridicule the background texts »but rather use them as standards by which to place the contemporary under scrutiny« (Hutcheon 57). Accordingly, Hutcheon defines parody not only as repetition that includes difference but as »imitation with critical ironic distance, whose irony can cut both ways« (37). Here is where Ben-Porat's idea concerning »indirect satiric parody« comes into play. In this scenario, *TCR* utilizes satire to draw viewership and parody as its main rhetorical device to criticize cultural dissemination and maintenance of narratives, both at individual and at collective levels.

The role of irony in parodic trans-contextualization causes confusion between labeling a media product as parody or satire. Being an inherently multilayered form of communication, irony can be characterized as working at the semantic level, or in other words, as occurring at the intratextual level. It provides one signifier and paradoxically communicates two signifieds (cf. Hutcheon 54). For example: *Fox News is fair and balanced.* This sentence has six signifiers {Fox} {News} {is} {fair} {and} {balanced}, though Fox News functions as a compound noun and therefore as a single signifier {Fox News}. Irony works by confusing what is stated and what is intended. The signifiers used, that Fox News *is* fair and balanced, might for some recipients of this message seem contradictory. This is because the signifier {Fox News} will for some conjure up signifieds such as fair, truth, and balance, which would all coalesce with the rest of the sentence, whereas for others, {Fox News} might conjure up signifieds such as biased, conservative, and lies, all of which are associations that would contradict the basic meaning of the sentence. It is here, at the crossroads of superimposition, where the recipient must make decoding choices. Because parody structurally works in a similar manner at the intertextual level, superimposing multiple texts and simultaneously confusing what is stated and what is intended, Hutcheon contends that irony »appears to be the main rhetorical mechanism for activating the reader's awareness of this dramatization. Irony participates in parodic discourse as a strategy [...] which allows the decoder to interpret and evaluate« (31).

After having discussed the parameters of parody, the next logical step is to look at the ramifications of parody on major themes found on *TCR*. One of the primary themes, which also relates directly to the constitution of the Colbert persona and the show's use of parody itself, is the maintenance of identity. The next section will look at how Colbert utilizes parody in constructing and in continually informing his television persona.

THE COLBERT PERSONA AND ITS CONSTITUTIVE VOICES

Being a parody, *TCR* itself does not create new stories. Instead, being a parody of the American news media system, the show is condemned to trans-contextualizing existing news stories, which is exactly what *TCR* does on a nightly basis. A sample story from *TCR* and its constitutive background texts will be analyzed. Before doing so, however, the status of a ›story‹ in the context of news media must be clarified. A story requires a combination of action and mishappening:

If nothing eventful happens, stories remain predictable, and it would be pointless to tell them: if Columbus had found his way to India without having discovered the new world, or if there had been no wolf at grandmother's house in *Little Red Riding Hood* [...] those would not have been stories worth telling. (Marquard, *Philosophie* 60-61; my translation)[3]

---

3   »Solange ihnen [Geschichten] nichts dazwischenkommt, sind sie voraussagbar, und es wäre witzlos, sie zu erzählen: wenn Kolumbus Indien amerikalos erreicht hätte, wenn Rotkäppchen die Großmutter wolflos besucht hätte, [...] wären das keine – richtigen – Geschichten gewesen.«

Odo Marquard is referencing a major historical event and a fairytale, yet I will present television news stories. In terms of media effects, communications researcher Charles Aust concludes that there is a link between the story from within literature and the story extant in the news context, and this link is drama. Within journalism, news traditionally serve to inform consumers of the risks and dangers that society poses (cf. Aust 513). News sustain one's effort in self-preservation, physically and existentially. However, Aust asserts that the motives serving self-preservation cannot solely explain why masses flock on a daily basis to read, listen to, and watch news information regarding the misfortunes of other people. In positing drama as the other integral ingredient making news a profitable product, Aust indicates that news must necessarily »rely on conflict and endangerment. As in drama, conflict is one of the essential and enduring themes of journalism« (Aust 515). The conflict in the following stories, however, will appear in very different forms. Each story deals with the 2009 nomination of Sonia Sotomayor to the U.S. Supreme Court and alleged controversial comments she made in a 2001 speech.

In the first background text, CBS, which could be considered the most ideologically neutral news provider compared to my other examples and whose audience breakdown is 36% conservative, 41% moderate, and 15 % liberal (cf. Rosenstiel 56), focuses on Sotomayor's word choice and the possible political consequences. Reporter Wyatt Andrews summarizes the situation involving the 2001 speech in which the controversial words were given and he reports as well on other media reports of this story. Thus the story of concern is that politically motivated stories that are destructive in nature could emerge, though they should have no impact on the results of the Senate confirmation hearing process.

Neutral: CBS's Evening News Correspondent Wyatt Andrews reporting

[Andrews] It's a line that has raised the most heat about the nomination of Judge Sotomayor. In a 2001 lecture on how ethnic experience can affect a judge Sotomayor said:

»I would hope that a wise Latina woman with the richness of her experiences would more often than not reach a better conclusion than a white male who hasn't lived that life.«

After three days of wishing the controversy away, the White House called it a poor word choice. [...]

While supporters insist that she was stating the facts, that experience impacts judging, Sotomayor's better than a white man comment has energized the conservative opposition. It has led to charges that she will be a liberal who favors minorities and led Rush Limbaugh and others to call her racist. [...] politically however, most Republicans think the racism charge goes too far.

[Clip of Senator John Cornyn] I just don't think it's appropriate. I certainly don't endorse it. I think it's wrong.

[Andrews] But what also happened this week is that Republicans did the math – they don't have the votes to defeat Sotomayor.

[John Dickerson, CBS News political analyst] The new position for Republicans is: Let's have a dignified hearing and let's stop the name calling and get to the issues at hand here. (Andrews)

Striving for the appearance of objectivity, CBS provides the viewer with the most primary source material aside from interviewing judge Sotomayor herself. The piece gains in objective appearance as the quote of concern is read aloud as well as displayed in textual form on screen. In contrast, the second background text, Fox News's *The O'Reilly Factor*, whose audience breakdown is 72% conservative, 21% moderate, and 3% liberal (cf. Rosenstiel 56), does not directly mention the speech by Sotomayor and delves directly into analysis. Commentator Bill O'Reilly does, however, present a more drama-filled story than does CBS. The lead begins by saying that Obama has maliciously created a precarious political situation for the Republicans by nominating a Latina.

Right-leaning: Fox News with Bill O'Reilly

[O'Reilly] Once again, President Obama has pulled off a shrewd political move by nominating a Latina, Judge Sonia Sotomayor, to the Supreme Court. [...] Republicans face a quandary. This morning on ABC, conservative Ann Coulter pretty much defined the problem:

[Ann Coulter from ABC News clip] Saying that someone would decide a case differently, better in fact, because she is a Latina rather than a white male. I mean that statement by definition is racist; I'm not saying she's a racist, but the statement sure is. (O'Reilly, »Supreme Court«)

O'Reilly's news lead is thus defined by the political peril in which the Democrats have placed the Republicans. O'Reilly, with whom the Colbert persona is often compared, typically begins his pieces with a provocative lead followed by him or his guests taking up conservative talking points.[4] A reason for comparing the two is that Colbert also employs a similar story structure, though he presents conservative talking points with satiric undertones and then moves beyond them.

Also employing similar storytelling methods, though with antithetical content when compared to Fox News, is MSNBC's Rachel Maddow, whose audience breakdown is 21% conservative, 40% moderate, and 35% liberal (cf. Rosenstiel 56). She visually and textually depicts the nomination of Sotomayor as a godsend for American culture. Similar to O'Reilly, she presents no source material from the Sotomayor 2001 speech and instead presents a provocative lead and then delves into what one might label liberal talking points.

Left-leaning: MSNBC's Rachel Maddow:

[Maddow] We begin with remarks in New York City by the President of the United States:

[President Obama in NAACP clip] No matter how bitter the ride, how stony the rope, we have always persevered. We have not faltered nor have we grown weary [...].

[Maddow] The nation's first African American president tonight speaking in New York City addressing an essentially all-black audience for the first time since he has been president. The occasion, of course, is the 100th anniversary of the founding of the NAACP, the nation's oldest civil rights organization. Beyond that huge anniversary, today was a landmark day for civil rights in America, as confirmation hearings ended for the person who is on track to be the first Latino elevated to the United States Supreme Court. [...] One prominent Republican who believes that the Republicans did not make enough of the

---

4   For example, in a fruitful exchange with O'Reilly, Colbert ironically comments on his character's dependency on O'Reilly's persona: »Colbert: Could you take [Sean Hannity] in a fight? O'Reilly: I don't want to fight. We're Irish guys. Colbert: You're Irish and don't want to fight? O'Reilly: This is a cliché, [...] I'm a feat, I'm not a tough guy. This is all an act. Colbert: You're breaking my heart. O'Reilly: I'm sensitive. I am. ... Colbert: If you're an act, then what am I?« (O'Reilly, »Stephen Colbert«).

issue of race at the Sotomayor hearings is my MSNBC colleague Patrick J. Buchanan, who argued [...] that the hearings should have been seized on even more by Republicans to try to win over white conservatives who feel aggrieved by racial issues. He says »These are the folks [...] who pay the price of affirmative action when their sons and daughters are pushed aside to make room for the Sonia Sotomayors.« [...] Pat are you happy that we're about to have a Latino on the Supreme Court for the first time? (Maddow)

All three stories deal with the perceived impact of Sotomayor in different but predictable ways and they all share the journalistic desire to show and tell the news consumer what is going on in his or her society. They are predictable, if one refers to my generic labeling of the different areas in the American political medial landscape – left, right, or neutral. All three stories also share another journalistic trait inherent to modern day newscasts: story analysis. In trying to remain objective, CBS uses its own political analyst John Dickerson, who does not convey his own political affiliations and who explains what the »new« situation for »Republicans« is by subsuming the political group and speaking for the Republicans: »let's [let us Republicans] have a dignified hearing and let's stop the name calling and get to the issues at hand here« (Andrews). Andrews draws on a single statement from Republican Senator John Cornyn with which Dickerson generalizes and postulates the actions »dignified« Republicans would follow if they wanted to »get to the issues at hand.« Neither Andrews nor Dickerson enlighten the viewer as to which »issues« should be discussed. O'Reilly and Maddow not only emulate and exaggerate the CBS story construction formula, but both shows also share an uncannily similar rhetorical strategy in promoting their political narratives by way of letting other voices, such as Ann Coulter, Dick Morris, Barack Obama, and Pat Buchanan,[5] serve both as reinforcement and as political straw men.

Two further tactics employed by the above stories are priming and framing. The idea of priming, which refers to the »capacity of the media to isolate particular issues, events, or themes in the news as criteria for evaluating politicians« (Ansolabehere, Behr, and Iyengar 148), calls into question the importance of a story and how the story's narrative is used in a more broadly political sense. MSNBC and Fox News

---

5   Left out of the O'Reilly story for reasons of length.

clearly prime the same story quite differently, while CBS mentions the White House's wish that this was a non-story. Similarly, analysis of framing sheds light onto how »surrounding features of the reporting discourse can influence the way in which represented discourse is interpreted« (Fairclough 82). Surrounding features can include usage of certain grammatical structures or even on-screen imagery. When the focus is shifted to comparing the visual presentation of each background text, one immediately encounters three contrasting narratives of Sotomayor.

CBS presents an undated and fairly unedited photo with reference to on-screen framing. In great contrast, however, Fox News presents an altered image whose meaning is twofold. On the one hand, and in conjunction with the story, O'Reilly highlights the dangers the Republican Party will encounter if they try to block Sotomayor's nomination. Yet, when looking at the on-screen graphics, one will see located behind a bright yellow ›danger ahead‹ sign a gray-scaled image of Sotomayor and Vice President Biden together at the White House. Such imagery can be visually connoted along the lines of Ann Coulter's comment insinuating Sotomayor to be dangerous and a racist. O'Reilly's *bête noire* can be found in MSNBC's former anchor Keith Olbermann (cf. Stelter) or Rachel Maddow. Instead of portraying President Obama's nomination of Sotomayor as ›danger ahead,‹ Maddow does the exact opposite by framing this story as being historically important and something positive through superimposition and transition from President Obama's NAACP speech to Sotomayor, visually interlocking the narratives with the word ›history,‹ which is poignantly highlighted.

If we accept the narratives coming from CBS, MSNBC, and FOX News, then Sotomayor, who poses reverse racism ›danger ahead‹ for the Republican Party, is a racist Latina who, mathematically, cannot be stopped on her march to make ›history.‹[6] *TCR* does more than accept the contrasting truths as presented by each background text: the show conjoins these medial narratives into one narrative that is the Colbert persona and, in what has become a routinized pattern, Colbert

---

6   After the nomination, both political parties knew that Sotomayor would receive enough votes during the Senate Confirmation Hearings, making her nomination virtually incontestable.

begins the story by letting the voices of others speak before he proceeds.

Parody: TCR's Stephen Colbert

[Colbert] Nation, during Sonia Sotomayor's confirmation hearings I learned something very important:

[CNN clip: news anchor] Here's what you've said about Sotomayor: »she appears to be racist.«

[Tom Tancredo in response] Everybody is afraid to challenge her on it for fear of themselves being called racist.

[Fox News clip with Rush Limbaugh] Here you have a racist, I mean, you want to soften that and say a reverse racist.

[MSNBC clip with Pat Buchanan] I do believe she is an affirmative action appointment. Affirmative action is to increase diversity by discriminating against white males.

[Colbert] As a white male, I am being reverse discriminated against. Thank you reverse civil rights leader Pat Buchanan. Now folks, I don't see race. People tell me I am white and I believe them […] Well, as proud white men, Pat and I cherish all the things our people have done for America.

[MSNBC clip with Buchanan] White men were 100% of the people that wrote the Constitution, 100% of the people who signed the Declaration of Independence, 100% of the people who died at Gettysburg and Vicksburg.

[Colbert] Yeah! Where were the black guys during the Civil War? Now, I'm not saying they all should have volunteered, just 3/5 of them. Now Pat and I aren't saying that being oppressed is all bad. For instance, now white people can call each other names that outsiders don't get to use, like Senator. Plus, now that white people are disadvantaged, that makes us the new black people. So, as a new black man, I was looking forward to hearing the first black president give a speech to an organization that has done so much for my people, the NAACP. But folks, I was bitterly disappointed.

[Obama] No one has written your destiny for you, your destiny is in your hands, you cannot forget that, that is what we have to teach all of our children. No excuses, no excuses.

[Colbert] No excuses! Oh, as soon as white people start being black he takes away the excuses. (»Episode 5096«)

Looking at *TCR*, Colbert overtly subsumes the voices coming from other outlets as he lets each cable news network literally speak for him, a strategy mirrored by Rachel Maddow's use of Barack Obama in her exposition, Bill O'Reilly's use of Ann Coulter in his opening, and by Wyatt Andrews's use of John Dickerson. This technique allows each respective anchor to distance her or his medial persona from the emotional description of extreme jubilation for the advancement of race relations on the one hand, or the claims of reverse racism on the other. Nevertheless, the distancing strategy indicates a conscious effort on the part of anchors such as Maddow, O'Reilly, and Andrews in trying to foster and then maintain an appearance of fairness and balance in the dispositions of the viewers. In contrast, Colbert differentiates himself from his background texts by creating critical ironic distance between his narratives and any media claims to authenticity.

The Colbert story rhetorically employs irony by alluding to cultural stereotypes such as African Americans having to rely on various excuses for living in deplorable living situations. For example, Colbert explains that »being oppressed isn't all bad. For instance, now white people can call each other names that outsiders don't get to use, like Senator« (»Episode 5096«). The cultural allusion of »Senator,« a word literally associated with many more whites than blacks, indirectly refers to the N-word, a term predominantly and exclusively used in black communities (cf. Parks and Jones). Of course he does not stop there. Typical Colbertian behavior is to feed his internalized narratives, a.k.a. the background texts, into his machine of narcissism and megalomania and draw them out to an illogical conclusion. We see this in the Colbert story above, as he is not only suffering from reverse racism, but, as a(n) (il)logical consequence, he becomes a new black man and then begins to look forward to Maddow's notion of a history-making speech from President Obama, to his dismay. This tactic can be seen in almost any episode in the majority of his skits, for it is part of his comedic approach. This approach also leads to many logical fallacies and philosophical conundrums, some of which are nicely elucidated in an edited collection on *TCR* by Aaron A. Schiller. However, the two topics the essays in Schiller neglect are comedy, namely parody and satire, and identity.

As a result of having instantly subsumed the background texts into his own story, Colbert consequently claims to have learned a great deal during the hearings without quoting and using any source material from the actual proceeding. Additionally, in not showing the 2001 Sotomayor speech, Colbert does not divulge why Sotomayor is a racist. Instead of conducting research and presenting documented images from our historical reality, Colbert shifts the focus away from actual cultural signs and events, such as Sotomayor's nomination, onto the storytellers who narrate these media stories. Consequently, by completely relying on the narratives and visual imagery of others, and by instantly internalizing the stories coming from other newscasts, structurally *TCR* becomes Ben-Porat's modeled reality of a modeled reality, whose focus is more on form (maintenance of stories) and less on content (Sotomayor). As David Kiremidjian writes, »parody has no form, structure, or mechanism of its own, but must adopt, by its very nature, the form of the original to which it refers and to which it owes its existence,« and such being the case, the Colbert persona would not exist save for the presence of the background texts. If *TCR* were indeed primarily a satire, the existence of background texts would be irrelevant. Instead, these texts, which themselves are modeled realities, provide *TCR* not only with vital sustenance, but also with the constitutive elements of a persona that cannot represent an identity that is stable, coherent, and singular.

PARODY AND THE DIALOGICAL SELF

Through continuous use of the address »Nation,« *TCR* parasocially includes a viewer position in its construction of stories.[7] In doing so, Colbert exaggerates a news person's ability to become a storyteller whose task it is to communicate narratives. *TCR* most clearly rejects any notion of objective reporting by addressing the viewer directly. »How can this be?« one may ask when one considers that many newscasters begin and end shows with personalized greetings aimed at communicating directly with the viewing audience and at building a rapport, something to which the title alludes, as both t's in *The Colbert Report* are not pronounced, as in the word rapport.

Following on from Jonathan Cohen's concept of the parasocial, Werner Wirth contends that »[f]rom a media-psychological perspective, there is no doubt that involvement is a psychological construct

---

7 Cohen writes that »identification with media characters [both real and fictive] is a process that impacts our involvement with, and interpretation of, media texts« and describes this interaction as parasocial (193).

located within the individual« (201). The jump from interaction to involvement is also fostered by the structural requirements found in parody. Parody necessitates decoder competence since the parodic text contains one or more target and background texts. For example, Colbert's reverse racism story is the parodic text whereas the aforementioned stories from CBS, Fox News, and MSNBC serve both as Colbert's target texts and his background texts. Hutcheon calls this required interaction an act of enunciation in which the encoder, Colbert, and the decoder, his viewer, must take part in an »amicable community« of common cultural knowledge for parody to function (94). Referring back to the reverse racism story, the addressee is labeled »Nation.« Not only is Colbert directly addressing his audience, he does so by speaking to a dominant facet of identity: nationality. This is worth noting because some of those whom Colbert parodies such as Bill O'Reilly, Pat Buchanan, Rachel Maddow, Glenn Beck, and Sean Hannity consider themselves to be partakers in culture wars concerning the identity of the nation, and, furthermore, that this war should be approached through the commercial promulgation of ideologies and ideas over the cable airwaves.

On the airwaves, issues are dealt with in a fragmentary nature whereby source materials are loosely intertwined with other imagery such as the ›danger ahead‹ next to Sotomayor and also with news commentary. In promoting his monotheistically influenced parodic text, in which Colbert conveys an almost absolute belief in religion as long as it suits his narcissistic needs, Colbert draws on the inclusionary power of relegating national identity as a primary facet in identity construction and accordingly he tries to overcome the fragmentary nature of the cable news culture war. Terry Eagleton writes that because cultures are intrinsically incomplete, they utilize »the supplement of the state to become truly themselves« (59). In this light, it is easy to see why Colbert et al. named their self-help book, which deals with how to be an American, *I am America (And So Can You!)*. Instead of being consumed and imprisoned by American identity, Colbert subsumes and imprisons America into his cult of personality.

Imprisonment in the bounds of culture is exactly how Marquard characterizes the role of stories in society: »Narrare necesse est [to narrate is necessary]: We humans must narrate. This fact was so and remains so, for we are our stories and stories must be told« (*Philoso-*

phie 60; my translation).[8] Drawing on a historical example to support his reasoning, Marquard describes the personage of Christopher Columbus and how Columbus must be understood through the bounds of story. Columbus is he who discovered America and the new world, and, eventually, it is the stories we tell that end up defining us (cf. Marquard, *Philosophie* 60). Columbus becomes what he discovered. That is his most dominant story. Though, at the other end of the personage spectrum, one can also examine the shortest of short stories that we humans tell, for example the story of a personal identification card. From discovering a new continent to the banalities of 21st-century cultures, such as having to provide a passport at an international airport and literally showing the story of your identity, cultures abound with different types of stories.

Marquard describes the precarious situation in which stories find themselves as polymythic (cf. *Abschied* 106). Precariousness arises out of the shifting balances of power amongst stories as not all stories are equally maintained. Within this imprisonment of narrative, Marquard looks at the relations amongst stories and their frequency of use in his attempt to map out a philosophical narratology. He begins by underscoring that those who actively partake in more stories have more narrative freedom for they have more stories and thus more options from which to choose self-constitutive information. Using Marquard's neologism, it is those who live polymythically that have more freedom (cf. *Abschied* 98). Conversely, those who engage life in a more finite, singular approach, especially with regards to stories, limit their narrative maneuverability. This approach to the stories available in a culture leads to monomythic tendencies, which can lead one to become entrapped in and even promote a monomythic *Gleichschaltung*. *Gleichschaltung*, a German word which equates to the standardization of various social institutions, usually in an authoritarian country, can be used to imply the power and corresponding possible danger of monomythic thinking. Marquard says that those who deviate from a socially-supported monomythic story are commonly labeled as being heretic, a traitor of history, a misanthropist, and a reactionary (cf. *Abschied* 100).

---

8 »Narrare necesse est: Wir Menschen müssen erzählen. Das war so und bleibt so. Denn wir Menschen sind unsere Geschichten, und Geschichten muß man erzählen.«

He contends further that this compulsion of blind acquiescence to the monomyth causes one, in identity formation, to succumb to narrative atrophy (cf. *Abschied* 98), an atrophy the Colbert persona comedically excoriates. Suffering from narrative atrophy can be characterized as identity's discontentment due to a fundamental lack of non-identity, or a lack of periphery stories with which one can sustain the psychological self. It is namely the compulsory nature of consent to monomyths that is prominent in parts of America's information dissemination system which Stephen Colbert utilizes and parodies via his self-mocking Christian conservative blow-hard persona. Once the parody has been decoded, beyond the singular, ultra-religious, and unified appearance of the Colbert persona, the decoder will experience Colbert's agglomeration of seemingly opposed self-constitutive narratives.

Dealing with a Colbert persona that one cannot easily identify with because of its dialogic nature and the fact that it has multiple voices that constitute the persona has made interpretation more difficult, and this should not be surprising. It is far easier to avoid the fractured Colbert persona and instead interpret Colbert in the singular, as a satirist who ridicules conservative mores. Yet, through ironic trans-contextualization, *TCR* pushes viewers away from narratives that are stable and singular in power while at the same time drawing viewers into his narcissistic, megalomaniacal, singularizing self. The Colbert persona toys with both the polymythic and monomythic. For interpretation, recipients must first create interpretive room for a newfound narrative maneuverability. Marquard writes that »the individual must explicitly constitute a notion of self with which the creative space needed for inner subjectivity can be supported, thus creating distance between the individual and the monotheistic story« (*Abschied* 108; my translation).[9] The creation of the free space in which individuality forms requires a »minimum of chaos« as well as a »certain measure of sloppiness which arises from the collision of the various divisions of power« in the form of various stories (*Abschied* 108; my translation).[10]

---

9   »da muß er sich ausdrücklich als Einzelner konstituieren und sich die Innerlichkeit erschaffen, um hier standzuhalten«

10 »Es braucht ein gewisses Maß an Schlamperei, die durch die Kollision der regierenden Gewalten entsteht, um diesen Freiraum zu haben; ein Minimum an Chaos ist die Bedingung der Möglichkeit der Individualität.«

Although the Colbert persona creates this free space by using the structures inherent in parody and the maintenance of news stories, the show stops short of elucidating how this process might work for recipients.

In unison with Marquard's prerequisite of identity formation being minimal chaos in the process of colliding stories, Halbertal and Koren suggest that when multiple identities coincide within one self, the emphasis should shift »from identity synthesis to identity coherence« (58). Monotheism created the situation in which individuality shines, in that it posed a narratological threat to the individual (cf. Marquard, *Abschied* 108). Yet, as just over three quarters of the U.S. population prescribe to religions that place narrative restrictions over identity, i.e. a good Christian would not engage in sodomy, changes to social mores in the United States are creating situations where individuals are neither able to adhere to popular monomyths in the form of religion nor to reconcile their identities within their cultural frameworks.[11] The 21st-century citizen is subject to the age of the polymyth, a time in which one can find many social forces in the form of stories vying for prominence within that entity we call the self.

Halbertal and Koren's study concerning identity formation among gay and lesbian Orthodox Jews found that these opposing selves neither synthesize nor find a resolution regarding their differences. Instead there is a »dialogical process of ever-intensifying communication and deepening mutual understanding [that] itself takes on the dimensions of a primary identification that creates the possibility for their [Orthodox Jewish *and* gay or lesbian identities'] viable coexistence« (42). Though the Colbert persona does not at all strive for identity coherence or even a viable coexistence, the common interpretation of *TCR* as satire does not allow for this dialogical process to arise. Instead, this erroneous interpretation grafts a net of monomytic coherence over the Colbert persona and results in a satirist who occupies the clear position of a liberal, who, for background texts, utilizes only those narratives stemming from the conservative right to ridicule. However, this is clearly not the case, as the Colbert persona does in fact utilize self-constitutive narratives from all over the political spectrum that do not coalesce into a simple, singular self that is free of

---

11 Cf. Raggatt; Halbertal and Koren; Cohler and Hammack.

troubles, despite the Colbert persona's grand and delusional efforts to do so.[12]

To counter cultural desire for an authentic, singular self, psychologist Hubert Hermans proposes the term the »dialogical self,« or a self that is intrinsically interwoven with history and culture, with time and space (»Mixing« 25). The dialogical self can be described as a constellation of self-positions, both internal, i.e. me as optimistic, me as sad, me as confident, and external self-positions, i.e. me the son, me the teacher, me the stranger and in this society of the self all of the self-positions are in constant dialogue. Working as a mini-society, there will be some characters in this constellation that might be bombastic and others that might be withdrawn. Relating to the example of gay and lesbian Orthodox Jews, the resultant conflicting selves come to represent the »discontinuous self,« though these incongruent selves, through dialogue, or in a process of ever-intensifying communication, »remain part of the same continuous self« (Hermans, »Construction« 100). He writes further that the »I fluctuates among different and even opposed positions, and has the capacity to imaginatively endow each position with a voice so that dialogical relations between positions can be established« (Hermans, »Construction« 100-01). By subsuming the narratives and voices of other news pundits, what the Colbert persona comes to medially embody is Hermans's neologism of the dialogical self. Yet this self that is constituted by contrasting narratives and voices continues to be interpreted by news media, academics, and Colbert's own megalomania alike through the visor of a singular self. Is Colbert really just a liberal satirizing conservative mores? Aside from the fact that it does not differentiate between Colbert the actor and Colbert the persona, it is thus not surprising that one of the few empirical studies conducted concerning *TCR* encountered problems interpreting its data. In trying to analyze how political ideology effects one's perception of comedy shows, and using an interpretation strategy labeled »biased processing,« or seeing what one wishes to see, to analyze the survey results, LaMarre, Landreville, and Beam are unable to ascertain if

---

12 The troubled self is also a running theme in the show's ›Formidable Opponent‹ segments, where the conservative Colbert persona often squares off with a liberal Colbert persona, where both represent facets of the same persona.

biased processing completely negates the perception of humor among those who think he [Colbert] genuinely means what he says [Is he really a conservative?] [...] or simply alters their perception of who the joke targets are. [...] Stated differently, it is unknown whether conservatives who engage in biased processing fail to see the humor at all. (219)

LaMarre, Landreville, and Beam assume the position that *TCR* is a satire, and that it's host, satirist Stephen Colbert, employs deadpan satire, meaning he always remains in character, which results in a type of ambiguous humor that both conservatives and liberals are able to interpret for themselves and enjoy (cf. 226). *TCR*'s parody of the American news media system and of singular notions of selfhood become themselves suppressed by the monomyth that *TCR* is a satire, while the dialogicality and polymyth the show presents are depluralized and displaced to the periphery. Parody, Hutcheon writes, »can call into question the temptation toward the monolithic in modern theory« (116), yet, taking *TCR* as a case study, parody does not have to be interpreted that way. As parodic elements fall victim to parochial interpretation and as viewers struggle to decode and come to terms with the Colbert persona's representation of the dialogical self, satire, according to many views on *TCR*, becomes the monolithic body of interpretation with which parody is monomythically consumed. Satire becomes the vehicle with which the media-induced multiplicity of partial and fragmented selves found on *TCR* is moulded together, transforming the Colbert persona into a singular, rational, authentic, presumably *liberal* self.

WORKS CITED

Andrews, Wyatt. »Sotomayor Controversy.« *CBS Evening News.* 29 May 2009.

Ansolabehere, Stephen, Roy Behr, and Shanto Iyengar. *The Media Game: American Politics in the Television Age.* New York, NY: Macmillan, 1993.

Aust, Charles F. »Factors in the Appeal of News.« *Communication and Emotion: Essays in Honor of Dolf Zillmann.* Ed. Jennings Bryant, David Roskos-Ewoldsen, and Joanne Cantor. London: Lawrence Erlbaum Associates, 2003. 511-25.

Ben-Porat, Ziva. »Method in Madness: Notes on the Structure of Parody, Based on MAD TV Satires.« *Poetics Today* 1.1/2 (1979): 245-72.

Bennett, Lance, Regina G. Lawrence, and Steven Livingston. *When the Press Fails: Political Power and the News Media from Iraq to Katrina.* Chicago, Il: U of Chicago P, 2007.

Berg, Jan. »Techniken der Medialen Authentifizierung Jahrhunderte vor der Erfindung des ›Dokumentarischen.‹« *Die Einübung des Dokumentarischen Blicks: Fiction Film und Non Fiction Film zwischen Wahrheitsanspruch und Expressiver Sachlichkeit 1895-1945.* Ed. Ursula von Keitz and Kay Hoffmann. Marburg: Schüren, 2001. 51-71.

Bryant, Jennings, and Peter Vorderer, eds. *Psychology of Entertainment.* London: Lawrence Erlbaum Associates, 2006.

Colbert, Stephen. Interview by Chris Cocoran. »A Conversation with Stephen Colbert.« *Harvard University Institute of Politics.* 1 Dec. 2006. Web. 10 Oct. 2011. http://www.iop.harvard.edu/Multimedia-Center/All-Videos/A-Conversation-With-Steven-Colbert2

Colbert, Stephen, et al. *I am America (And so Can You!).* New York, NY: Grand Central Publishing Hatchette Book Group, 2007.

Cohen, Jonathan. »Audience Identification with Media Characters.« Bryant and Vorderer 183-94.

Cohler, Bertram J., and Phillip L. Hammack. »Making a Gay Identity: Life Story and the Construction of a Coherent Self.« McAdams, Josselson, and Lieblich 151-73.

Dowd, Maureen. »America's Anchors: Jon Stewart and Stephen Colbert Faked It until They Made It. Now They May Truly Be the Most Trusted Names in News.« *The Rolling Stone.* 31 Oct. 2006. Web. 14 Jan. 2008. http://www.rollingstone.com/news/coverstory/jon_stewart_stephen_colbert americas_anchors/page/1

Eagleton, Terry. *The Idea of Culture.* Oxford: Blackwell, 2000.

»Episode 1001.« *The Colbert Report with Stephen Colbert.* Comedy Central. 17 Oct. 2005.

»Episode 3028.« *The Colbert Report with Stephen Colbert.* Comedy Central. 1 Mar. 2007.

»Episode 5096.« *The Colbert Report with Stephen Colbert.* Comedy Central. 20 July 2009.

Fairclough, Norman. *Media Discourse.* London: Edward Arnold, 1995.

Halbertal, Tova Hartman, and Irit Koren. »Between ›Being‹ and ›Doing‹: Conflict and Coherence in the Identity Formation of Gay and Lesbian Orthodox Jews.« McAdams, Josselson, and Lieblich 37-62.

Hermans, Hubert J.M. »The Construction and Reconstruction of the Dialogical Self.« *Journal of Constructivist Psychology* 16 (2003): 89-130.

——. »Mixing and Moving Cultures Require a Dialogical Self.« *Human Development* 44 (2001): 24-28.

Hutcheon, Linda. *A Theory of Parody: The Teachings of Twentieth-Century Art Forms.* 1985. Urbana, IL: U of Illinois P, 2000.

King, Larry. Interview. »Interview with Stephen Colbert.« *Larry King Live.* CNN. 11 Oct. 2007.

Kiremidjian, David. *A Study of Modern Parody: James Joyce's* Ulysses, *Thomas Mann's* Doctor Faustus. New York, NY: Garland, 1985.

LaMarre, Heather L., Kristen D. Landreville, and Michael A. Beam. »The Irony of Satire: Political Ideology and the Motivation to See What You Want to See in *The Colbert Report.*« *International Journal of Press/Politics* 14.2 (2009): 212-31.

Maddow, Rachel. »Maddow Challenges Buchanan on Race.« *The Rachel Maddow Show.* MSNBC. 16 July 2009.

Marquard, Odo. *Abschied vom Prinzipiellen: Philosophische Studien.* Ditzingen: Reclam, 1986.

——. *Philosophie des Stattdessen.* Stuttgart: Reclam, 2000.

McAdams, Dan P., Ruthellen Josselson, and Amia Lieblich, eds. *Identity and Story: Creating Self in Narrative.* Washington, DC: APA, 2006.

»Megalomania.« *Oxford English Dictionary Online.* Nov. 2010. Oxford UP. n.d. Web. 19 Mar. 2011. http://oxforddictionaries.com/definition/megalomania

Mnookin, Seth. »The Man in the Irony Mask.« *Vanity Fair.* Oct. 2007. Web. 15 Aug. 2011. http://www.vanityfair.com/culture/features/2007/10/colbert200710

Ogborn, Jane, and Peter Buckroyd. *Satire.* Cambridge: Cambridge UP, 2001.

O'Reilly, Bill. »Stephen Colbert Enters the No Spin Zone.« *The O'Reilly Factor.* Fox News. 19 Jan. 2007.

——. »Supreme Court Celebration.« *The O'Reilly Factor*. Fox News. 27 May 2009.

Parks, Gregory S., and Shayne Jones. »›Nigger‹: A Critical Race Realist Analysis of the N-word Within Hate Crimes Law.« *The Journal of Criminal Law & Criminology* 98.4 (2008): 1305-52.

Raggatt, Peter T.F. »Multiplicity and Conflict in the Dialogical Self: A Life-Narrative Approach.« McAdams, Josselson, and Lieblich 15-36.

Rosenstiel, Tom. »Ideological News Sources: Who Watches and Why – Americans Spending More Time Following the News.« *Pew Research Center for the People and the Press. Online-Only*. 12 Sept. 2010. Web. 18 Apr. 2011. http://www.people-press.org/files/legacy-pdf/652.pdf

Schiller, Aaron Allen, ed. *Stephen Colbert and Philosophy: I am Philosophy (And so Can You)*. Chicago, IL: Open Court, 2009.

Stelter, Brian. »Comedy Central's Satirists To Return Despite Strike.« *The New York Times*. 21 Dec. 2007. Web. 22 May 2011. http://query.nytimes.com/gst/fullpage.html?res=9D02E3DC153BF 932A15751C1A9619C8B63

Stanley, Alessandra. »Bringing out the Absurdity of the News.« *The New York Times*. 25 Oct. 2005. Web. 22 May 2011. http://www.ny times.com/2005/10/25/arts/television/25watc.html

Wirth, Werner. »Involvement.« Bryant and Vorderer 199-213.

Authentic Bodies

Genome(s) vs. Gender Norms in *Oryx and Crake,*
The Year of the Flood, and *BioShock*

SVEN SCHMALFUSS

Science fiction is never intended to be an authentic representation of our world. Science fiction is a thought experiment. Sci-fi authors pick up contemporary socio-political issues and relocate them in a what-if situation. They create a world coherent with or mainly focused on the topic at hand. As with a scientific experiment in a laboratory, most of the disturbing influences from the outside, which do not affect the main issue, are excluded (cf. Degani-Raz). Such stories are not snapshots of society but carefully crafted worlds in which to observe the developments and interactions of an idea. Science fiction can create an optimistic, hope-inducing world of tomorrow or can serve as a warning of the possible outcome of today's actions. Thus the speculative fiction set in a near future of Margaret Atwood's two »simultaniels«[1] *Oryx and Crake* (2003) and *The Year of the Flood* (2009) or the retro-futurism of Irrational Games's[2] *BioShock* (2007) present us with encapsulated worlds in which to observe the relations between genetic engineering and the perception of a gendered body as authentic.[3]

---

1 Atwood calls her two novels »simultaniels« rather than pre- or sequels, since both narratives focus on roughly the same time frame (Q TV).

2 Irrational Games was renamed 2K Boston shortly before the release of the game but acquired its original name back in 2010 (cf. »Brief History«).

3 The *BioShock* franchise comprises Irrational Games's *BioShock*, two re-imaginations of parts of the first game for mobile phones (*BioShock* devel-

The (human) body and its boundaries, quite often in a gendered perspective, is one of the staple topics of science fiction. The genre has always been interested in the question of what constitutes an authentic body. Can artificially created bodies be authentic, or do bodies have to be natural, at least to a certain degree, to be authentic? And if so, what should be the threshold between a machine or a monster and a human? Is a form of bodily authenticity at all possible in a world inscribing norms and rules on our bodies? Must we see the dissolved monolithic body as a threat or can we also see it as a possibility, especially to tread gendered grounds outside of the essentialist dichotomy?

The Marxist-Feminist Donna Haraway uses the cyborg, a mythical creature developed in science fiction stories, as a powerful metaphor for a new ›monstrous aesthetic‹ to tackle this dichotomy. In the following pages I want to discuss the above-mentioned novels by Margaret Atwood and the game *BioShock* as parables on the dangers and possibilities involved in genetic engineering for a new form of ›authentic‹ cyborg bodies from a gender perspective.

THE INFORMATICS OF DOMINATION OR LIBERATION

Information has become one of the defining *über*-metaphors of life in the beginning of the 21st century. Our entire existence is structured and dominated by information and informatics. However, the metaphor of information is not only limited to computer-mediated social interaction, but even our conception of biology is shaped and defined

---

oped by Starwave and *BioShock 3D* developed by Studio Tridev), 2K Marin's *BioShock 2* (2010) together with its viral marketing campaign *Something in the Sea* (www.somethinginthesea.com), and Irrational Games's forthcoming *BioShock Infinite*. I will focus in the following on the original game, as it represents Irrational Games's creative intentions for the underwater city of Rapture. *BioShock 2* is both a pre- and a sequel to the original game, thus adding quite substantially to Rapture's history. For the sake of the argument's coherence and for space restrictions, a discussion of these new aspects unfortunately has to be postponed. *Infinite*, from what is known at the time of writing, presents a whole new story, set in a different time (1912) and place (the airborne city Columbia).

by the field of genetics, by the implied information stored in the genes. Donna Haraway summarized these changes back in 1985 in her essay »A Cyborg Manifesto« as a »movement from an organic, industrial society to a polymorphous, information system – from all work to all play, a deadly game« (523). She called this system the »informatics of domination« (524), which, in her eyes, will succeed the old capitalist system as the means of exploitation.[4] In her eyes,

communications sciences and modern biologies are constructed by a common move – *the translation of the world into a problem of coding*, a search for a common language in which all resistance to instrumental control disappears and all heterogeneity can be submitted to disassembly, reassembly, investment and exchange. (524; emphasis in the original)

This translation is the actual core of genetics. The assumed basis for life in general has moved from a deity beyond our perception to two complementary base pairs and their combinations. This offers at least the possibility of a glance behind life's veil, of understanding the code from which we are all created. The genetic code and the chance factor of evolution have driven all mythical powers from our bodies, now conceived as biomechanical machines. Furthermore, this translation into code allows us humans to become gods, as code is a form of language and therefore can be learned and used in powerful ways, or as Haraway phrases it: »perfect communication, [...] the one code that translates all meaning perfectly, the central dogma of phallogocentrism« (532). Haraway uses the term »phallogocentrism« to describe the combination of a (patriarchal) economy of power with a specific symbolic system, which can also be found in contemporary genetics. Most fields of genetics, and especially genetic engineering, are still high-end technologies, mostly restricted to larger corporations or universities. Companies have genetically modified crops patented and licensed, thus increasing their market shares, revenues, and economic influence. As many other science fiction stories, *Oryx and Crake*, *The*

---

4   Haraway actually refers to the »informatics of domination« as the successor of »white capitalist patriarchy« (523): »The actual situation of women is their integration/exploitation into a world system of production/reproduction and communication called the informatics of domination« (524). I took the liberty of broadening her focus.

Year of the Flood, and *BioShock* pick up on these real scenarios and enlarge them with companies monopolizing genetic technologies and a civilization suffering as a consequence.[5] These fictional firms sell information – applied information, corporealized information – and the right to use this information. The societies depicted in the novels and the game are completely dependent on genetic engineering, to the extent that the companies controlling the genetic economy also control the respective societies. They accumulate political power not through the official channels but through their economic influence on body politics. They sell the best, or best-advertised genetic products, so people start buying and using their products. The society's assumed ›moral‹ threshold to the level of bodily alteration is lowered with every product, and thus society ends up being totally dependent on these companies. Atwood and Irrational Games both draw dystopian connections between genetics and drug trafficking. The genetic economies in the novels and the game have a small group of producers on the upper end, who can afford a secluded life of luxury, and a huge group of users, who live in dismay and try to satisfy their basic needs. This is even heightened in *BioShock*, where characters who have not yet turned completely crazy can mostly only be heard over the radio or be seen through windows. Roaming the halls and walkways of Rapture are the insane Splicers, who have lost all control over their body through their need for ADAM, the game's genetic currency. ADAM is a form of trans-genetic matter that destroys native cells and replaces them with unstable stem versions, thus allowing for numerous bodily transformations like psychokinetic abilities (cf. audio diary »Brigid Tenenbaum: ADAM Explained«).[6] Rapture, though built on an ideology to end all exploitation, has become the site of an enormous system

---

5   Margaret Atwood dislikes the idea of her novels being described as science fiction, as she sees this genre linked to stories of space travel and alien encounters. She categorizes her novels as being speculative fiction (cf. for example, Rothschild). *BioShock* can more specifically be filed under the header of retro-futuristic biopunk/dieselpunk (cf. Wikipedia; ›Piecraft‹ and Ottens; Taylor). I will return to the discussion of the novels and the game as entities of the biopunk genre further on.

6   All audio diaries can be accessed through the game's menu, once found by the player. A collection of all diaries with transcripts can be found under »*BioShock* Audio Diaries« on the *BioShock Wiki*.

of slavery and addiction, even including an element of gendered exploitation in the form of the Little Sisters.

Donna Haraway offers a way out of this asymmetric power structure by turning the informatics of domination into an informatics of liberation through a self-confident reappropriation of the system. She uses the fictional concept of the cyborg, a hybrid life form with biological and cybernetic elements, and turns it into a metaphor for political struggle in this new age of oppression. Cyborg politics are the only way to counter the aforementioned phallogocentrism. They

> insist on noise and advocate pollution, rejoicing in the illegitimate fusion of animal and machine. These are the couplings which make Man and Woman so problematic, subverting the structure of desire, the force imagined to generate language and gender, and so subverting the structure and modes of reproduction of ›Western‹ identity, of nature and culture, of mirror and eye, slave and master, body and mind. ›We‹ did not originally choose to be cyborgs, but choice grounds a liberal politics and epistemology that imagines the reproduction of individuals before the wider replications of ›texts.‹ (Haraway 532)

The cyborg, in Haraway's terms, defies the distinction into two separate spheres of nature and culture and reverses the notion that there is an origin (in nature) to which we can return. Whereas the hegemonic powers create a cloned sheep that looks like a sheep, the cyborg wears its fracturedness and constructedness on the outside, even seeing it as the main source of its political cause.[7] The cyborg is a monster in so far as it is inauthentic from a naturalistic perspective – it does not comply with the hegemonic aesthetic norms – but is proud of this status, as it sees authenticity only in the acceptance of the constructed state of being, which is always an interpretation and reinscription of biology (cf. Haraway 532-33). The cyborg thus creates its own, fragmented form of aestheticism. Haraway conceptualizes the cyborg in a highly metaphorical way, to include as many ›cyborg‹-situations as possible.

As I have argued elsewhere, there is a quite obvious application of Haraway's concept which offers insights into the construction of a

---

7   The sex and gender of cyborgs is often ambiguous, even multiple (cf. the quote from Haraway above). For simplicity's sake, I will always refer to them with neutral gender.

(gendered) gamer identity in/with digital games (cf. Schmalfuß). *Bio-Shock* can be seen as a prime example for the possibilities and limitations of the application of a cyborg entity encompassing both the player and their in-game avatar.[8] Players and their representation in the game world, i.e. their avatar, are cybernetically linked through two interconnected input-feedback-loops of controller-commands and visual realization (cf. Schmalfuß 218-20). The connection is even heightened in first-person shooters like *BioShock*, as the avatar's and the player's point-of-view are merged (cf. Mosel 70-71). Except for the ending, in *BioShock* this perspective is maintained even in the pre-rendered cut-scenes, so as to create a far-reaching emotional bonding between the player and the game's protagonist Jack. As will be seen further on, this bond is used very effectively to ponder on the relationship between player and avatar, while other parts of the game hinder this arousal of cyborg awareness, along Haraway's lines. But first I want to focus on three even more obvious forms of cyborgs, the end-products of the genetic splicing in the two fictional worlds and the gendered implications of their creation.

EVERY BOY AND EVERY GIRL, SPLICE UP YOUR LIFE

Atwood's unnamed city on the eastern coast of the USA and *Bio-Shock*'s Rapture are both highly satirical dystopias of a world apocalyptically transformed through bioengineering. Whereas Atwood's catastrophe is global and decimates a large portion of humanity, the ›downfall‹ in *BioShock* is limited to the underwater city of Rapture, and only affects the rest of the world if the player acts, in the game's terms, unethically.[9] The novels and the game therefore can be seen as

---

8 As a consequence it would be more appropriate to talk about the player/avatar-continuum throughout the essay. For reasons of readability I will only address the element relevant for the respective argument. Still, it should be kept in mind that the players choose the avatar's actions while they are experiencing the game through the avatar's eyes.

9 *BioShock* features a system of moral choices which is an element of the game mechanics and influences the outcome of the game's storyline. If the player chooses to harvest the Little Sisters, Jack takes over control of the

part of the science fiction sub-genre biopunk. Where its namesake cyberpunk revolves around the collision of biology and cybernetics, biopunk focuses on the biological embodiment of informatics (cf. Taylor §4). Biopunk stories are not about the relation between organic bodies and machines or mechanical parts, but they treat bodies as biological machines that can be reworked. A main topic therefore is the question what constitutes an authentic body and what does not. »A typically distinguishing feature of biopunk is its willingness to stretch […] aspects of the digital zeitgeist to their limits. […] biopunk refashions sentiments of unease with physical immediacy to take the form of nauseating disgust with the biological *per se*« (Taylor §15; emphasis in the original). This disgusting element is exemplified in *BioShock*'s horrendously disfigured Splicers (cf. *BioShock: Breaking* 11-12), which are the game's main enemies, and in Atwood's monstrous creations like the ChickieNobs, huge, sea anemone-shaped chickens consisting only of breast meat (cf. *Oryx* 202). These examples would point to a rather easy distinction between what is seen as an authentic and thus normatively ›good‹ body and what as a ›bad,‹ because inauthentic, monstrous body. Yet, the novels and the game allow for this clear-cut dichotomy only in specific ways. More often, the position of these newly created life forms in the narrative worlds is portrayed in far more complex ways. This becomes obvious when we consider the two men mostly responsible for the respective disasters the novels and the game portray: their main antagonists. Both universes center on paradisiacal dreams of self-proclaimed rational idealists and their ideas spinning out of control and into mayhem. Both Crake's, whose actual name is Glenn, and Andrew Ryan's original plan is to create a perfect society through the extraction and refinement of the world's best elements (which are not confined to human elements), and shutting the rest of the corrupted world out. Ryan sought refuge in a complete exile from the rest of the world, which was heading from World

---

Splicers and attempts to conquer the whole world through the use of nuclear warheads. I will come back to this moralizing end-sequence. Through this system the game designers tried to create a closer link between the players' decisions and the influence they have on the world and thus on their avatar. This ultimately fails, as it is based on purely aesthetical premises, only affecting the video after the game, and has no ›real‹ in-game repercussions.

War II into the Cold War.[10] He persuaded some of the world's best and brightest minds to come to Rapture by offering them a place to freely – in an extreme libertarian definition of the word – follow their trades. Crake, as becomes evident from Snowman's memories, would never leave anything to chance in building a new and ›better‹ society.[11] Never one to give in to passions, he wants to keep the reins in his own hands. He literally builds his new race, later named Crakers by Oryx (cf. *Oryx* 311), from the genetic material he considers the logically best for a better humanity, regardless of the gene's origin, be it from humans, other animals, or even plants (cf. *Oryx* 302-06). The rest of humanity Crake plans to eliminate by means of what he sees as its own vices and immorality. He creates a pill, BlyssPluss, that:

a) would protect the user against all known sexually transmitted diseases, fatal, inconvenient, or merely unsightly;

b) would provide an unlimited supply of libido and sexual prowess, coupled with a generalized sense of energy and well-being, thus reducing the frustration and blocked testosterone that led to jealousy and violence, and eliminating feelings of low self-worth;

c) would prolong youth. (Oryx 294)

Apart from these effects, which are publicly advertised, the pill has two other effects. The first, which Crake reveals to Jimmy in their first discussion of the pill, is that BlyssPluss acts »as a sure-fire one-time-does-it-all birth-control pill, for male and female alike, thus automatically lowering the population level« (*Oryx* 294). This allows for the pill to be marketed effectively to political authorities to lower population density in certain areas. If this effect has to be reversed in other areas, the components of the pill can be altered (cf. *Oryx* 294). Apart from this morally already very dubious form of reducing population numbers, BlyssPluss has another effect, one even Oryx and Jimmy

---

10 This is a direct link to *Atlas Shrugged* by Ayn Rand and this is not the only connection. Ryan especially shares Rand's Objectivist ideology. Unfortunately these influences cannot be discussed here (cf. fn. 20).

11 Snowman is the name Jimmy gives himself when he shows himself to the Crakers for the first time. I will refer to him as Snowman in events after this event and as Jimmy in events happening before this, or in events related to the Gardeners (as he is known to Ren as Jimmy).

only find out when the disease is already rapidly spreading. The pill contains a genetically modified, fatal virus, timed to break out at nearly the same time all over the world, thus causing a maximum of social upheaval and preventing the creation of an antidote for as long as possible (cf. *Oryx* 346-47). Crake's choice of words (»blocked testosterone«) is not only indicative of the product's main target group, men, but it also sheds light on his own conceptions of sexuality, which are self-centered and full of machismo. Through the BlyssPluss pill Crake plans to clear the slate for his own new and ›better‹ version of humanity, the Crakers. Still, ›humanity 1.0‹ proves to be far more resilient than Crake had anticipated. Especially in the countryside but also in urban spaces, people survive the »Waterless Flood,« as the God's Gardeners call the epidemic in accordance with their gospel (*Flood* passim). What Crake achieves, is to throw the whole world into a state of anarchy. All political systems and infrastructures are destroyed. The survivors team up in small groups to fight for survival against the forces of nature (including animals designed by humans to serve specific commercial ends, like *pigoons* or *liobams*, which are now roaming the streets freely) or even other humans. In this violent environment, it is more likely for the peaceful Crakers to become extinct than for the ›older‹ humankind.[12]

This peacefulness is part of their genetic programming. Crake's aim in designing ›his children‹ is the eradication of all human misery. They are built to withstand the hardships of a post-climatic-change society devoid of any of the ›harmful‹ inventions of civilization. They feature »a UV-resistant skin, a built-in insect-repellent, an unprecedented ability to digest unrefined plant material,« and an advanced immune system (*Oryx* 304). Their brains are genetically altered to eradicate the »destructive features« which Crake believes to be »responsible for the world's current illnesses« (*Oryx* 305). Racism is circumvented by the Crakers not being able to register skin color. The neurological structures necessary to create hierarchies have been removed. As they are dependent neither on hunting nor on agriculture, Crake hopes that they will not develop a concept of territoriality. And through a rationalized system of sexuality and reproduction even jeal-

---

12 Both novels are open-ended, thus denying an authoritative answer to the Crakers' possibility of survival.

ousy is supposed to be erased (cf. *Oryx* 165). Crake's hopes do not stop here:

[A]s there would never be anything for these people to inherit, there would be no family trees, no marriages, and no divorces. They were perfectly adjusted to their habitat, so they would never have to create houses or tools or weapons, or, for that matter, clothing. They would have no need to invent any harmful symbolisms, such as kingdoms, icons, gods, or money. Best of all, they recycled their own excrement. (Oryx 305)

Crake tries to eradicate the »G-spot in the brain,« as he calls God, because »God is a cluster of neurons« (*Oryx* 157). Crake is a »numbers person« (*Oryx* 74), a man of the natural sciences; for him metaphysics, symbolism, and especially emotions are the root of all evil (cf. *Oryx* 361). As with the timing of the genocide, Crake takes a risk in the design of the Crakers and their education. He cannot carve all of the »G-spot« from the Crakers' brains, as they would either turn into zombies or psychopaths (cf. *Oryx* 157) and he leaves them in the hands of Jimmy (cf. *Oryx* 328-29), who can only conceptualize his world in words and metaphysics, not logic and numbers. The Crakers approach everything in a curious, innocent, friendly, and child-like manner. Snowman, as the only creature in their small cosmos they can converse with, is their center for advice, their guide. Even though he recalls Crake's warnings against symbolism now and then, Jimmy's first words to the Crakers are already a lie: »My name is Snowman« (*Oryx* 348). Jimmy wants to leave his old life behind and thus creates a persona for himself. Together with the questions raised during the Crakers' exodus from Paradice, his lie spawns a web of new lies to build a coherent and sound explanation for the existence of the Crakers, Snowman, and their surroundings. Snowman creates a complex theology centered on Oryx and Crake, with him acting as a messenger. He borrows heavily from different religions but he also needs to incorporate what Oryx and Crake have left behind. Oryx, who acts as a teacher for the Crakers in their Paradice habitat, explains all the plants and animals to them, so they associate these areas with her (cf. *Oryx* 309). She also tells them that they were made by Crake (cf. *Oryx* 311). This lays the basis for two distinct spheres in the newly emerging theology: the Children of Crake, i.e. the Crakers, and the Children of Oryx, i.e. the other animals and plants (cf. *Oryx* 96). With the Crakers' erection of an idol of Snowman, the gendered dichotomy between masculine culture and feminine nature is revitalized in the new theology (cf. *Oryx* 360-61).

An asymmetric gender hierarchy is restricted not only to a meta-physical level. Crake exploits female bodies for reproductive purpos-es, which is central to his genetic design of the new race. From his perspective of minimizing disputes between the individuals of the group, this form of organization seems logic. In the end, this leaves the whole upbringing of the children to the women and lets men off the hook. Crake changes so many aspects of the Crakers' genome, even far-ranging ones like the diet-change from omnivore to herbivore, but he leaves the basics of the reproduction cycle untouched. He removes all pleasurable aspects of sexuality to minimize jealousy and regret and he disguises, through the Crakers' group-matings, who the father of a child is, so as to eradicate family trees and inheritance (cf. *Oryx* 305). All these elements remove nearly all anxieties for heterosexual males. Women, on the other hand, do not partake of this liberation. Through the cycle of heat female Crakers go through every three years, they are more slaves to their wombs than their human counter-parts (cf. *Oryx* 164). This becomes evident in the actual sexual en-counter. Sexual behavior is only triggered when a woman is in heat. Her abdomen will turn blue and she emits certain pheromones. The men pick up on this and start a rather complicated courtship ritual. The woman elects four men and they retreat to a reclusive space. The other men's libido is automatically regulated down and they return to their normal lives. The ›fivesome‹ start to have sex, with the men taking turns, until the woman is pregnant and the blue of her belly fades. At this point the men also lose their sex-drive. As these sexual acts can take hours, Crake has equipped the women with extra muscles and skin in their vulvas to sustain these acts (cf. *Oryx* 164-65). Snowman tries to rationalize this passion-free take on sexuality with the ruling out of explicit sexual violence against women. »No more *No means yes*, [...] [n]o more prostitution, no sexual abuse of children, no hag-gling over the price, no pimps, no sex slaves. No more rape« (*Oryx* 165; emphasis in the original). Snowman, who, as Jimmy, has taken part and enjoyed all means of sexual exploitation of women, seems to have found a new moral high ground since his messianic call to guide the Crakers. Still, this observation is true only on an individual level. No singular Craker man will take sexual advantage of, or exploit a

Craker woman. The sexual hierarchy has been moved by Crake onto a more basic, biological level. Still, the whole description of the group-mating matches a gang-bang from a pornographic film or even a gang-rape rather than the mating behavior of animals. This rape serves no personal lust or power-cravings but a genetically built-in reproductive drive based on a strong gender asymmetry.

Atwood uses the Crakers to display harsh criticism of morally un-fettered genetics. Still she refrains from describing them as monsters of any sort. All the ›monsters‹ in the two novels are ›normal‹ humans, the Painballers in *The Year of the Flood*, for example, or even Crake and the other natural scientists. The Crakers in all their inauthenticity, in their aggravated form of sexist gender ideals, in their embodied ef-ficiency, create a new form of innocence which needs to be protected. They are cyborgs but not yet in an empowered sense of the word. This is what they learn through Snowman and the conclusion of *The Year of the Flood* leaves open to what end the Crakers will use his teach-ings.

Rapture's economy of genome alteration is grounded in a similar system of exploitation of female members of society, the Little Sisters. *BioShock*'s Brigid Tenenbaum sends the protagonist Jack on the quest to restore the Little Sisters' innocence, allowing them to flee their state of slavery (for which Tenenbaum is responsible) and live a free life. The game, as will be seen later on, also allows the avatar to encounter the Little Sisters in the ultimate form of exploitation, by killing and harvesting them. All Little Sisters roaming Rapture are accompanied by a (male) Big Daddy, their protector, while they extract ADAM from corpses. Throughout the early conceptual phases of *BioShock*, the pairs of gatherers and protectors were not gendered. The gatherers were slugs, native to the deep sea (cf. *Welcome*; *BioShock: Breaking* 40-42), which collected genetic material from corpses and could turn this material, through digestion, into ADAM. Irrational Games had to realize that using a slug undermined the system of moral choice and the notion of a bonding between the gatherer and the protector – who had been »a guy in a diving suit« for roughly the whole production time – as »nobody cares about a slug.« The more humanoid the char-acters became, the better the bonding seemed to work. So when Robert Waters, Irrational Games's concept artist, came up with a picture of an »incredibly creepy looking little girl,« the team knew they had found a gatherer to whom the player could have an emotional attachment. Irrational Games was aware of the fact that they were challenging a boundary of moral norms, at least in digital games' terms, with these little girls and their function in Rapture (*Welcome*).

The exploitation of the Little Sisters can on some level be compared to Oryx's history of being forced to participate in child-pornography (cf. *Oryx* 138-44). The young girls' innocence is willfully destroyed to cater for capitalist greed. Oryx has to participate in sexual encounters on video, to be sold over the internet to a society which is always in search of the latest extremes. *BioShock*'s Little Sisters are symbiotically joined with the sea slugs Tenenbaum found to mass-produce ADAM (cf. audio diary »Brigid Tenenbaum: Mass Producing ADAM«), which can be purchased and turned into Plasmids, i.e. genetic alterations of the body.[13] The Little Sisters are the key factor in the genetic economy that drives Rapture. The child-porn actresses struggle to keep up their childhood against the invading powers of the porn-industry, be it even in a way as crude as giggling at the sight of a porn-actor losing his erection (cf. *Oryx* 140). The traumatic, psychological effects of the situation are also evident in Oryx's retelling of her story to Jimmy. She leaves out the events that took place in front of the camera. The game's Little Sisters unconsciously cling to a quite similar final straw. »Even with those things implanted in their bellies, they are still children. They play, and sing. Sometimes they look at me [Tenenbaum], and they don't stop. Sometimes they smile« (audio diary »Brigid Tenenbaum: Functional Children«). They see the Big Daddies, to which they are genetically bound through pheromones, not only as their protectors but also as some kind of playmate: they lead them around Rapture, pointing out items which have captured their interest.[14] They even have a pet-name for the Big Daddies: »Mr. Bubbles.«

The Big Daddies, on the other hand, are huge, hulking, tank-like creatures purpose-built to protect the Little Sisters. They once were humans but their skin and organs are directly grafted into the suit (cf. audio diary »Dr. Suchong: Cheap Son of a Bitch«), a process which

---

13 The Freudian link implied in the sea slugs seems obvious.

14 Tenenbaum mentions this in a radio message to the avatar when he enters an area called »Little Wonders.« A transcript can be found on the *BioShock* Wiki, along with all other radio messages, under »Radio Messages: Point Prometheus.«

cannot be reversed (cf. audio diary »Dr. Suchong: Protector Smell«). A Big Daddy nonetheless has emotions, even though these are completely focused on the genetically imprinted bond with the Little Sisters. They sound enraged if a Splicer or the avatar attacks the gatherer. In contrast to the Little Sisters, Big Daddies ›respawn‹ to a game level. So when the avatar has ›dealt‹ with every gatherer in a level, either through harvesting or rescuing them, one or more Big Daddies will wander the halls of this area, banging on every vent, in hope for a Little Sister to climb out of it. Their grunts even sound slightly frustrated when no ›little one‹ comes to greet them. Neither the Little Sisters nor the Big Daddies, however, are complete monsters.[15] Both of them have an innocent side, comparable to the Crakers. They are crafted, inauthentic life forms which form the real basis for Rapture's economy but they both can find a new authenticity. They are an authentic representation of Rapture's inauthenticity.

This inauthentic displacement of Rapture's society is exemplified most strikingly in the level »Proving Grounds.« The area had once been a museum for natural history with exhibits of deep-sea life still adorning the walls. After Rapture's fall, the complex had been turned into a testing facility, a proving ground, for the newly developed pairs of gatherers and protectors.[16] After turning into a Big Daddy, the avatar is guided through this area by a Little Sister who has to be protected. The avatar has finally become a part of Rapture's economic system and now has to destroy it from within.

If the player acts ethically right, in the game's terms, the symbiont can be removed from all Little Sisters and they can start a new life, outside of Rapture. The Big Daddies, on the other hand, are doomed to walk the ruins of Rapture until they die. Like Andrew Ryan or Sander Cohen, Rapture's best-known artist and Ryan's main instrument of propaganda, they are so intrinsically – one might say corporeally – linked with Rapture and its ideology that they cannot escape from this decaying place.

---

15 Tenenbaum draws the comparison to the Golem and Frankenstein's creature in a radio message, which can be heard when the avatar walks into an area called »Failsafe Armored Escorts« (cf. *BioShock Wiki*, »Radio Messages: Point Prometheus«).

16 Cf. the article on »Proving Grounds« on the *BioShock Wiki*.

DR. STEINMAN'S AESTHETIC IDEALS SURGERY[17]

The inhabitants of Rapture have become addicts to ADAM, turning the whole city into a battleground as they are fighting over the scarce resources.[18] As Dr. Tenenbaum explains,

ADAM acts like a benign cancer, destroying native cells and replacing them with unstable stem versions. While this very instability is what gives it its amazing properties, it is also what causes the cosmetic and mental damage. You need more and more ADAM just to keep back the tide. From a medical standpoint, this is catastrophic. From a business standpoint, well [...] Fontaine sees the possibilities. (audio diary: »Brigid Tenenbaum: ADAM Explained«)

Genetic engineering, in the hands of all citizens, brings about the same effects as drug use. The use of ADAM leads to the need for the next shot. While the people had thought they would be improving themselves, they were actually driving themselves into bodily mutilation and mental insanity. The game delivers its socio-critical message in satirical tones: A society focused solely on self-perfection without moral, i.e. socially conscious, restraints is actually rotten to the core. According to the internal ethical logic of the game's narrative, self-improvement which is singularly powered by egoistic greed leads to degeneration. The moment a cyborg turns against its equals, it becomes a monster. This is most visible in the case of the Splicers and

---

17 For reason of space I have to restrict my focus on aesthetic body ideals, as they are pondered on in the works under scrutiny. A discussion of the links between art design and the use of music in these works to these bodily norms can be found in an extended chapter entitled »A Rupture in Rapture« in the publications-section of my website: www.svenschmalfuss.net.

18 In comparison to the Splicers, the avatar is only very limitedly influenced by the heavy use of Plasmids. The player also sees the ghosts of the people who were the involuntary DNA-donors for a Plasmid (cf. audio diary: »Bill McDonagh: Seeing Ghosts«) but is, apart from this, not affected by the same psychotic developments as the other Splicers. This might be explained by Jack's genetically engineered origin.

their deformed bodies.[19] Plastic surgery had already been an important business in Rapture before the full-fledged ADAM use started but has become far more important afterwards, to correct the negative effects the splicing had on the body. This is even expressed in the visual design of the Splicers, which is based on real bodies constructed through plastic surgery. Irrational Games used photographs taken from the website accompanying Paddy Hartley's *Project Fascade*, which show soldiers from World War I who had received horrible facial wounds and were treated by Sir Harold Gillies. This adds another layer of irony to *BioShock*'s aesthetics; whereas these soldiers received their wounds involuntarily in action and Gillies tried to reconstruct a ›normal,‹ authentic face for them to allow them to live a ›normal‹ life, the Splicers in *BioShock* mutilate themselves through their overdosing of ADAM. Gillies sought to help the soldiers but his findings built the foundation not only for reconstructive but also for modern aesthetic cosmetic surgery. Plastic surgery always refers to a certain aesthetic ideal from which the patients are thought to deviate. As they could not choose their physical features, they see them as inauthentic representations of themselves. It is the patients' wish to comply with the ideal and thus to make their body a more authentic representation of themselves. The patients are, or at least feel, criticized or even rejected by their social surroundings for the corporeal features of the body they have been born with or with which they must live after an accident. For trans-genders, plastic surgery even offers a gendered ›coming home‹ in form of a sex-change. Cosmetic surgery thus can cater for a form of cyborg authenticity as it allows patients to represent themselves authentically – as true to themselves – but it also always features the inauthentic influence of society through the application of hegemonic body ideals.

Plastic and especially aesthetic cosmetic surgery has been at the core of Rapture from the beginning. In the city's hospital district, Medical Pavilion, Dr. Steinman's Aesthetic Ideals Surgery constitutes the center area.[20] J.S. Steinman has sealed off the Medical Pavilion

---

19 *BioShock 2*'s multiplayer allows for players to experience the development of their character from a ›normal‹ human to a ›mutilated‹ and crazy Splicer.

20 This level-layout is also based on a form of architectural hierarchy. Steinman is the end-boss of this level and the surgery is his den, thus located

from the rest of the city and has turned it into a territory over which he rules. Steinman has been driven to insanity by the ADAM-assisted search for perfect beauty. He sees Aphrodite walking the halls (cf. audio diary: »Dr. Steinman: Aphrodite Walking«), who advises him to do »something about symmetry« (audio diary: »Dr. Steinman: Symmetry«). Symmetry seems to be no longer the perfect beauty ideal for Steinman. He describes the three crucified women in the triptych over his head, as one being too fat, one being too tall and the one in the middle as being too symmetrical. Steinman admires Picasso and the creativity of Cubism. In one of his audio diaries (»Dr. Steinman: Surgery's Picasso«) he asks: »Wouldn't it be wonderful if I could do with a knife what that old Spaniard did with a brush?« The Splicers living in Rapture are the result of this maniac Cubistic take on the human form. Steinman himself sees in ADAM the means to achieve his true aesthetic ends. The whole Medical Pavilion is plastered with photographs of Steinman's patients, smeared with blood and decorated with a pair of scissors as goggles. The walls and floors are also covered with his main motifs, written in blood. Most prominent of them: »ADAM denies us any excuse for not being beautiful.« With ADAM, he insists, »the flesh becomes clay« and therefore: »What excuse do we have not to sculpt, and sculpt, and sculpt, until the job is done?« (audio diary: »Dr. Steinman: Higher Standards«). ADAM leaves imagination as the final and only limit to aesthetic refinement (audio diary: »Dr. Steinman: Limits of Imagination«). According to Andrew Ryan's philosophy, even morality is no hindrance any more. Steinman sees Ryan and ADAM as the final liberators of his art:

Ryan and ADAM, ADAM and Ryan [...] all those years of study, and was I ever truly a surgeon before I met them? How we plinked away with our scalpels and toy morality. Yes, we could lop a boil here, and shave down a beak there, [...] but could we really change anything? No. But ADAM gives us the means to do it. And Ryan frees us from the phony ethics that held us back.

---

centrally to the whole level. The »Medical Pavilion« level also consists only of rooms themed by ›scary‹ medical traits, like dentistry and cosmetic surgery. The only non-medical area is the crematory. Thus it complies with typical ›ghost train‹- and dungeon-like structures of digital game levels.

Change your look, change your sex, change your race. It's yours to change, nobody else's. (audio diary: »Dr. Steinman – ADAM's Changes«)

The combination of scientific discoveries which allow for almost any form of bodily transformation and a political climate which permits the neglect of any moral implication opens up the possibility of perfect self-expression. With Steinman falling ever deeper into a maniac state of mind, it is not the patients who can express themselves through the operation but rather Steinman as the operator.[21] He longs to be a great artist, Aphrodite's lover, creating extraordinary works for which he will be remembered but he fails his own aesthetic ideals. He is never satisfied with his own work, thus spiraling ever more deeply into lunacy.

Dr. Steinman is *BioShock*'s caricature of modern cosmetic surgery. A failed, self-proclaimed artist who seeks to find a higher form of beauty but only creates monsters. In the consumerist society of Rapture he finds a willing counterpart. Most of Rapture's citizens are blinded by the bliss promised by ADAM and turn voluntarily into zombies, always craving for their next shot. Still the game's moral impetus cannot be reduced to a simple distinction between authentic natural bodies and inauthentic genetically altered bodies, as there are, apart from Ryan, Tenenbaum, and the rescued Little Sisters, nearly no unaltered bodies in the game. As much as this would create a hierarchy between these unaltered characters and their crazy opponents, this is counterbalanced through their isolated position and especially though the game's protagonist Jack.[22] He, as the game's chief moral agent, is genetically modified himself. Only if he can rid himself of Fontaine's mind-control-system and turn into a Big Daddy, he can save the Little Sisters. This depiction of the avatar as an empowered cyborg has ramifications for the cyborgian connection between player and avatar, as will be seen in the following part of this essay.

---

21 Cf. his jabbing of the corpse on his operation table during the encounter with the avatar and the audio diary which can be found on this corpse: »Dr. Steinman: Not What She Wanted.«

22 Ryan has locked himself in his office, only communicating with the outside world via radio massages. Tenenbaum is only visible to the player behind glass or on a balcony, and thus always out of reach. The rescued Little Sisters live in a safe-house Tenenbaum has built for them.

The Crakers' identity between authenticity and inauthenticity has been discussed above. During their design process, Crake, like Steinman, tries to create new aesthetics which are based on an attempt to rule out any imperfections. So the Crakers »look like retouched fashion photos, or ads for a high-priced workout program« (*Oryx* 100). The Crakers have no need for, and therefore do not wear any, clothes, which lets Crake's design decisions appear to be following an aesthetic ideal that could best be described as ›porn chic.‹ The text describes the female Crakers through Snowman's astonished eyes:

They're every known colour from deepest black to whitest white, they're various heights, but each one of them is admirably proportioned. Each is sound of tooth, smooth of skin. No ripples of fat around their waists, no bulges, no dimpled orange-skin cellulite on their thighs. No body hair, no bushiness. (*Oryx* 100)

Crake's beauty ideals are Atwood's satire of the over-sexualization of the media and especially advertising. The irony of Crake's concept is that he actually tries to create a new aesthetic standard as all Crakers will be improved in this way, and there will be no sexually driven humans left in his plan who could be attracted by these ideals. There is nothing to sell, no product, not even lust that could be exploited by these porn-aesthetics. Crake uses these beauty concepts, with which he grew up, as the basis for what he sees as a whole new conception of beauty, based on a complete tabula rasa of older, in his eyes outfashioned standards. Still he simply resurrects old, sexist ideals. This adds one more aspect to Crake's totalitarian approach to ethical improvement.

THE CIRCUS OF VALUES

In Crake's eyes humankind is rotten to the core and therefore annihilation is the only way to save Earth. Only through an all-encompassing reboot, i.e. the Crakers' ›humanity 2.0,‹ all failures of the past can be rectified. In a world with very low ethical standards for the sciences, he takes the ultimate step to eradicate humanity and start anew. In his view, the world can only be saved through the destruction of authentic humankind and its replacement with an inauthentic humanity, the

Crakers. Thus, he acts immorally to achieve what he considers as a moral end. The God's Gardeners, on the other hand, see the only hope for the world in a return to a more authentic state of coexistence with nature. They live a morally good life, seek seclusion during the »Waterless Flood« and want to set an example in moral behavior after it has ebbed. Snowman thinks he is the last human on earth and thus has to save humanity's cultural heritage. He tries to align this with his other duty, the guidance of the Crakers. By combining the task he set for himself, i.e. rescuing culture through word-keeping, with the one Crake set for him, i.e. looking after the Crakers, he introduces the Crakers to religion as it seems to be the only coherent and morally valuable system of explanation he can offer them. Jimmy is thus the missing link between Crake's nihilism and the Gardeners' spirituality. He is even turned into a quasi-deity by the Crakers when they start worshipping the idol they built of him (cf. *Oryx* 360-61). He has made the moral choice to care for the Crakers and they have realized the gravity of this decision. Whereas the Crakers, who combine in themselves features of biology and technology, are an example of a cyborg in a very literal definition, the Gardeners and especially Snowman are examples of cyborgs in Haraway's terms. The Gardeners confront the ›informatics of domination‹ with their own mixture of religious beliefs and scientific knowledge. They combine passion and rationality in comparison to Crake's cold rationality. They are not trying to go back to simpler times but try to incorporate a more sustainable way of life. Nevertheless, it is far too simplistic to reduce Crake to this. Crake is extensively linked with the Gardeners, especially through his connection to Pilar, one of the Gardeners' Eves (cf. *Flood* 178; 187). The Gardeners and Crake fight for the same cause but with totally different means. Jimmy, standing on neither side, might be the prime example for a Harawaian cyborg in the two novels. He is the one irrational element in Crake's system, yet, ironically, central to it. He is not exclusively Jimmy, the man he was born as any more, but also Snowman, the self-styled prophet of Crake, who has to serve a function in the theological system he built himself. He embodies all the aspects of life Crake is not capable of, like passion, empathy, a feeling for the beauty of cultural products, etc. He is the ›words person‹ in Crake's world of ›numbers persons.‹ Whereas Crake envisioned a world that could function after the BlyssPluss-Holocaust, Snowman brought life – in cultural terms – back to it.

The characters are not the only cyborgian element in Atwood's novels. During late 2009 and 2010 Atwood went on a rather unusual book tour. She traveled from city to city, mostly via public transport, to participate in staged readings from the book.[23] The only constant elements of these performances were Margaret Atwood, the text, and the music, but the shows were staged every time by a different group of actors and musicians. Sometimes these shows were even staged in churches with real clergymen (e.g. the performance in St. John's Church in Edinburgh on 30 August 2009 with Bishop Richard Holloway as Adam One; cf. Atwood »Day One«). These happenings seem to be comparable to the Gardeners' Tree of Life Natural Materials Exchanges (cf. *Flood* 140-44) or their public processions (cf. *Flood* 39). They are ways for the Gardeners' ideas to reach out to new audiences through mutual exchange. Even the combination of real-world Christianity and the books' cult is possible and beneficial to both sides. The God's Gardeners' approach seems to be more acceptable in our post-industrial, Western world, while the Church gives the Gardeners the link to an institution which is roughly two thousand years old.

Atwood includes another dimension to this moral cyborgian outreach to reality in her two novels. She auctioned off the names of two of the novels' characters for charity. The two names are Amanda Payne and Rebecca Eckler (cf. *Flood* 433-34). The writer Rebecca Eckler met with Atwood after the publication of *The Year of the Flood* to talk about the character based on her name (cf. Eckler). She had to find out that her character is actually very different from her: »One of my character's first quotes is, ›Praise the Lord and spit. I'm too black and ugly for him...‹ There you have it. Rebecca Eckler is no longer skinny, neurotic and Jewish.« Eckler as a reader and a fictional character is the closest we get to Haraway's cyborgs in Atwood's novels. In her article, Eckler, a long-term, die-hard fan of Atwood, describes the child-like fun she had encountering her own name in the book, nearly identifying with the character of her name. »I feel something like a shock of electricity every time I see it. There's my name! (I've made turnip pie?) There's my name! (I helped kill someone?) There's my

---

23 Cf. the »Events« page on the webpage *Margaret Atwood: The Year of the Flood*. http://www.yearoftheflood.com/. There is also a documentary of this book tour, *In the Wake of the Flood* directed by Ron Mann, available on DVD.

name! (Did I really just say, ›Once he's stuck his pole in some hole, he thinks it's his?‹)« (Eckler). This mixture of Eckler's curiosity as a reader and her immersion into the story turns her into an entity that is fictitious and real at the same time. This allows for a different connection to, and examination of, the text by this one reader. The bodily differences, even in a literary text, are the most striking to Eckler. Unfor-Unfortunately, she does not see, or at least describe, the possibilities of a different, fictional body. Her short self-description as being »skinny, neurotic and Jewish« in real life says more about her self-conception than about the character Atwood created from her name. So this cyborg entity can create options which a reader might or might not take.

A comparable cyborgian connection is at the basis of a player's experience of *BioShock*. The player sees the world through the avatar's eyes, thus a higher degree of immersion and immediacy for the player is achieved. Even pre-rendered cut-scenes are quite often experienced from the avatar's perspective. In *BioShock* only the end-sequences are narrated from a different point of view; for the rest of the game the player *is* Jack. *BioShock* uses this not only to increase the excitement but also for one of the most interesting metafictional plot-twists in a game, by challenging the ontological connection between player and avatar. All through the first half of the game, the avatar tries to get either to Atlas or to kill Ryan. During this time one has to perform tasks which no rational person would perform. Why take refuge in an underwater city in turmoil after a plane crash, as the avatar does in the beginning of the game? Which sane person would self-inject a gene-altering substance? And most of all, does it make sense to kill Andrew Ryan? The player's answer to all these questions during game-play might be: I do it, because the game wants me to. One knows that one is supposed to fight enemies with all available weapons in hostile surroundings in a first-person shooter, therefore all these actions seem reasonable in this particular place created by the game and governed by specific game rules. The player is aware of the factitiousness of the rules and the playing field. The use of vaudevillian haunted-house effects like spatially triggered light-outs or scenes taking place behind unbreakable glass play into this fun-ride experience.[24]

---

24 A level set in Rapture's amusement park, which might have played more on this idea, was cut from the game and is only available through the *PlayStation 3* version's downloadable content. Levine states Walt Disney

These elements have become a certain standard for the first-person shooter genre. The game picks up on the player's knowledge of this and turns it into a plot device. Shortly before the avatar confronts Ryan, he enters a room which is dominated by a wall plastered with notes. Photos are pinned to this wall of most of the influential people in Rapture and of Jack. All these photos are linked through red yarn. Across the whole wall the words »Would you kindly« are painted in bright red. Atlas, the self-proclaimed freedom fighter, who is actually Ryan's antagonist and main business rival Frank Fontaine, had used these exact words quite substantially up to this moment to get the avatar – or in other words the player – to do certain things, like picking up a weapon. With the help of two audio diaries (»Dr. Suchong: Mind Control Test« and »Dr. Suchong: Baby Status«) in front of the wall, the player realizes that Jack was the result of a genetic experiment and that he, and thus the player, has been manipulated to play a part in a broader scheme. The full extent of the influence on the avatar's will becomes evident during the scene in Ryan's office. Ryan starts talking about the structures of slavery. Slavery stands in stark contrast to Ryan's libertarian beliefs, his Objectivist world view. »A man chooses. A slave obeys.« These words, uttered by him during the encounter in his office and found on propaganda posters throughout Rapture, are central to his political and social ideology. Ryan is aware that his freedom is based on another person's exploitation. Ryan created the player's avatar, Jack, to be his slave but he recognizes that Jack is now used by Fontaine to kill him. When Ryan asks the avatar to step into his office, the game breaks the connection between the player and the avatar. Ryan has taken control over Jack and the player is forced to watch the unfolding events through Jack's eyes, without the possibility to intervene. Ryan demands:

World's influence on his approach to game design himself: »I'm fascinated with Disney World. I'm less fascinated in [sic] the individual characters. If you are a videogame developer and you don't understand the influence Walt Disney World should have on you as a videogame developer, and those rides, the Haunted Mansion and the Pirates of the Caribbean [...] you're not doing your job. They were the proto-videogames, those semi-interactive, environmental experiences. The opening of *BioShock* is one of those rides« (Russo 31).

Stop, would you kindly? (Jack reacts instantly, and obeys the command invol-
untarily) »Would you kindly.« … Powerful phrase. Familiar phrase? (Jack ex-
periences a cascade of memories of Atlas including the phrase in his
›suggestions‹) Sit, would you kindly? (Jack obeys) Stand, would you kindly?
(Jack obeys) Run! Stop! Turn. (Jack obeys) A man chooses, a slave obeys.
(Ryan hands Jack his golf club) Kill! (Jack obeys, striking him with the club)
A man chooses! (Jack strikes again) A slave obeys! (Jack strikes again)
OBEY! (Jack kills Ryan with a final, deadly blow). (»A Man Chooses«)

During the entire murder the player has no influence over the avatar's
body. Only after Ryan's death does the player take over control again.
Due to his remote-controlled mind, Jake is as limited in his actions as
the player is through the game's rules. And as much as Jack is used by
Ryan and Fontaine to achieve their respective goals, the player is directed through the rules the designers set to experience the events in
the way they planned it. Both the player and the avatar are given the
illusion of a world in which they can decide on how to act, and both
are entangled in a web of controlling methods. Only when left without
the supposed control over the events, when the corporeal connection
with Jack is broken, the player becomes aware of these influences (cf.
Sicart 156-58). Players are not only performing according to typical
game mechanics because they know about the game's rules, but because the story wants them to, as it is based exactly on an attempt to
rid oneself (i.e. the avatar) of similar influences:

> *BioShock* requires ethical players to understand the design decision of depriv-
> ing them of control at a specific point but also of forcing them to reflect upon
> the meaning of the previous actions taken in the game, all in accord with play-
> er repertoire but clearly unethical in the context of the game narrative. (Sicart
> 158)

Unfortunately the game cannot deliver on the ramifications of this interesting dilemma during the rest of the game, even though the second
half offers areas which are slightly more open for the player to experiment. The main objective remains to bring down Fontaine for his betrayal and to break the mind control. The only aspect which has
changed is that from this point on Tenenbaum convinces the avatar to
act for moral reasons, instead of Fontaine forcing him. Players, during
the revelation of the mind control, are reminded of their status as one

of Haraway's cyborgs, an entity with fictional and ›real‹ moral agency, but unfortunately the story cannot build up on that.

Another moral element in *BioShock*, which has been widely advertised, is not as much a real choice as it pretends to be (cf. Sicart 158-61). Every time the avatar captures a Little Sister, he, and through him the player, is asked whether to harvest or to rescue her. Harvesting will kill her and give the avatar more ADAM than he will get for rescuing her. Saving her will break the symbiotic connection between the girl and the slug, thus ›freeing‹ her from her life as an ADAM producer. Harvesting or rescuing the Little Sisters is, apart from the end-sequence, unimportant to the game. The game's narrative seems to follow mostly the assumption that the player will do the right thing and free the innocent girls. Even if the player harvests only one Little Sister, a sad version of the bad end video sequence will follow the final fight. The console versions of the game award the rescuing of all Little Sisters with a special trophy. Still this decision has no influence on the game-play. Even though the avatar will receive more ADAM for killing the girls, for every third Little Sister rescued, Tenenbaum will send a present for Jack, which includes an amount of ADAM roughly equal to the difference between rescued and harvested Little Sisters, some Plasmids and other goodies like EVE-potions.[25] »The problem with this mechanic is that it trivializes the moral capacities of the player to reflect on her actions by depriving the choice of any consequence to her relation with the world« (Sicart 160). The avatar's surroundings do not react to these moral decisions in any way (cf. Sicart 160). One is neither punished for exploiting the Little Sisters, nor does one have to make do with less ADAM in exchange for a clear conscience. Therefore this moralizing aspect appears rather superficial, clearly marking it as game mechanics with nearly no ramifications in the game's world. Thus it breaks the immersion, reminding the players that they are exactly that, persons playing a game.

Both these ethical design decisions, the mind-control feature and the harvest-rescue feature, cut the connection between the player and the avatar, highlighting the cyborgian nature of this entity. Whereas

---

25 The stereotypically gendered basis of these acronyms should be mentioned here, as ADAM, the ›masculine‹ version of the substance, is the creative force, while EVE, the ›feminine‹ one, restores the avatar's ›genetic‹ energy. (My thanks go to Irmtraud Huber for pointing this out to me.)

the first does so decisively to inspire players to reflect on their own actions, the second one creates an alienation from the game-play and thus the game's world, as players' decisions are not grounded on ethical reflections but rather on a decision over which ending they want to see.

OH LET ME NOT BE PROUD, DEAR 'BORG

BioShock and the Margaret Atwood novels allow for certain forms of self-confident cyborgs in Donna Haraway's terms. On the surface all three works tell stories of good authentic bodies versus bad and corrupted inauthentic bodies. *BioShock* and *The Year of the Flood* are centered on the rescue of the innocent, the rescued Little Sisters, who can finally live a normal life, and the God's Gardeners, who have decided to live in accordance with nature instead of ruling over her. Even *Oryx and Crake*'s Crakers could be seen in this light but they are also part of a more troubling notion underlying this simplistic distinction. The Crakers are genetically engineered creatures, thus inauthentic, and still they are more innocent than any of the humans in the novels, even the God's Gardeners. In *BioShock*, Jack finds a »family,« as Tenenbaum proclaims in the game's end-sequence, through the rescue of the Little Sisters. He somehow has become the father figure in this very inauthentic family. This family of sorts still cultivates the stereotypic gender roles. Jack is the protecting father; Tenenbaum, although she had always rejected this role, has assumed the caring role of the mother, and both help their step-children, the rescued Little Sisters. The game's narrative constructs this as a form of authentic love, a love the Splicers and Big Daddies will not find. They might be monsters without an authentic body, mere enemies in game terms but they also appeal to the player's pity. The remnants of their former lives as ›normal‹ citizens of Rapture are still visible. The Splicers wear rugged costumes from the New Year's party or even torn versions of their everyday clothes. They seem to be encapsulated through their madness in short behavioral loops, cut from their everyday routines. A Daddy's sorrow is more than obvious when he wanders the halls, searching for his Sister. One is rather inclined to help than to kill him. The avatar learns more and more about these characters' tragic lives but still has to fight them to leave Rapture alive. They are still his enemies but they also found a new form of authenticity, a new reason to stay alive, even though they are doomed to die.

Oryx and Crake, *The Year of the Flood*, and *BioShock* argue against a *laissez-faire* approach to genetic engineering and for a more cautious attitude towards nature and society by respectively portraying dystopian worlds, which can only be redeemed through love for the environment and fellow humans. The novels and the game seem to assign more intrinsic value to authentic bodies but they also remind us of the responsibility we have for the inauthentic bodies we create. Maybe these inauthentic bodies, the cyborgs, are the ones to show us a way to contend with the informatics of domination.

WORKS CITED

Atwood, Margaret. »Day One: A Restaurant Baptism, and a First Performance.« *The Globe and Mail*. 1 Sept. 2009. Web. 12 Apr. 2011. http://www.theglobeandmail.com/news/arts/books/atwood-on-tour

——. *Oryx and Crake*. London: Bloomsbury, 2003.

——. *The Year of the Flood*. London: Bloomsbury, 2009.

BioShock. 2K Boston [Irrational Games], together with 2K Australia, 2K Marin, and Digital Extremes. Take-Two Interactive, 2008. (PlayStation 3 version).

BioShock: *Breaking the Mold*. Take-Two Interactive. n.d. Web. 29 Mar. 2011. http://downloads.2kgames.com/bioshock/artbookhigh .zip

The BioShock Wiki. n.d. Web. 1 Apr. 2011. http://bioshock.wikia.com/ wiki/BioShock_Wiki.

»A Brief History...« *Irrational Games*. 2010. Web. 31 Mar. 2011. http://irrationalgames.com/studio/

Degani-Raz, Irit. »Beckett's Worlds as Thought Experiments.« *Drawing on Beckett: Portraits, Performances, and Cultural Contexts*. Ed. Linda Ben-Zvi. Tel Aviv: Assaph, 2003. 141-58.

Eckler, Rebecca. »Margaret Atwood Didn't Kill Me: Rebecca Eckler Paid to Get Her Name in the Novelist's New Book, but What Would Atwood Do with Her?« *Macleans.ca*. 23 Sept. 2009. Web. 11 Mar. 2011. http://www2.macleans.ca/2009/09/23/margaret-atwood-didn%E2%80%99t-kill-me/.

Haraway, Donna. »A Cyborg Manifesto: Science, Technology, and Socialist-Feminism in the Late Twentieth Century.« *The New Media Reader.* Ed. Noah Wardrip-Fruin and Nick Montfort. Cambridge, MA: MIT Press, 2003. 516-41.

Hartley, Paddy. *Project Facade.* n.d. Web. 11 Apr. 2011. http://www.projectfacade.com/index.php?.

»A Man Chooses, a Slave Obeys.« *The BioShock Wiki.* n.d. Web. 13 Apr. 2011. http://bioshock.wikia.com/wiki/A_man_chooses,_a _slave_obeys

Mosel, Michael. *Deranged Minds: Subjektivierung der Erzählperspektive im Computerspiel.* Boizenburg: Werner Hülsbusch, 2011.

›Piecraft‹ and Nick Ottens. »Discovering Dieselpunk.« *Gatehouse Gazette* 1/1 (2008): 3-9. Web. 30 Mar. 2011. http://www.ottens.co.uk/ gatehouse/Gazette%20-%201.pdf

Q TV. »Margaret Atwood on Q TV.« *Q with Jian Ghomeshi* 2/11. CBC Radio, 22 Nov. 2009. Web. 31. Mar. 2011. http://www.youtube.com/watch?v=cQkuMe2-X3Y

Rand, Ayn. *Atlas Shrugged.* 1957. New York, NY: Signet, 2007.

Rothschild, Matthew. »A Progressive Interview with Margaret Atwood.« *The Progressive* 74.12 (2010): n.p. Web. 30 Mar. 2011. http://www.progressive.org/rothschild1210.html

Russo, Tom. »The Many, Irrational Lives of ... Ken Levine.« *Electronic Gaming Monthly* 246 (2011): 22-31.

Schmalfuß, Sven. »›Ghosts of Sparta‹: Performing the God of War's Virtual Masculinity.« *Performing Masculinity.* Ed. Rainer Emig and Antony Rowland. Basingstoke: Palgrave Macmillan, 2010. 210-33

Sicart, Miguel. *The Ethics of Computer Games.* Cambridge, MA: MIT Press, 2009.

Taylor, Paul. »Fleshing Out the Maelstrom: Biopunk and the Violence of Information.« *M/C: A Journal of Media and Culture* 3.3 (2000). Web. 30 Mar. 2011. http://journal.media-culture.org.au/0006/ biopunk.php

Welcome to Rapture: BioShock ›Making Of.‹ *BioShock.* 2K Boston [Irrational Games], together with 2K Australia and 2K Marin. Take-Two Interactive, 2007. (PC version, Collector's Edition).

Wikipedia. »*BioShock 2.*« n.d. Web. 30 Mar. 2011. http://en.wiki pedia.org/wiki/BioShock_2

Contestations

»The Real Thing«

Authenticating Strategies in Hemingway's Fiction

MELANIE EIS[1]

In 1932, Ernest Hemingway published *Death in the Afternoon*, the first study of the Spanish bullfight in the English language. It is also the book which develops Hemingway's famous iceberg theory, or theory of omission:

> If a writer of prose knows enough about what he is writing about he may omit things that he knows and the reader, if the writer is writing truly enough, will have a feeling of those things as strongly as if the writer had stated them. The dignity of the movement of an iceberg is due to only one-eighth of it being above water. A writer who omits things because he does not know them only makes hollow places in his writing. (182)

This confident tone mirrors that of anthropologists publishing at the same time: underlying Hemingway's quasi-ethnographic account of the Spanish bullfight is the claim that it is possible for the Western writer to make universally true statements about his ›primitive‹ object of study.[2] Strikingly, in Hemingway's novels and short stories as well

---

1   Much of the original research for this article goes back to my unpublished *Magisterarbeit* (master's thesis), handed in at Bremen University 29 May 2008.

2   As Marianna Torgovnick remarks in her acclaimed analysis of the primitivist discourse pre-eminent in ethnographic studies published at the beginning of the 20th century, this discourse fortifies a duality between the

as in the non-fiction publication *Death in the Afternoon*, this ›truth‹ is often located in places and with people which are both depicted as somehow more ›primitive‹ than the author and his protagonists. Apparently, this is where »the real thing,« which is »valid in a year or in ten years or, with luck and if you stated it purely enough, always« can be found (*Death* 6). In this article, I will try to dissect how this »real thing« stands in for a truth which has claimed particular authenticity through a primitivist discourse.

Not only Hemingway's texts and protagonists are part of this discourse of authenticity, but also his public persona and many scholarly texts concerning his work. I argue that the myth it produces is one of »whiteness as a particular authenticity« (152), as it »connect[s] the particular situation of young white men at a certain point in U.S.-American history to a seemingly archetypal collective psyche of ›real men‹« (161), as Sabine Broeck remarks in her intriguing reading of two more recent U.S.-American novels.[3] Concerning the myth around the person Ernest Hemingway, I can only point out a couple of the countless biographies and articles concerned with presenting the author as ›the real thing,‹ that is, a man sparkling with virility. Among them is, famously, Scott Donaldson's *By Force of Will*, which relies on anecdotes such as an incident where after receiving a disapproving review, Hemingway wrestled down the critic responsible for the magazine article when encountering him at his publisher's (cf. 186-87).[4] Another example would be A.E. Hotchner's well-known *Papa Hemingway*, which informs readers on one of the first pages of Hemingway's daiquiri-drinking record. He is quoted to have told Hotchner: »Made a run of sixteen here one night« (7). One could even argue that ›Ernest Hemingway‹ has by now reached the status of a brand that sells masculinity. However, in the last decades, another story has come

---

observer at the top and the observed at the bottom of the cultural hierarchy (cf. 8). For a further critique of the anthropologic ethos, cf. Clifford and Marcus. One could further argue that the thinking which made such a primitivist discourse possible already started during Enlightenment with the invention of the concept of race (cf. Bernasconi).

3   My concept of myth refers to Roland Barthes's *Mythologies*. The conception of this essay has relied on his analyses of modern cultural phenomena as semiotic systems.

4   For a list of Hemingway biographies, cf. Trogdon.

to the fore: that of the suffering author.[5] More interesting for the purpose of this article, this development also seems to be true for the discussion of Hemingway's texts.

If, as I argue, the »real thing« the author as well as his protagonists hunt for is the display of ›true‹ masculinity, then the question regarding this discourse of authenticity is: how is raced-gendered identity in Hemingway's texts and those revolving around them (written by his critics and by journalists) displayed as ›true‹ masculinity?[6] Whose truth is it, and which preconditions are necessary for the display of this particular truth? Consequently, I am not only interested in the question of what is represented as truth, but also in the question of ›Who speaks?‹ in the discourse that encompasses Hemingway's texts, those of Hemingway scholarship, and the (self-)representation of the author himself (a discourse I will call ›Hemingway text‹). However, the focus of this article excludes the public persona and can, due to limited space, naturally only outline examples in Hemingway's fiction and scholarly readings of Hemingway's texts.

In their influential discussion of the significance of the concept of authenticity in the 20th century, Susanne Knaller and Harro Müller remark that its high profile can be seen as expression and symptom of a crisis of the modern subject (cf. 10). It is this crisis which has played

---

5   The examples are numerous and easy to be found. As biography is not my aim here, reference to one very recent example has to suffice: an article by Matthias Matussek to commemorate the 50th anniversary of Hemingway's death in the German magazine *Der Spiegel*.

6   My analysis of the construction and representation of a white, virile heterosexual masculinity in the texts by Ernest Hemingway and the literary critical discourse about his texts relies on the theoretical breakthrough which was brought to Gender and Cultural Studies by the concept of intersectionality (cf. Crenshaw; Brah and Phoenix). It is important to note that the current theoretical debate about intersectionality sometimes tends to overlook the long tradition of practical and theoretical groundwork by women of color (cf. Davis; bell hooks; Hull et al.; Lorde; Mohanty; Moraga and Anzaldúa). Furthermore, I would like to stress that an analysis of sexual identity is always already part of these considerations. Following Judith Butler's *Gender Trouble*, it cannot be thought of as apart from gender identity. Both are no longer ontological categories, but have to be imagined as produced by a matrix of heteronormativity.

a major role in Hemingway's fiction and Hemingway scholarship. A good starting point from which to probe into the prevailing discourse of crisis is the old but still widespread idea that at the center of every fictional text by Ernest Hemingway stands a ›code hero‹ or ›Hemingway hero.‹ What makes these characters code heroes are the strict rules of performance they follow. They are, according to influential Hemingway critic Philip Young

made of the controls of honor and courage which in a life of tension and pain make a man a man and distinguish him from the people who follow random impulses, let down their hair, and are generally messy, perhaps cowardly, and without inviolable rules for how to live holding tight. (63)[7]

Suffering, but never without showing »honor and courage,« seems to be the only way for a Hemingway character to perform an accepted version of masculinity. Anyone who does not know how to »live holding tight« against pain belongs to the other side, that of the »messy« people »who follow random impulses« and are not proud enough to endure silently. This idea of a code hero's ideal performance has for many critics become an essence of Hemingway's texts, as Philip Young has been, while one of the first, by far not the only promoter of this concept. For instance, a relatively recent monograph on Hemingway by Peter Messent still sees Hemingway's protagonists as suffering from a »problematic of identity,« which »is a major concern in Hemingway's fiction« (44). Similarly to Young, Messent connects the identity anxieties in Hemingway's texts to »the actual conditions of a modernized world marked by increasingly strong patternings of rationalisation and bureaucratisation« (44-45). Both for Young and Messent, Hemingway's characters are marked by endurance, which can be called a leitmotif of the critical perception of Hemingway's protagonists. Other examples are John W. Aldrige, who agrees that the world for Hemingway characters is »enemy territory« (123) in which they have to learn to move around carefully and knowingly, and Michael

---

7   Young's psychological and biographical work *Ernest Hemingway: A Reconsideration* was published 1966, five years after Hemingway's death. For an account of the controversy that took place earlier between him and the author, who sought to prevent psychological criticism of his work, cf. Young's »Foreword: Author and Critic – A Rather Long Story.«

Reynolds, who sees the protagonist of *The Sun Also Rises*, Jake Barnes, as »impotent in more ways than one« (64). His »injury is omnipresent« (Wagner-Martin, »Introduction« 5).

However, we have to be aware of the danger of a one-sided argument when this crisis discourse provides Hemingway's protagonists' white male identity with authentication strategies through what Robyn Wiegman calls »particularity.« As Wiegman states, there is always a »tension between particularity and universality that [has characterized] [...] the changing contours of white power and privilege in the last three centuries« (270-71). In the case of the Hemingway text, an emphasis on the particular struggle of the white male subject tends to render invisible its generally privileged status. This means that what remains unmentioned in a reading such as Messent's is that changes in the world of the white male subject, which took place at the time Hemingway was writing, might also be summed up as claims for recognition as well as political interventions by those people in relation to whom white male hegemony had been (and still often is) in a position of social superiority. The disillusionment Messent refers to in this context seems rather like nostalgia for a past in which the white male's hegemonic position was not threatened by the claims to social participation and equality of marginalized groups and was closer to the power to define the universal. However, Messent is only one scholar in a crisis discourse which has added up, so recent Hemingway critic Debra Moddelmog, to a »lengthy history of masculinity in crisis« (24). The number of Hemingway protagonists alone who have been wounded in war strikingly underlines this thesis: examples are Nick Adams (the protagonist of several short stories), Jake Barnes of *The Sun Also Rises*, Robert Jordan of *For Whom the Bell Tolls*, Colonel Cantwell of *Across the River and Into the Trees*, Harry Morgan of *To Have and Have Not*, and Frederic Henry of *A Farewell to Arms*. Their crisis discourse bespeaks nostalgia for a masculine virility from some unknown past. I argue that, paradoxically, Hemingway's white male protagonists are still equipped with universal power of definition, made possible by appropriating the particularity, or, put differently, authenticity of racialized Others. This authentication is enabled through a primitivizing discourse in the Hemingway text.

This is true for example for the posthumously published novel *The Garden of Eden*. The protagonists, a newly-wed U.S.-American couple on honeymoon in France, unfold a complicated scene of sexual role-playing on a screen of, as Toni Morrison calls it, »Africanist« imaginary. In her celebrated collection of essays, *Playing in the Dark: Whiteness and the Literary Imagination*, Morrison points out that the novel's »voluptuous illegality is enforced by the associations constantly made between darkness and desire, darkness and irrationality, darkness and the thrill of evil« (87). For the protagonists Catherine and David Bourne, Africa is a place of yearning, a primitive place where time stands still and where sexuality unhampered by civilizing influences exists. It arguably outlines a dichotomy between white civilized restraints and black sexual authenticity.[8] This imaginary depends on »Africanism – the fetishizing of color, the transference to blackness of the power of illicit sexuality, chaos, madness, impropriety, anarchy, strangeness, and helpless, hapless desire« (81). Catherine wants to be David's »African girl« (Hemingway, *Garden* 29); they refer to this role-playing as »the dark magic of the change« (20). Their excitement is heightened by the introduction of another layer of taboo when Catherine not only tries to change her race, but also her gender: »You don't really mind being brothers do you?« Catherine asks her husband. He does not: »›You're awfully dark, brother,‹ he said. ›You don't know how dark.‹« Catherine comforts him: »Truly you don't have to worry darling until night. We won't let the night things come in the day« (22-23).

The fact that until Morrison's analysis, the discussion of *The Garden of Eden* had focused almost exclusively on the novel's representa-

---

8   Linking the ideas of free sexuality and the ›primitive‹ is not only innate to most of Hemingway's texts, but part of the discourse of primitivism which sprang from as well as fostered Eurocentric political and discursive hegemony. Discrimination against and ideal identification with Africans or Native Americans (or any culture represented as primitive) are not necessarily a contradiction in this tradition, but derive from one and the same line of thought: that those who represent the Other are desirable and detestable at the same time (cf. Ickstadt 252). What makes the Other desirable is the myth of a sexuality that is uninhibited by power structures. If Catherine and David perceive African sexuality as free from cultural constraints, they do so through their own cultural lens. Moreover, they use a sexualized imaginary for a representation of Africa, which provides them with a vocabulary to refer to those of their own desires which would threaten their identity if not displaced on an Africanist Other.

tion of gender and sexuality shows how Hemingway scholarship has found it difficult to undergo an analysis of how Hemingway's fiction not only raises questions of gender identity but of the raced-genderedness of its protagonists. For example, the prohibition Catherine and David play with has been ascribed to Catherine playing David's »split off feminine half« (Eby 204), or to Hemingway's »androgynous dilemma« (Spilka 2).[9] Nancy Comley and Robert Scholes, who with the title *Hemingway's Genders: Rereading the Hemingway Text* have raised expectations of a critical reassessment of gender and identity in Hemingway's body of work, attribute the experiments Catherine and David engage in to »a metamorphic shift of race and gender« (93). However, Catherine and David are not really interested in changing their race; they might be »blacked-up« (Morrison 87) but only if it serves their own sexual excitement. And although Debra Moddelmog emphasizes Catherine and David's racism, she still contends that they »represent the possibility for change« (85), at least concerning a rigid gender order. Moddelmog's argument is convincing insofar as especially Catherine demonstrates that gender is performed and fluid; but the fact that her performance depends on an inherent racism of course questions the ethical value of this demonstration. It also only tells part of the story. The question which still needs to be answered is how their Africanist primitivism serves the authentication of David and Catherine Bourne's white, U.S.-American identification.

Catherine's longing to become David's »African girl« represents a search for a lost origin that Hemingway's fiction deals with regularly. As Hemingway critic Suzanne Del Gizzo suggests, Africa in Hemingway's texts often »holds the promise of an experience now lost in America forever« (511). This becomes even clearer when Catherine and David's relationship starts to unravel as David frees himself from the woman who has claimed to be his brother and thus endangered his heterosexual identification.[10] As Moddelmog puts it, he »has recog-

---

9   Cf. Gajdusek.

10 With Catherine, David became a man who desired a masculine libidinal position. As he seems unable to rethink his own identity outside the confines of psychoanalytic discourse, which has no place for homosexual desire as part of masculinity, he is now confronted with doubts about his own identity. As Judith Butler asks, »what would masculinity ›be‹ were it not

nized the complexity of their night time games all along, but has been even less able than Catherine to accept the presence, much less the enjoyment, of his own homosexual desire« (79). Thus he not only exchanges Catherine for another woman who is more happy with making it her mission to take care of him, Maria, but he also starts writing a story he locates in Africa, the story of the elephant hunt.

It is only when he has finished writing the story that Catherine asks David about it and he explains where it is set: »It's a story about Africa back before the 1914 war. In the time of the Maji-Maji War. The native rebellion of 1905 in Tanganyika« (Hemingway, *Garden* 157). What really seems to matter in the story »that for years he had put off facing« is a tale of male bonding and of the changing relationship between his father and himself while he grew up (123). »This was when I got to know [my father]« (154), he tells Maria. Now *The Garden of Eden* probably has to be read as a co-production of Ernest Hemingway and Scriber's editor Tom Jenks.[11] The manuscript has not been published yet, but Comley and Scholes quote from it in the above mentioned *Hemingway's Genders*. It is most revealing concerning David's perception of himself as a writer about Africa, although Comley and Scholes do not cite it to support the argument I am making here. David thinks,

> You have no precedent to help you and you write about a country where no one has written truly to guide you. They've written well about South Africa but not about the highlands on the equator where you were a boy. They will of course but so far it is yours to do as well with it as you can. (75)

Even though readers of the novel never get such an explanation for why the »Elephant Hunt« is such a difficult story to write, David in the novel is working with the same assumptions as David in the manuscript. While he writes, David creates his very own Africa, which seems strangely depopulated except for his father, himself, and an African hunting guide, all three of them out on an expedition that only serves David's ends: to establish his coming of age as a virile, white

---

for this aggressive circuit of renunciation [of both femininity and homosexuality] from which it is wrought?« (*Gender Trouble* 31).

11 Cf. Moddelmog as well as Comley and Scholes for a discussion of the changes Jenks made to the manuscript.

man. David presents his alter ego resisting his father for the first time. For a rebellion of his own, the ›native rebellion‹ he tells Catherine about is mere background. Morrison notes that Africa means a lot to David, maybe more than it means to Catherine. »Its availability as a blank, empty space into which he asserts himself, an uncreated void ready, waiting, and offering itself up for his artistic imagination, his work, his fiction, is unmistakable« (88-89). Africa in David's story lacks its own history and culture – he only reluctantly names specific places and people – and therefore provides ideal grounds for him to find what he is looking for: a page that has not been written on yet, which he can fill with his own words. It does not seem so much that, as Comley and Scholes comment, »the source of his creativity lies in what for him is the forbidden territory of the feminine« (60), but rather that it lies in authenticating his voice through the search for the ›real thing‹ in Africa. The novel claims authenticity for its white, virile, heterosexually identified protagonist through a primitivist discourse.

This is not only the case in *The Garden of Eden*. For example, in the short story »Fathers and Sons,« one of Hemingway's so-called Nick Adams stories, Nick Adams's midlife crisis of identity is intertwined with nostalgia for lost innocence and purity, the loss of which is inextricably linked to the Native Americans he has spent his youth with.[12] This nostalgia is triggered not only by Nick's sense of his father's ultimate failure (as evidenced by his suicide), but also by a premonition of his own death and inability to give his young son the answers he needs. Although his apologetic perception of his father's death as »in a trap that he had helped only a little to set« helps Nick to keep seeing his father in a good light, he has to admit to the fact that his father was »sentimental« and that he could only offer his son two things to learn from him, »fishing and shooting,« at least abilities Nick highly valorizes (463). However, what he has learned concerning interpersonal relationships and sexuality, he has learned from his Ojibway friends and especially from his Ojibway girlfriend Trudy. A longing reminiscence of a scene from his youth ironically makes the narrator appear just as »sentimental« as he accuses his father to have

---

12 There has been disagreement in Hemingway criticism on which of his short stories are to be deciphered as dealing with Nick Adams, a discussion that is explained in more detail in Flora's introduction to *Hemingway's Nick Adams* (11-16).

been. Nick is roaming the woods with his Ojibway friend Billy and Billy's sister Trudy:

But there was still much forest then, virgin forest where the trees grew high before there were any branches and you walked on the brown, clean, springy-needled ground with no undergrowth and it was cool on the hottest days and they three lay against the trunk of a hemlock wider than two beds are long, with the breeze high in the tops and the cool light that came in patches, and Billy said:
»You want Trudy again?« (466)

For Nick Adams, a fulfilling sexuality seems only possible at a primitive place similar to that described above, in a »virgin forest« which is now gone. Trudy »did first what no one has ever done better«, but now everything that has ever been is in decay: »They all ended the same. Long time ago good. Now no good« (471). Susanna Pavloska in her study *Modern Primitives: Race and Language in Gertrude Stein, Ernest Hemingway, and Zora Neale Hurston* attributes this lament to Hemingway's more or less »›realistic‹ attitude towards Native Americans« as he is »representing Native American culture as time-bound as any other« (59). However, I would rather stress how the Ojibway had served Nick Adams for his identification with white masculinity as authenticity. Then Nick Adams's statement seems less realistic in the sense that it considers the Ojibway point of view, but maybe more realistic in the assessment that Native Americans do not serve for his romantic self-definition any more.[13]

For Nick Adams, the key to his truth about his own identity is located in what is displayed as a primitive time and place. Something similar happens in a passage from Hemingway's autobiographical account of his first safari, *Green Hills of Africa*, which is quoted regularly in scholarly discussions of his work and evokes the notion of the U.S.-American myth of Manifest Destiny as applied to Africa. The narrator claims that »[o]ur people went to America because it was the place to go then. It had been a good country and we had made a mess of it and I would go, now, somewhere else as we had always had the

---

13 For a more detailed account of how a primitivist discourse has shaped the representation of Native Americans and what this meant for white U.S.-American self-definition, cf. Carr.

right to go somewhere else and as we had always gone« (236). Hemingway's comment about going »somewhere else« now that »we« have made America »a mess« shows his investment in the U.S.-American exceptionalist, nation-founding Frontier myth (cf. Turner). But not only that: It also shows an investment in a Western colonialist discourse, which has a long history of appropriating those places and people it has marked as racialized Others. If the »good country,« which the enduring Puritan myth of the New World Garden of Eden America symbolized for its white settlers, has been corrupted, then a mythic new home needs to be found »somewhere else« to meet the recreational needs of America's white male population. This need to ›go home‹ to what they perceive as simple, more comfortable and authentic places haunts Hemingway's protagonists. »In Hemingway's fiction, America – once boyhood is over – generally signifies not ›home,‹ the place where private desire and communal codes can fall into comfortable alignment, but the alien. There is a recurrent sense of cultural failure in his American stories« (Messent 128).

By now it might have become clearer how white male focalizers in Hemingway's fiction establish their claims to white male authenticity by speaking about a primitivized »somewhere else.« As already remarked upon above, not only the African continent, but also rural pre-World War II Spain serves as a »good country« where the white male subject restores his claims to authenticity. Hemingway's first successful novel *The Sun Also Rises* (1926) sets the tone for Hemingway's reverence of rural Spain as a return to mythical, long lost origins. As I have already mentioned, the protagonist of this novel, Jake Barnes, is one of Hemingway's war-wounded protagonists. The nature of Jake's wounding could not be more telling concerning the crisis discourse of white male subjectivity in the Hemingway text: he has probably been castrated – at least it is clear from the text that his wounding prevents him from heteronormative sexual acts such as penetration.[14] A symbol for his questioned virility, his wound can be seen as standing in for the threats Jake's claims to white male privilege encounter throughout the novel: Brett Ashley, the woman he is in love with, but who is too independent to stay with him; the relative openness of the bohemian scene of Paris in the 1920s, where the first part of the novel is set,

---

14 For a further discussion of this theme and how it affects Jake's heterosexual identification, cf. Fantina; Comley and Scholes; Moddelmog.

which allows for homosexuality to be an option; and Robert Cohn, who is Jake's direct competitor – as a writer and for Brett's affection. The misogyny, the homophobia in the portrayal of Brett's homosexual Parisian friends, as well as the anti-Semitism in the representation of Robert Cohn are blatant. In this case, they all seem to serve at least one common goal, and that is to authenticate the narrator's identity through marking the others as abject. Of course the histories and functions of misogyny, anti-Semitism, and homophobia are not to be generally equated, and their respective functions are much more complex than I could account for here.[15] However, in this context, they all add up to an animosity towards anything that is, from the focalizer Jake Barnes's point of view, endangering the virility he struggles hard to hold up. The reason why he hates Robert Cohn is not that Cohn is Jewish, but that he is more successful as a writer and with Brett than himself; the reason why he hates Brett is because she makes him feel his hampered virility through preferring other, more able men; the reason why Brett's homosexual friends make him feel »sick« (Hemingway, *Sun* 18) is because they show him how similar he is to them. As Ira Elliott contends, what scares Jake is »[t]he very existence of the gay man« because it »calls into question [...] naturalized sex/gender roles« (68). »[H]is anger is self-hatred displaced onto the homosexual, for Jake has lost (physically and psychologically) his signifying phallus« (69). Jake understands that he would be hard-pressed trying to find any differences between himself and the homosexuals, and to cover this fact, he aggressively distances himself from them. The same is true for his relationship with Robert Cohn: to veil the fact that Robert is more successful than Jake (he does, for example, succeed in sleeping with Brett), Robert is portrayed with such anti-Semitism that it seems a mystery how Hemingway scholarship could have avoided announcing this fact in any account of the novel.[16]

Jake Barnes's whiteness as well as heterosexual masculinity could be clearly marked as constructions by these challenges to Jake's

---

15 For a history of U.S.-American anti-Semitism from the late 19th century to the early 20th century, cf. Brodkin Sacks.

16 While many of the Hemingway scholars cited above do not even mention the problematic portrayal of Robert Cohn, or others were apologetic about it (cf. Meyerson; Reynolds), Jeremy Kaye offers a more balanced point of view.

claims to white male authenticity. However, these challenges are dismissed when the setting of the novel moves to rural Spain and its rituals, which serve as a recreational space for Jake to assert himself. In the Spanish outdoors, Jake openly shows his deep affection for his best friend Bill, now apparently without allowing doubts to his own heterosexual identification. A »schism in the male-homosocial spectrum created by homophobia« helps Jake to construct this male-to-male friendship as radically different from homosexuality (Sedgwick 201). This schism is represented as being reliable in the Spanish outdoors but questioned in Paris, where Jake is reminded that he is not so different from the homosexuals he despises as their performance puts into doubt those ontological categories that grant him his heterosexual male identification. Not surprisingly, Hemingway scholarship has mostly chosen to focus on the homosocial bonding taking place during Jake and Bill's fishing trip at Burguete and mark it as a heterosexual haven, as for example the much-cited Hemingway scholar Scott Donaldson: »[a]s almost every commentator on the novel has noticed, the interlude at Burguete stands in idyllic counterpoint to the sophisticated pretentiousness of Paris« (»Humor« 37). Donaldson, just as Jake Barnes, seems to delight in the traditional values of Spanish peasants: affection, duty, and honor. They are shown as an antithesis to modern society in Paris, sharing everything from food to wine to stories. When Jake and his friend Bill are on a bus with them, »[T]hey all wanted us to drink from their leather wine-bottles« (Hemingway, *Sun* 91). Scott Donaldson remarks that »Spaniards, unlike Frenchmen, were likely to be friendly for no good financial reason at all« (»Humor« 95). The Spanish peasants' companionship gives Jake a sense of belonging: »as representatives of the traditional world, [they] are part of a collective existence, connected through the rituals of the Catholic church […] to their past and to each other« (Pavloska 61). Rural Spain is thus ascribed with recreational qualities for Jake Barnes and helps his claims to masculine authenticity.

The ritualized bullfight Jake and his friends attend several times while in Pamplona proves to be another recreational environment for the protagonist's virility. It is presented as an example of perfect and unquestioned virile masculine conduct, and Pedro Romero, the young star matador, as a »model of what Jake wishes he could be« as David Blackmore contends in his 1998 article on masculinity anxiety in *The Sun Also Rises* (55). However, the line between wanting to be like

Romero and desiring to have Romero proves to be slim. Put differently, Jake's intention to prove a real man might take him just a little bit
further than he plans. He admires Romero's display of masculinity so
much and tries so hard to seem as virile as possible that he sometimes
steps over the line of what is safely considered as part of the heterosexual realm. This becomes apparent in several instances. For example, as the narrator Jake describes what he sees during a bullfight, he
slips into a sexualized »language of erection, penetration and orgasm«
(Blackmore 57). Thus, in the last two decades of Hemingway criticism, the fact that both participants in the dance-fight between the bull
and the matador are male has lead several scholars to express their
doubts whether the text really does remain as safely within the constraints of heterosexual fiction as the novel has been sold as.[17] Among
them is, as already mentioned, Blackmore, who follows Moddelmog's
assessment that »Jake's descriptions of the meeting of the bull and
bullfighter imply more than flirtation; the encounter evokes images of
sexual foreplay and consummation« (Moddelmog 96). First to comment on the thin line between the aficionados of the bullfight's desire
to be like the boy who woos the bull flirtatiously into his death and a
desire to have him were probably Davidson and Davidson in 1987.
They even go as far as to state that »the whole ethos of *afición* resem-
bles a sublimation of sexual desire« (95, emphasis in the original).
And indeed, one could become suspicious considering how Pedro
Romero's fighting is described: »[t]he bull wanted it again, and
Romero's cape filled again« followed by »the sword went in, and for
just an instant he and the bull were one« (Hemingway, *Sun* 191-93).
Moreover, are not even the aficionados themselves taking part in the
sexuality of the bullfight when, after the fight, they are now satisfied
and as Brett states, »limp as a rag« (149), or having »that disturbed

---

17 A good example is the blurb on the back of the 1994 Arrow paperback
    edition, which reads as following: »Jake is wildly in love with Brett Ash-
    ley, aristocratic and irresistibly beautiful [...]. When the couple drift to
    Spain to the dazzle of the fiesta and the heady atmosphere of the bullfight,
    their affair is strained by new passions, new jealousies, and Jake must fi-
    nally learn that he will never possess the woman he loves.« It is remarka-
    ble how the novel is reduced to the one aspect of the heterosexual
    relationship between Jake and Brett, even though it is never even con-
    summated.

emotional feeling that always comes after a bull-fight, and the feeling of elation that comes after a good bull-fight« (145)? All this induces Comley and Scholes to assert that »no other cultural context available« to Hemingway could have provided him with the grounds »to explore aspects of manliness, including male desire directed toward other males« as much as the bullfight (109). In other words, the safety of the representation of rural Spain as a primitive place loosens the tight constrictions of white, heterosexual male conduct and makes space for the masculine assertion of a character as hampered in his virility as Jake.

No matter how blatantly sexualized Hemingway's presentation of the bullfight might seem now, Jake's membership in the club of aficionados and his identification with the bullfighters who are admired for their virile performance has been taken to remain in the heterosexual realm by Hemingway scholarship for a long time. In this line of thinking, Jake's gaze on the bullfighter Pedro Romero does not mean he desires him, but that he desires to be like him. Furthermore, his role as an aficionado of the bullfight who is »[w]atching and evaluating grants Jake a measure of authority in scenes where men compete against and test each other,« as Thomas Strychacz contends (79). But Jake's relationship with the bullfighter is more ambiguous than that, which becomes apparent even when they first meet. Jake is smitten with the boy:

His black hair shone under the electric light. He wore a white linen shirt and the sword-handler finished his sash and stood up and stepped back. Pedro Romero nodded, seeming very far away and dignified when we shook hands. Montoya said something about what great aficionados we were, and that we wanted to wish him luck. Romero listened very seriously. Then he turned to me. He was the best-looking boy I had ever seen. (Hemingway, *Sun* 143-44)

However, there are precautions taken against the masculinity anxieties a desire for Pedro might trigger in Jake. Hemingway represents the bullfight as a fetishized ritual that displaces homosexual desire: except for the passage cited above, Jake's gaze might be following the matador's body, but his movements are attached to the ritual of the bullfight. Most of the time, Jake does not comment on Pedro's physical attractiveness, but on his artistry in the ring. When explaining the bullfight to Brett, Jake comments,

I had her watch how Romero took the bull away from a fallen horse with his cape, and how he held him with the cape and turned him, smoothly and suavely, never wasting the bull. She saw how Romero avoided every brusque movement and saved his bulls for the last when he wanted them, not winded and discomposed but smoothly worn down. She saw how close Romero always worked to the bull [...]. Romero's bull-fighting gave real emotion, because he kept the absolutely [sic] purity of line in his movements and always quietly and calmly let the horns pass him close each time. (Hemingway, *Sun* 147-48)

For Jake, if it is done well, the ritual of the bullfight signifies authentic, »real emotion.« Positioning himself as omniscient observer of the ritual of the Spanish bullfight, he is represented as a figure of authority. Spain as a symbol of the primitive functions primarily as a displacement of his homosexual desire and for the authentication of a naturalized masculinity. While Jake is subject to agonizing self-doubt, Pedro Romero is Jake's hero of virility, who never questions himself: »He knew everything when he started. The others can't ever learn what he was born with« (Hemingway, *Sun* 148). So can't Jake – but he is the one from whose point of view we perceive the story. He has the power to define, and he feels powerful through his participation in what he takes as Romero's authenticity.

My symptomatic reading of the Hemingway text recognizes these practices of authentication as white male claims to hegemonic truth. As other Hemingway scholars have asserted, these claims come as a reaction to changes in a modernized world – changes which have questioned them and against which assertions of white male authenticity unfold in the Hemingway text. Hemingway's white, male heterosexual protagonists are cast as injured – in the novels and short stories themselves as well as in the scholarly discussion. They seek remedy in taking part in what is displayed as the authenticity of minorities and thus re-establish their own claim to truth, or, put differently, authenticity.

WORKS CITED

Aldridge, John W. »Afterthoughts on the Twenties and *The Sun Also Rises*.« Wagner-Martin 109-29.

Barthes, Roland. *Mythologies*. 1957. London: Vintage, 2009.

Bernasconi, Robert. »Who Invented the Concept of Race?« *Race*. Ed. Robert Bernasconi. Malden, MA: Blackwell, 2001. 11-36.

Blackmore, David. »»In New York It'd Mean I Was a ... ‹: Masculinity Anxiety and Period Discourses of Sexuality in *The Sun Also Rises*.« *Hemingway Review* 18 (1998): 49-67.

Brah, Avtar, and Ann Phoenix. »Ain't I A Woman? Revisiting Intersectionality.« *Journal of International Women's Studies* 5 (2004): 75-86.

Brodkin Sacks, Karen. »How Did Jews Become White Folks?« *Critical White Studies: Looking Behind the Mirror*. Ed. Richard Delgado and Jean Stefancic. Philadelphia, PA: Temple UP, 1997. 395-401.

Broeck, Sabine. »Grounds of Whiteness: White Male Claims to Authenticity.« *The Pathos of Authenticity: American Passions of the Real*. Ed. Ulla Haselstein, Andrew Gross, and MaryAnn Snyder-Körber. Heidelberg: Winter, 2010. 151-62.

Butler, Judith. *Gender Trouble: Feminism and the Subversion of Identity*. New York, NY: Routledge, 1990.

Carr, Helen. *Inventing the American Primitive: Politics, Gender and the Representation of Native American Literary Traditions, 1789-1936*. Cork: Cork UP, 1996.

Clifford, James, and George Marcus, eds. *Writing Culture: The Poetics and Politics of Ethnography*. Berkeley, CA: U of California P, 1986.

Comley, Nancy R., and Robert Scholes. *Hemingway's Genders. Rereading the Hemingway Text*. New Haven, CT: Yale UP, 1994.

Crenshaw, Kimberlé. »Mapping the Margins: Intersectionality, Identity Politics, and Violence Against Women of Color.« *Identities: Race, Class, Gender and Nationality*. Ed. Linda Martin Alcoff and Eduardo Mendieta. Malden, MA: Blackwell Publishing, 2003. 175-200.

Davidson, Arnold E., and Cathy N. Davidson. »Decoding the Hemingway Hero in *The Sun Also Rises*.« Wagner-Martin 83-107.

Davis, Angela. *Women, Race and Class*. New York, NY: Vintage, 1981.

Del Gizzo, Suzanne. »Going Home: Hemingway, Primitivism, and Identity.« *Modern Fiction Studies* 49 (2003): 496-523.

Donaldson, Scott. *By Force of Will: The Life and Art of Ernest Hemingway*. New York, NY: Viking Press, 1977.

——. »Humor in *The Sun Also Rises*.« Wagner-Martin 19-41.

Eby, Carl P. *Hemingway's Fetishism: Psychoanalysis and the Mirror of Manhood*. Albany, NY: State U of New York P, 1999.

Elliott, Ira. »Performance Art: Jake Barnes and ›Masculine‹ Signification in *The Sun Also Rises*.« Wagner-Martin 63-80.

Fantina, Richard. *Ernest Hemingway: Machismo and Masochism*. New York, NY: Palgrave Macmillan, 2005.

Flora, Joseph M. »Introduction.« *Hemingway's Nick Adams*. Baton Rouge, LA: Louisiana State UP, 1982. 1-17.

Gajdusek, Robert. »Elephant Hunt in Eden: A Study of New and Old Myths and Other Strange Beasts in Hemingway's Garden.« *Hemingway Review* 7 (1987): 14-19.

Hemingway, Ernest. *Across the River and Into the Trees*. London: Cape, 1950.

——. *Death in the Afternoon*. 1932. Harmondsworth: Penguin, 1966.

——. *A Farewell to Arms*. 1929. London: Arrow, 1994.

——. »Fathers and Sons.« *The First Forty-Nine Stories*. 1939. London: Arrow, 1993. 462-72.

——. *Fiesta: The Sun Also Rises*. 1927. London: Arrow, 1994.

——. *For Whom the Bell Tolls*. 1941. London: Arrow, 1994.

——. *The Garden of Eden*. New York, NY: Charles Scribner's Sons, 1986.

——. *Green Hills of Africa*. 1935. Harmondsworth: Penguin, 1966.

——. *To Have and Have Not*. 1937. Harmondsworth: Penguin, 1955.

hooks, bell. *Ain't I a Woman: Black Women and Feminism*. Boston, MA: South End Press, 1981.

Hotchner, A.E. *Papa Hemingway: The Ecstasy and Sorrow*. New York, NY: William Morrow and Company, 1983.

Hull, Gloria T., et al., eds. *All the Women are White, All the Blacks are Men, but Some of Us Are Brave: Black Women's Studies*. Old Westbury, NY: Feminist Press, 1982.

Ickstadt, Heinz. »Die Amerikanische Moderne.« *Amerikanische Literaturgeschichte*. Ed. Hubert Zapf. Stuttgart: Metzler, 1997. 218-303.

Kaye, Jeremy. »The ›Whine‹ of Jewish Manhood: Re-reading Hemingway's Anti-Semitism, Re-imagining Robert Cohn.« *The Hemingway Review* 25 (2006): 44-60.

Knaller, Susanne, and Harro Müller. »Einleitung.« *Authentizität: Diskussion eines ästhetischen Begriffs*. Ed. Susanne Knaller and Harro Müller. Munich: Fink, 2006. 7-16.

Lorde, Audre. *Sister Outsider: Essays and Speeches*. Freedom, CA: Crossing Press, 1984.

Matussek, Matthias. »Die wahren Sätze.« *Der Spiegel* 26 (2011): 98-103.

Messent, Peter. *Ernest Hemingway*. New York, NY: St. Martin's Press, 1992.

Meyerson, Robert E. 1982. »Why Robert Cohn? An Analysis of Hemingway's *The Sun Also Rises*.« *Critical Essays on Ernest Hemingway's* The Sun Also Rises. Ed. James Nagel. New York, NY: G. K. Hall & Co., 1995. 95-105.

Moddelmog, Debra A. *Reading Desire: In Pursuit of Ernest Hemingway*. Ithaca, NY: Cornell UP, 1999.

Mohanty, Chandra Talpade. *Feminism Without Borders: Decolonizing Theory, Practicing Solidarity*. Durham, NC: Duke UP, 2003.

Moraga, Cherríe, and Gloria Anzaldúa, eds. *This Bridge Called My Back: Writings by Radical Women of Color*. 1981. New York, NY: Kitchen Table, 1984.

Morrison, Toni. *Playing in the Dark: Whiteness and the Literary Imagination*. Cambridge, MA: Harvard UP, 1992.

Pavloska, Susanna. *Modern Primitives: Race and Language in Gertrude Stein, Ernest Hemingway, and Zora Neale Hurston*. New York, NY: Garland, 2000.

Reynolds, Michael. »The Sun in Its Time: Recovering the Historical Context.« Wagner-Martin 43-64.

Sedgwick, Eve Kosofsky. *Between Men: English Literature and Male Homosocial Desire*. New York, NY: Columbia UP, 1985.

Spilka, Mark. *Hemingway's Quarrel with Androgyny*. Lincoln, NE: U of Nebraska P, 1990.

Strychacz, Thomas. *Hemingway's Theaters of Masculinity*. Baton Rouge, LA: Louisiana State UP, 2003.

Torgovnick, Marianna. *Gone Primitive: Savage Intellects, Modern Lives.* Chicago, IL: U of Chicago P, 1990.

Trogdon, Robert W., ed. *Ernest Hemingway: A Documentary Volume.* Detroit, MI: Gale Group, 1999.

Turner, Frederick Jackson. *The Frontier in American History.* New York, NY: Holt, 1921.

Wagner-Martin, Linda. »Introduction.« Wagner-Martin 1-18.

——, ed. *New Essays on* The Sun Also Rises. New York, NY: Cambridge UP, 1987.

Wiegman, Robyn. »Whiteness Studies and the Paradox of Particularity.« *The Futures of American Studies.* Ed. Donald Pease and Robyn Wiegman. Durham, NC: Duke UP, 2002. 269-304.

Young, Philip. 1966. *Ernest Hemingway: A Reconsideration.* University Park, PA: Pennsylvania State UP, 1996.

——. »Foreword: Author and Critic – A Rather Long Story.« Young 1-28.

Real Lives – Living Wild

Authenticity, Wilderness, and the Postmodern Robinsonade in James Hawes's *Speak for England* and Jeanette Winterson's *The Stone Gods*

FRANCESCA NADJA PALITZSCH

The question ›What is authentic?‹ is both a fashionable and a tricky one; it is this question that has triggered ongoing academic discussions about the nature, experience, and, not least, aesthetics of authenticity. Writings on authenticity span a huge number of philosophical traditions and scientific theories, entailing that ›authenticity‹ has been conceptualized as a socio-cultural ideal and has been controversially discussed in terms of representational strategies (cf. Vannini and Williams, »Authenticity« 2-3; Ferrara 21). Without going into greater detail here, I would like to introduce a few essential points concerning the notion and treatment of authenticity in literary criticism, which are vital for the discussion of the relationship between authentic representation, wilderness motifs, and the postmodern Robinson story in the two novels at hand.

The idea of being close to a notion of originality or reality, or in more recent terminology of being authentic, has been a key factor in human history and thought as it concerns individual uniqueness and interpersonal relationships, the subjective and the objective (cf. Kuhry vi). As the notion of authenticity is not a stable concept with regards to the bounds of time and culture as well as personal convictions, a brief glance at the historical development of the term authenticity reveals it to be »struggling […] against two perceived sources of the inauthentic

– convention and imitation« (Haselstein, Gross, and Snyder-Körber 10; cf. Vannini and Williams, »Authenticity« 2-3). Efforts to grasp or even vaguely define authenticity call for not only a close examination of the term in association with the concept of sincerity, but also for the incorporation of its opposites and how these relate to the question of what is real. Hartman provides an impressive list of contrastive key words that set a frame for a tentative attempt at defining authenticity: »imitation, simulation, dissimulation, impersonation, imposture, fakery, forgery, inauthenticity, the counterfeit, lack of character or integrity« (25). When one enumerates this catalogue of key words, however, it seems essential to pinpoint the paradoxical nature of the concept of authenticity, since the authentic experience is never truly unspoiled and genuine, but always tainted through mediation and commentary. As Virginia Richter aptly remarks, »authenticity has been thoroughly deconstructed and discarded as the product of an impossible nostalgia for ›pure origins‹« (60; cf. Milnes and Sinanan 17), a purity never inherent or provable when it comes to the aesthetics of authenticity. As concerns the origins and the nature of the authentic, there remains one vital quality to be discussed, namely in how far being authentic, being ›real,‹ is something artificially attained and attributed, or whether everyone and everything has an innate authenticity that cannot be removed, negotiated, or manipulated: »Authenticity cannot be stripped away, nor can it be appropriated. In short, the object, person or process in question either *is* authentic or is *not*, period« (Vannini and Williams, »Authenticity« 2; emphasis in the original).

Due to this paradoxical nature of authenticity, the concept has become very prominent in the discussion of both contemporary culture and postmodernism. As the modern individual is confronted with a culture of copies and simulacra, of dispensable grand narratives and genuine experiences, of instable identities and volatile cultural traditions, authenticity seems strangely out of place – at first glance: »Contemporary industrial and information societies are being commodified and virtualized, with every day becoming saturated with ›toxic levels of inauthenticity‹« (Vannini and Williams, »Authenticity« 1). At second glance, however, this indictment is premature since the notion and academic discussion of authenticity has made a significant comeback »in the guises of memory, ethics, religion, the new sincerity, and the renewed interest in ›real things‹« (Haselstein, Gross, and Snyder-

Körber 14). The ›new authenticity,‹ as it is labelled in the introductory chapter to *The Pathos of Authenticity* by Ulla Haselstein, Andrew Gross, and MaryAnn Snyder-Körber, no longer stands as an outright rejection but rather a challenge to postmodernist scepticism and theories:

> It [the new authenticity] offers a revision of postmodernism based on 1) the reconceptualization of culture and cultural history as memory, 2) the redefinition of authentic feelings as cultural products (rather than ›merely‹ personal experiences), and finally 3) a reassessment of the role played by materiality in the construction of subjectivity and social structure. (19)

In view of this, authenticity still works in terms of being a significant »value judgment« as regards the analysis of social norms, subjective opinion, and the symbolic production of culture (Richter 59). Or, as Salmela and Mayer put it, authenticity can be regarded as a »moral compass to our lives« (2), thus proclaiming an ethics of the authentic as a means for orientation in a world marked by globalization, displacement, and uncertainty. Accordingly, in such a world the focus lies on how subjectivity, identity construction, and personal independence can be appreciated and analyzed in relation to social predicaments and positions, which entails that »contemporary authenticity [...] seems more concerned with re-establishing connections between individuals and society than in advocating individual protest and autonomy« (Haselstein, Gross, and Snyder-Körber 18).

Indeed, the issue of authentic representation in the two novels to be analyzed in the following offers some interesting points of departure: both entertain distinct postmodern narrative techniques and ideas of popular culture; both are Robinsonades of sorts; both contain numerous adventure stories that show a particular dystopian streak; both involve a conflict of the individual with society; most importantly, both are set – at least partially – in wilderness surroundings. The latter especially serves as the red thread to be followed in the analysis of authenticity in both James Hawes's *Speak for England* (2005) and Jeanette Winterson's *The Stone Gods* (2007).

(IN)AUTHENTIC LIFESTYLES, WILD LIVES, AND DYSTOPIAN ROBINSONS

As concerns the notion of authenticity and its fictional demonstration, James Hawes's *Speak for England* has a lot to offer in terms of character presentation, plot line, and cultural references. The novel features Brian Marley, a middle-aged, divorced, and disillusioned English teacher, who risks his life and sanity for the sake of winning Britain's ultimate, even diabolical survival reality TV show, *Brit Pluck*, set in the jungle of Papua New Guinea. From the very beginning, the reader is able to see that Hawes's novel is indeed an exquisitely and harshly satirical comedy about popular and postmodern (British) culture which is ruled by spin doctors, sensationalist media hordes, and the loss of traditional values – an impression that becomes more intense as the narrative progresses. As the main events of the jungle adventure are set around Christmas, Brian, possibly named after Jacob Marley in Charles Dickens's *A Christmas Carol* (cf. Holmes) and easily recognizable as the quintessential English everyman, encounters both past, present, and future versions of England and Englishness, as *Speak for England* and the ›journey‹ of its protagonist combines three distinct dystopian settings: 21st-century Cool Britannia culminating in the depiction of the survival camp in the jungle wilderness, a utopian colony modeled on pre-1960 English traditions, and eventually Great Britain being corrupted (or rescued?) after the repatriation of the colonists (cf. Clements).

The first chapter of *Speak for England* is strangely reminiscent of a classical Robinsonade. Though not invoked directly in the novel and lacking the typical shipwreck story, the parallels to the Robinson story are striking as Marley undergoes an adventurous and grueling ordeal of his own. All necessary and recognizable elements are found: total seclusion from society and confinement on an island, decline in health, keeping a diary, challenge to the castaway's mental sanity and convictions, and appearance of a servile companion (cf. Barberet 115-19; Fisher 130-32). But does this make Marley's tale a truly postmodern Robinson story? Hawes's fifth novel merges elements of high and low culture: it features remarkable resemblances to famous TV shows such as *Survivor*, *Lost* or *I'm a Celebrity – Get me out of Here* and combines these with traditional motifs of the Robinsonade as found in Golding's *Lord of the Flies* or *Pincher Martin*. As Alfred Hickling aptly states, *Speak for England* presents us with a »scintillating parody of a horribly plausible TV concept« (Hickling; cf. also Berberich 395). What makes the Robinson scenario in *Speak for England* both a bogus and recognizable version of Defoe's Ur-Robinsonade is the fact that the novel creatively combines conventional elements of the castaway narrative with embellishments of modern culture. Marley is not the victim of a shipwreck but rather of a helicopter crash which leaves him with just a camera and knife and without any provisions or means of establishing contact to the mainland. Retreating even deeper into the jungle and thus into the heart of the dark, croc-infested wilderness, he is not only bruised and battered but also slowly descends into madness. Despite his plight, Marley's sole intention is to send proof of his survival to his baby son with the digital satellite camera he managed to retrieve from the site of the chopper crash. Even the last of the main characteristics of the Robinson story is met as a dazed and disoriented Marley hears an evil voice that urges him on to pluck up his courage and live, a voice that he varyingly identifies as »his invincible other self« or as a »mad bastard« (4), but which can easily be interpreted to be an imagined Friday figure.

Similarly, the jungle experience itself appears rather like a popular, stylized TV series than the believable description of the tropical forest and several times in the text this description borders on the ludicrous. The respective text passages abound in superlatives and are adjective-ridden, thereby pinpointing the exaggerated manner of the horror awaiting Marley. To give a short but expressive sample from the novel:

[...] the horrid forest night had fallen with its usual awful, equatorial speed. As the last light faded, Marley, frantically scanning the fast-darkening patch of sky above his head for any sign of approaching aircraft [ ], had finally been driven from the crash site by nightmarish hordes of enormous, slavering crocodiles, drawn out of their depthless, Jurassic swamps by the scent of flame-grilled Western flesh. [...] he had escaped those lunging, prehistoric jaws only by a despairing scramble up into trees filled with horrific, thigh-wide snakes, unbearable clouds of mosquitoes, hordes of ticks, armies of leeches, vast, clattering moths, small but inconceivably deadly frogs and spiders the size of dinner plates. (11)

Tellingly, the jungle scenario is presented as if to fit the title of the survival show or even to outdo it: it is a »Green Hell« like no other, endless and invincible – or so Marley thinks. Accordingly, it remains debatable whether the report provided by a confused and fearful man can actually be verified as a convincing jungle situation. All the same, the colorful images of unconquerable wilderness flashing at the reader can be interpreted as an author's postmodern play with the reader's expectations and prejudices. Similarly, just as the wilderness descriptions seem exaggerated or even fake, so the protagonist does not appear to be an ›ideal‹ Robinson facing the situation head on; rather he is a self-loathing, pitiful, cowardly wimp, who at times appears not only dazed but literally scared out of his wits and sense of self:

Which? How? Who?
Marley's body stood frozen before the soaring rock face, but his mind staggered with internal vertigo as he stared into the endless, meaningless blackness of his own self. Where his voice should have been, where *he* should have been, there was nothing but a dizzying void. […]
With his shivering finger poised over the button in case he should miraculously hit the *authentic* tone of himself, he tried to begin speaking to his *real* three-year-old son at the *imagined* age of twenty-six, across the gap of twenty or more post-mortal years.
Christ, if only he was Irish. They know how they sounded. Or Scots. No problem for them. Welsh, whatever. Anyone who knew exactly what they were supposed to sound like and just did it without thinking. Someone who knew exactly who they were. A Geordie, a Scouser, even a Brummie for fuck's sake, there, see, *for fuck's sake*, that was not him, that was not how *he* spoke, that was something to do with Ireland or Australia or something, that was someone else, that was learned, taken on, taken up, borrowed. A caveman, that would be real. A lump of unthinking primate. He would just look at the camera and smile and wave goodbye. (20-21; emphases in the original)

The passage above deserves closer attention for several reasons. Faced with a seemingly insurmountable cliff, Marley finally realizes the hopelessness of his situation, alone, lacking resources and a plan to escape. Trapped in this feeling of utter despair he begins to question his own identity: as a father who cannot relate to his son, as a Western European stuck in an inimical wilderness, and also as an Englishman who is unable to claim a distinct cultural heritage or identity. The choice of words in this passage makes Marley's internal turmoil all the more poignant. Similar to the description of a measureless and untamable jungle, his inner chaos and confusion is termed »endless, meaningless,« and »dizzying,« while his struggles to be or even sound ›authentic‹ or to relate to his only son are thwarted. Family roles, nationality, and even identity are assumed and borrowed. Accordingly, in answering the opening questions of which/how/who he is, Marley sees himself as a caveman or primate, a real savage, who just follows his baser instincts to survive and thus eclipses everything else. But are we dealing with genuine emotional reactions here? For once, feelings of confusion and panic are to be expected; also Marley's need to imagine his baby son all grown up and happy is understandable; yet the sudden rush of anger when considering his inability to feel proud of his own nationality materializes out of nowhere and seems oddly out of place. It may even be a superfluous addendum to an otherwise believable scene, inserted strategically by the author to show Marley's (and thus England's) lack of cultural orientation, a void which will and can only be filled by the antiquated, yet powerfully convincing, moral and social values of the non-native inhabitants of the jungle, a camp of British citizens who survived a plane crash decades earlier and who are led and controlled by a man calling himself ›the Headmaster.‹

Most interestingly, however, it is in the deepest and darkest heart of New Guinea, this »place utterly hostile to human life, let alone civilisation« (7), that Marley gets closer to England than ever before in his life. Climbing the Hindenburg Wall and leaving behind the dystopian jungle world, he stumbles on what can at first glance only be described as an Englishman's utopia, complete with »cricket, rugger, decent chaps and pretty girls, brought up on a diet of Dan Dare and the strip cartoons of the Eagle, certain of their place in the world« (Clements). Moored on this island out of time and place, the inhabitants of the tiny colony (the Headmaster and his willing disciples) are survivors of a 1958 Comet IV aircraft crash, who have managed to uphold their archaic version of England according to a pre-1960s prep-school model, with the Headmaster Quartermain as the chief of the village. Thus, both Marley and the readers find themselves confronted with a bunch of settlers who

have staunchly upheld old-fashioned, traditional notions of Englishness. They have raised the British Standard and, with stiff upper lips, braved the dangers

of their castaway existence while propagating, from generation to new generation, politically *in*correct images and ideas of English supremacy and superiority over other countries and races. (Berberich 395-96; emphasis in the
original)

Thus, the way of life in this community of adept and resourceful Crusoes is fascinating when it comes to a study of authenticity and how
the villagers perceive and conduct themselves. Michael Seidel's study
on Defoe's novel identifies one important step that Crusoe takes in
order to accommodate himself to his new surroundings: he »names
things that pertain to his condition in such a way that he builds a repli-
cate universe in isolation. [...] It gives him a civilized veneer in so
natural a place« (191). This process of replicating the real is exactly
what the colonists have done – to a stunning degree:

At the far end of the hut was a small raised stage. Above its centre, two
crossed bamboo staves carried a large Union Jack and an Australian flag of
exactly equal size, the reds aged to pink, the deep navy shades faded to sky
blue like the ragged, blood-rusty colours of regiments long amalgamated or
disbanded, hanging in the still, dusty, wood-polished air of a quiet English
country church. Between the banners hung a framed and faded portrait of the
young Queen Elizabeth and her dashing Duke of Edinburgh. (Hawes 110-11)

This »shrine of Englishness« (396), as Christine Berberich calls it, can
be seen as a site of memory and tradition, both of which have faded
over time and have more or less truthfully been reconstructed from the
few documents, books, and paraphernalia that were rescued from the
crash. Considering Vannini and Williams's almost lyrical comment
that the »authentic stands against replicas, pretense, and posing« (»Authenticity« 2), the villagers' ceremonial customs appear to be not only
an utterly inauthentic strategy to keep alive memories and traditions,
but also contrary to any ideas of cultural and social evolution. In order
to keep England alive and the wilderness at bay, the colonists have
modeled their village along the lines of conservative and outdated, if
not outright mythical, ideas of Englishness, creating for themselves a
version of the Sceptred Isle that is as far away from reality as their re-
mote sanctuary home is from the actual island. And while all the
members of the colony appear to be fully brainwashed and indoctri-
nated by the impressively manipulative Headmaster, the latter is anx-

ious to hear Marley's report of England's present situation and status in the world, only to be frustrated and clearly infuriated by the truth he hears: »That all sounded pretty damn good at first, about the rugger and everything, went down very well, you made England sound like a fine place. But then you damn nearly blew it, you silly sod« (207). Accordingly, the colonists' attempt to authentically reconstruct or rather resourcefully simulate real England is threatened by the arrival of the mediocre English everyman and with him the unexpected and indeed unwanted reality of 21st-century Britain.

To remedy this situation and to prove that their ›sheltered‹ version of England is the more authentic and desirable one, the colonists leave behind their not so paradisiacal Garden of Eden and after their repatriation turn Blairite Cool Britannia into a dystopian and reactionary distortion of former English glory. Consequently, the tyrannical Headmaster ousts the British government and eradicates democracy by means of his repressive, even »draconian policies« (Clements). To name only the most important alterations in the name of ›real‹ and ›proper‹ Englishness: immigrants are sent back, civil rights are suspended, the presumption of innocence is abolished, the European Union is abandoned, Scotland and Wales are granted independence, and Britain becomes a colony of the United States. The brutal reality of the island utopia/dystopia has descended upon the English as the conservative Robinsons exact revenge on a post-secular and postmodern society: Great Britain is transformed from a democratic, multicultural society to a xenophobic and repressive semi-autocracy under the leadership of the Headmaster. Clearly this dystopian story is both delightful and frightening when it comes to the author's inventiveness in forging an alternate reality and it stands as a »fine piece of satiric craftsmanship, complete with a warning about the dangers of nostalgia« (Edmonds). Accordingly, while the two stories about Marley's stay in the wilderness and the colonists enjoying their secluded little Britain sound relatively believable, this third segment could be easily read as yet another playfully postmodern and dystopian story of the *1984* variety.

WILDERNESS SPACES, DYSTOPIAN PANORAMAS, AND NEW ›AUTHENTICITIES‹

Concerning both its plot and major motifs, Jeanette Winterson's novel *The Stone Gods* can be seen as an evident continuation of and challenging contradiction to her earlier oeuvre, especially as regards attempts to discuss or define ideas of authenticity. The author herself provides a number of suggestions on her webpage when she describes *The Stone Gods* as »love-cum-survival story« and rejects any notions of the novel as an ecocritical »pamphlet or a docu-drama or even a call to arms« (Winterson, *Webpage*). Still, even in discarding these aspects of her novel, both reader and critic will quickly find these categories essential when trying to come to terms with this skillfully fragmented and playfully satirical postmodern story. As many of the rather controversial reviews of *The Stone Gods* have pointed out, this tale of love and survival is genuinely Wintersonian in its portrayal of gender twists and brilliant use of language as well as exceptional with regards to its pronounced science fiction elements and political and ecological concerns so far unprecedented in Winterson's oeuvre (cf. Onega 274).

In terms of authentic representation, *The Stone Gods* also holds a lot in store. Already the innovative and overly stylized structure of the narrative is telling: Billie/Billy Crusoe, whom Winterson describes as »our guide through the novel« (*Webpage*) is the protagonist in every of the four sections of *The Stone Gods*, respectively impersonating a rebellious and disillusioned PR consultant on Planet Orbus (chapter one), a marooned sailor on Easter Island shortly after the arrival of James Cook's expedition in 1774 (chapter two), and finally a disobedient scientist specialized in building human-like robots (chapters three and four). T he first two episodes present sample cases of environmental decline and ecological exhaustion. Especially the story about the islanders, who ravage their territory and its flora in order to produce and honor their massive idols, the stone gods, works as the center- (and title-)piece of Winterson's ecological tale because it stands apart from the other stories both in plot and motif. Chapter one, set 65 million years ago, tells of the death song of Orbus and the ill-fated attempt to colonize Planet Blue and can well be regarded as a counterpart of the microcosmic ecological disaster on Easter Island, on a yet larger, even interstellar scale. Still, both stories are only fictitious renderings of our own environmental situation; or, as Susana Onega aptly puts it, »*The Stone Gods* is primarily a work of fiction aimed at imagining into being new possibilities of reconfiguring the deeply diseased, terminal condition of our polluted and overexploited planet« (275).

In terms of authenticity this scenario offers several interesting starting points for analysis. Firstly, by naming the protagonist Billie/Billy Crusoe, Daniel Defoe's Ur-Robinsonade is invoked as a fascinating intertext to this novel, creating a futuristic sci-fi but also believable »pseudo-Robinsonade« (Fisher 130). One might even go as far as stating that the protagonist can be placed in what Owen calls the tradition of »postmodern, female Crusoes« (259). Indeed, in each part of *The Stone Gods* the protagonist appears stranded or even tossed into an unknown, hostile, and challenging world/planet/island: in section one Billie finds herself marooned in a freezing wilderness during a colonizing-mission to Planet Blue; in section two Billy is stranded on an exotic yet dying island; in sections three and four, Billie leaves behind the security of the Tech City compound to explore the surrounding wasteland areas, a secluded district inhabited by banned outlaws and victims of nuclear radiation. The parallels between the seemingly unconnected stories thus become obvious and highlight Winterson's own thoughts when she characterizes *The Stone Gods* as a »story of repeating worlds, repeating mistakes, chances for change« (*Webpage*).

When trying to analyze this fictitious yet believable rendering of Earth's possible future, one has to consider several aspects and motifs of the novel. As has been observed in most reviews, Tech City can easily be recognized as a near-future London, thus turning the presentation of planet Orbus and its inhabitants into »a distinctively British hell full of bureaucrats and media wannabes, [which] prompts unexpected thoughts of Alasdair Gray and Philip K. Dick« (Lake). By means of including notorious Big-Brother-techniques such as surveillance and CCTV, media overkill, repression of civil rights, and corporations replacing elected governments, this sterile, post-atomic »Rent-me-Rent-me world« is strongly reminiscent of the bestseller dystopias of the previous century, such as Orwell's *1984*, Huxley's *Brave New World*, and Atwood's *The Handmaid's Tale*, to name but a few (*Stone Gods* 164). But the text also lists keywords and motifs of well-known utopian texts:

The new world – El Dorado, Atlantis, The Gold Coast, Newfoundland, Ply-mouth Rock, Rapanaui, Utopia, Planet Blue. Chanc'd upon, spied through a glass darkly, drunken stories strapped to a barrel of rum, shipwreck, a Bible Compass, a giant fish led us there, a storm whirled us to this isle. (8; cf. 94, 150, 238)

The narrator toys with the issue of utopian/dystopian worlds and baits the reader with stock motifs of castaway and discovery narratives, thereby highlighting yet another leitmotif of this only seemingly loose-ly structured novel.

Leaving aside the question whether Winterson has managed to draw a convincing end-of-days scenario, I would like to focus again on the easily recognizable intertext at work, namely Defoe's Ur-Robinsonade. Julie Ellam fittingly describes *The Stone Gods* as a »purposeless derivative of *Robinson Crusoe*« (220), and indeed it is not only the family name of the protagonist that makes this analogy worth considering. Although each chapter has its own Billie/Billy, each of whom faces surroundings that show severe ecological prob-lems, one fact never changes: Billie/Billy Crusoe is paired either with a fellow sailor, the ›female‹ *Robo sapiens* Spike – a friend-cum-lover Friday figure – or a mysterious male guide called Friday. Compared to the original Crusoe story, in which the castaway is accompanied by a native, the story of *The Stone Gods* reveals a gender-inverted Robin-sonade that alternates between lesbian desire and assumed heterosexu-al love. It comes as no surprise, therefore, that Ursula K. Le Guin speaks of an »ironic comedy« since the lesbian lover is eventually re-duced to a talking (and licking) head and Billie finds herself drawn to her ultra-male, sure-footed rescuer. Yet the parallels between Defoe's castaway narrative and Winterson's dystopian version of it cannot on-ly be indirectly inferred by unmistakable similarities in name and plot; the novel also directly invokes *Robinson Crusoe* in order to foreshad-ow the events to come or to highlight a particular thought of the pro-tagonist: »*I was born in the year 1632 in the city of York, of a good family, tho' not of that country...* That's not me, that's Robinson Cru-soe. Birth is a shipwreck, the mewling infant shored on unknown land« (146; emphasis in the original). Inquiring into her uneasy, if not totally ruined childhood, the Billie of chapter three links the story of her birth to Defoe's *Robinson*, thus merging two tales of loners strand-ed in a world they neither know nor fully comprehend.

Additionally, aspects of liminality are prominent in *The Stone Gods* since the story abounds in descriptive detail of enclosed, un-known, or fantastically embellished spaces. The Billie Crusoe of chap-ter one is an outlaw from society in every sense of the word: she has not undergone age-fixing, she has supported protesters, and she lives in the very last ›normal,‹ rural patch of land to be found on Orbus, complete with live animals and a weathered cottage. Billie enjoys in-habiting this »last farm-cum-museum« (Onega 295), which preserves a tiny bit of authenticity from the past. However, she is continually made aware of the consequences of defying social and political princi-ples. She herself describes her abode as follows: »My farm is the last of its line – like an ancient ancestor everyone forgot. It's a bio-dome world, secret and sealed: a message in a bottle from another time« (13). In identifying the idea of the ›message in the bottle‹ as another of the multiple leitmotifs of *The Stone Gods*, this idea of being trapped in a secluded spot out of place and time reminds the attentive reader once again of the Robinson story, thus highlighting the »sense of alone-ness« of the archetypical lonesome individual fighting for survival in a hostile, and in this case completely dehumanized, world (Ellam 220; cf. Dennison). Consequently, it is not surprising that Orbus's bureau-crats take every step necessary to ensure the cessation of Billie's status *extraordinaire*, which eventually leads to her forceful re-allocation to Planet Blue, and thus to an actual wilderness.

In effect, the wilderness topic deserves a closer look when it comes to the discussion of the aesthetics of authenticity in Winterson's novel. As the plot »jump-cuts to several other locations, each with its own Billie and each with its own ecological problems« (Holgate), I will examine two sample passages depicting ›wilderness,‹ both of which are genuine renderings of uninhabited or desolate space, yet al-so defy any such clear-cut definition of the wild. At the beginning of the novel, the reader is confronted with a wilderness image of Planet Blue that is not only anti-realistic and anti-naturalistic in presentation but most likely faked and even propagandistic:

Trees like skyscrapers, and housing as many. Grass the height of hedges, nuts the swell of pumpkins. Sardines that would take two men to land them. Eggs, pale-blue-shelled, each the weight of a breaking universe. And, underneath, mushrooms soft and small as a mouse ear. A crack like a cut, and inside a million million microbes wondering what to do next. Spores that wait for the wind and never look back. Moss that is concentrating on being green. (3)

Indeed, this crafted, exaggerated image of Planet Blue is part of a media coup to sell the discovery mission to the public as well as to barter away miles and miles of the yet uninhabited planet to well-off customers. However, it is made clear in the novel that taking possession of the yet pristine and healthy planet will involve massive changes in this world's ecological set-up, most prominently the extinction of the giant reptiles that vaguely resemble dinosaurs. Most interestingly, no one seems to consider these plans to be immoral or counter-productive since the »[m]onsters will be humanely destroyed« (6) so that the »new planet will be home to the universe's first advanced civilisation« (7).

 Still, all of this is in line with the major ideologies underlying the social and political institutions of Orbus. Everything is controlled by monetary considerations; global corporations have taken over and tightly control everything and everyone, creating a synthetic world dependent on biotechnological inventions and artificial intelligence to safeguard the survival on a planet which is slowly falling apart. This consumerist attitude is exemplified in a short, but very telling dialogue between Billie and a shop assistant, Tasha. Having just purchased an evening dress and related articles, Billie is electronically charged with the sum and decides to make »a voluntary donation to Charity of the Month, which this month is Apes in the Wild. ›There isn't any Wild,‹ I [Billie] say. ›Exactly so,‹ says Tasha. ›The money is to create a strip of Wild, and then put Apes in it‹« (29). Having no identifiable wilderness areas left on Orbus, the wild – or at least some fake version of it – has to be recreated, being turned into both a media stunt and a means to soothe the environmental conscience of a population on the brink of extinction. When one considers the fact that this wilderness is not only something entirely inauthentic and refashioned, but also something that can be controlled through technology and human zeal, the involuntary landing in the »odd, mythopoetic wildness« (Lake) of Planet Blue seems all the more striking, unexpected, and frightening to those stranded in this hostile environment: »We landed in a jungle dense as night. The noise was deafening. Out of the green darkness we heard whistles and woops, yelps and cries of creatures we had never even had nightmares about« (84). This time, however, the wild creatures are real, nightmarish, uncontrollable, and give the distinct impression of an untarnished and prehuman proto-wilderness.

But even at this point, Planet Blue is on its way to turning – rapidly – into a planet equally hostile to human life as Orbus. And again it is human intervention, i.e. the miscalculated attempt to get rid of the dinosaurs that triggers a mini ice age, which leads to the imminent death of most lifeforms on Planet Blue – including Billie and Spike. Instead of paradise regained, the sublime and pristine beauty of Planet Blue is turned into an inimical, freezing hell-hole, creating an atmosphere of desperation and longing for the two stranded survivors:

It's dark now; the dark is cold and the cold is dark. [...] It will be a long time before anyone comes back to Planet Blue. And I remember it as we had seen it on that first day, green and fertile and abundant, with warm seas and crystal rivers and skies that redden under a young sun. (110-11)

The chance for a new start in a promising and abundant utopian paradise suddenly morphs into a dystopian and fatal nightmare.

There remains one further illustration of wilderness to be analyzed, namely Billie and Spike's trip to the wasteland area surrounding Tech City, aptly called Wreck City, which is a »No Zone – no insurance, no assistance, no welfare, no police. It's not forbidden to go there, but if you do, and if you get damaged or murdered or robbed or raped, it's at your own risk. There will be no investigation, no compensation. You're on your own« (179). Accordingly, Wreck City is a place outside civilization, outside jurisdiction, outside technology; it is a multicultural, multifaceted loophole that allows a captivating glimpse of Orbus's pre-atomic past and bleak future at the same time. It is there, in the ruins and filth of this outlaw district, that Billie encounters the survivors of the last atomic war, a meeting which is strikingly different from the depiction of the fathomless wild beauty of Planet Blue. Yet, the sites of nuclear destruction and radioactive pollution are also depicted in an intriguingly lyrical, if not lamenting fashion, yet not entirely lacking a realistic tinge:

In front of me, barring my way, was a petrified forest of blackened and shocked trees, silent, like a haunted house. I moved towards it, frightened of what I would find, with an instinct for danger that only happens when there really is danger.

I moved through the first rows of trees. Their bark had a coating – like a laminate. Further in, deeper, I could see that these trees were glowing. Was this place radioactive?
Underfoot was soggy, not mossy soggy, not water-logged, but like walking on pulped meat.
It wasn't only that the forest was silent – no bird noise, animal sound, tree cracking, it was that I had become silent. My footsteps sank into the pulp, and because I was afraid, my whole body had quietened itself, like a child hiding in a cupboard, afraid of the adult outside. (191-92)

This passage gives the impression of a perverted, poisoned jungle world, as images of fertile wilderness and teeming life are substituted by illustrations of the horrific damage being done to nature and man: instead of bustling life there is dead silence and irritating inactivity. Susana Onega observes in this context that »the nostalgic and sentimental tone of the narration of Billie's entrance into the Dead Forest [...], with its sweating trees and hairless and deformed mutant children, progressively develops into an overtly elegiac style, reaching a climax with Billie's programmatic crying for the death of the planet« (297):

Above me, the sky is drilled with stars, ancient light, immense distances, new worlds. If we found another planet, we could leave everything behind, start again, be safe. It would be different, wouldn't it? Another chance. [...]
And my tears are for the planet because I love it and because we're killing it, and my tears are for the wars and all this loss, and for the children who have no childhood, and for my childhood, which has somehow turned up again, like an orphan on my doorstep asking to be let in. But I don't want to open the door. (238-39)

With that, it seems, the adventure story about Billie Crusoe, her lover and friend Spike, her guide Friday, comes to an end. Confronted with ecological and personal disaster, Billie ponders the possibility of starting all over again on a different planet and mourns the willful destruction of her own world. In view of this, the manuscript about the sailors stranded on Easter Island left behind on the tube and the message recorded by the dying Billie and Spike on Planet Blue some 65 million years ago connect the stories effectively and hint at the circularity of the plotline. Going back to Robert Kuhry's statement that »authentici-

ty is a process of *unfolding*« (vii; emphasis in the original), the factor
›time‹ is significant in the individual's realization of what is real and
believable. Thus it is not surprising but rather logical that the Billie of
chapter three finds the manuscript of a short novel called »The Stone
Gods.« This found piece of writing essentially provides the story of
Billy the Sailor of chapter two. As the short Easter Island story would
appear – at first glance – oddly out of place in-between two detailed
stories of personal vanity, environmental failure, and scientific misfortunes, letting Billy stumble upon the lost piece of writing effectively
incorporates the shortest of the stories of Winterson's novel into the
general dystopian frame narratives. Moreover, this narrative strategy
enables the reader to recognize the circularity of time and unavoidable
repetition of every perceived reality, which must end in total extinction, no matter which millennium, planet, or way of thinking:

I took the manuscript out of my bag, dropped the pages, picked them up again,
shuffled as a pack of cards.

»What's that?« Spike asked.

»It's what I told you about, today, yesterday, when I don't know when, it
seems a lifetime ago. The Stone Gods.«

»I wonder who left it there?«

»It was me.«

»Why, Billie?«

A message in a bottle. A signal. But then I saw it was still there […] round and
round on the Circle Line. A repeating world.

Is this how it ends?

It isn't ended yet.

»The book isn't finished, but this is as far as I could go.«

»What shall I do with it?«

»Read it. Leave it for someone else to find. The pages are loose – it can be
written again.« (241-42; emphases in the original)

As messages from a past that is not so different from Billie's present
situation, the recorded message and the manuscript provide the reader
with an idea of what is about to happen, for every reality is a »repeating world – same old story« (59). Accordingly, the fact that a working
version of Winterson's novel was actually found at Balham tube station by Martha Osten can be interpreted as an uncanny, real-life enactment of the fictional tale or just a very clever media stunt to

promote the novel (cf. Onega 294-95); either way it hints at the circular and palimpsestic character of Winterson's narrative, indicating that stories, worlds, and identities are not static but continually rewritten and relived and re-imagined.

»THAT'S THE OFFICIAL STORY. WHAT'S THE REAL STORY?«

This quote, taken from *The Stone Gods* (73), seems to be quite handy for a summary of how ideas of authenticity influence any reading of James Hawes's *Speak for England* and Jeanette Winterson's novel. Both novels skillfully use fractured plot constructions and postmodern narrative techniques of adeptly replicating existing motifs in order to create compelling dystopian tales. As I have tried to demonstrate, however, there is more to these cleverly envisioned novels than just that. Both writers take up the castaway theme to generate stories of identity troubles and wilderness struggles: In *The Stone Gods* Winterson manages to weave an intriguing tale of ecological plight and of ill-fated attempts to tackle the wild, a tale which is repeated in different eras but with the same result – complete environmental decline and enforced relocation. In *Speak for England*, too, the scenario of a survival show gone awry, which in all probability could be true, is quickly but convincingly turned into a ravishingly funny satire about the reconstruction of jolly old England in the middle of a jungle wilderness before morphing into what can only be called an exaggerated dystopian vision of Great Britain corrupted and transformed into a mere shadow of its former splendor. Since the novels are postmodern takes on the Robinson story, their plots depart from the classical frame by means of using conventional elements of the castaway narrative in order to embellish two critical analyses of personal anxieties, ecological worries, and doubts about the accomplishments of popular culture at the beginning of the 21st century. But what about the issue of authenticity in both novels? The question of what is authentic and what is not can be traced in both Marley's and the colonists' nostalgia for what is essentially British as well as in Billie's sincere emotional turmoil when faced with the imminent death of the planet. The protagonists' ability to eventually recognize the true nature of the situation works not only as the satirical backdrop to the stories, but also as the moral compass for both Marley and Billie – and the reader. Having returned to Britain and being confronted with the rapid and massive changes taking place under the new leadership of the Headmaster, Marley begins to grasp the true and appalling nature of the situation. And eventually the extent of the loss of personal and cultural reliability dawns on him. Equally, when facing the inevitable clash of a disobedient individual with the repressive social system, Billie's determined protest against and seclusion from mainstream society culminates in her realization of the interconnectedness of worlds, human beings, and experiences. That is the real story – maybe.

WORKS CITED

Barberet, John. »Messages in Bottles: A Comparative Formal Approach to Castaway Narratives.« Novak and Fisher 111-21.

Berberich, Christine. »Whose Englishness Is It Anyway? James Hawes' Post-Modern Take on Englishness in *Speak for England*.« *Englishness Revisited*. Ed. Floriane Reviron-Piégay. Cambridge: Cambridge Scholars Publishing, 2009. 389-400.

Clements, Toby. »I'm English, Get Me out of Here? Toby Clements Reviews *Speak for England* by James Hawes.« *The Telegraph*. 16 Feb. 2005. Web. 20 Feb. 2011. http://www.telegraph.co.uk/culture/books/3636951/I%27m-English%2C-get-me-out-of-here%E2%80%A6.html

Dennison, Matthew. »*The Stone Gods* by Jeanette Winterson.« *The Times*. 22 Sept. 2007. Web. 20 Mar. 2011. http://entertainment.timesonline.co.uk/tol/arts_and_entertainment/books/fiction/article2503936.ece

Edmonds, Curtis. »Review: *Speak for England* by James Hawes.« *The Bookreporter*. n.d. Web. 20 Feb. 2011. http://www.bookreporter.com/reviews2/1596921412.asp

Ellam, Julie. *Love in Jeanette Winterson's Novels*. Amsterdam: Rodopi, 2010.

Ferrara, Alessandro. »Authenticity Without a True Self.« Vannini and Williams 21-35.

Fisher, Carl. »The Robinsonade: An Intercultural History of an Idea.« Novak and Fisher 129-39.

Hartman, Geoffrey. *Scars of the Spirit: The Struggle against Inauthenticity*. Basingstoke: Palgrave Macmillan, 2002.

Haselstein, Ulla, Andrew Gross, and MaryAnn Snyder-Körber. »Introduction: Returns of the Real.« *The Pathos of Authenticity: American Passions of the Real*. Ed. Ulla Haselstein, Andrew Gross, and MaryAnn Snyder-Körber. Heidelberg: Winter, 2010. 9-31.

Hawes, James. *Speak for England*. San Francisco, CA: Lawson, 2005.

Hickling, Alfred. »All for Empire: Alfred Hickling is Pleased to Discover that James Hawes Has Matured into a Wonderful Satirist with *Speak for England*.« *The Guardian*. 8 Jan. 2005. Web. 20 Mar. 2011. http://www.guardian.co.uk/books/2005/jan/08/features reviews.guardianreview24/print

Holgate, Andrew. »*The Stone Gods* by Jeanette Winterson.« *The Times*. 7 Oct. 2007. Web. 20 Mar. 2011. http://entertainment .timesonline.co.uk/tol/arts_and_entertainment/books/fiction/article 2584107.ece

Holmes, Andrew. »Enid Blyton meets the Blairites.« *Scotland On Sunday*. 2 Jan. 2005. Web. 20 Feb. 2011. http://living.scotsman. com/features/Enid-Blyton-meets-the-Blairites.2591888.jpg

Kuhry, Robert. »Prologue.« *Authenticity: The Being of the Self, the World, and the Other*. Ed. Robert Kuhry. Saratoga, CA: R & E Publishers, 1987. v-x.

Lake, Ed. »It's a Miracle – Another Planet for Us to Break: Jeanette Winterson, *The Stone Gods*.« *The Telegraph*. 29 Sept. 2007. Web. 20 Mar. 2011. http://www.telegraph.co.uk/culture/books/fiction reviews/3668240/Its-a-miracle-another-planet-for-us-to-break.html

Le Guin, Ursula K. »Head Cases: Ursula K. Le Guin Admires Jeanette Winterson's Complex and Cautionary Science-fiction Tale, *The Stone Gods*.« *The Guardian*. 22 Sept. 2007. Web. 20 Mar. 2011. http://www.guardian.co.uk/books/2007/sep/22/sciencefictionfantas yandhorror.fiction

Milnes, Tim, and Kerry Sinanan. »Introduction.« *Romanticism, Sincerity and Authenticity*. Ed. Tim Milnes and Kerry Sinanan. London: Palgrave Macmillan, 2010. 1-28.

Novak, Maximillian E., and Carl Fischer, eds. *Approaches to Teaching Defoe's* Robinson Crusoe. New York, NY: MLA, 2005.

Onega, Susana: »The Trauma Paradigm and the Ethics of Affect in Jeanette Winterson's *The Stone Gods*.« *Ethics and Trauma in Con-*

temporary British Fiction. Ed. Susana Onega and Jean-Michel Ganteau. Amsterdam: Rodopi, 2011. 265-98.

Owen, C.M. *The Female Crusoe: Hybridity, Trade and the Eighteenth-Century Individual.* Amsterdam: Rodopi, 2010.

Richter, Virginia. »Authenticity: Why We Still Need It Although It Doesn't Exist.« *Transcultural English Studies: Theories, Fictions, Realities.* Ed. Frank Schulze-Engler and Sissy Helff. Amsterdam: Rodopi, 2009. 59-74.

Salmela, Mikko, and Verena Mayer. »Introduction.« *Emotions, Ethics, and Authenticity.* Ed. Mikko Salmela and Verena Mayer. Amsterdam: John Benjamins, 2009. 1-7.

Seidel, Michael. »*Robinson Crusoe:* Varieties of Fictional Experience.« *The Cambridge Companion to Daniel Defoe.* Ed. John Richetti. Cambridge: Cambridge UP, 2008. 182-99.

Vannini, Phillip, and J. Patrick Williams. »Authenticity in Culture, Self and Society.« Vannini and Williams 1-18.

——, eds. *Authenticity in Culture, Self and Society.* Farnham: Ashgate, 2009.

Winterson, Jeanette. *The Stone Gods.* London: Hamish Hamilton, 2007.

——. »*The Stone Gods.*« *The Jeanette Winterson Webpage.* n.d. Web. 10 Mar. 2011. http://www.jeanettewinterson.com/pages/content/in dex.asp?PageID=471

Monica Ali and the Suspension of Disbelief

MELANIE METTLER[1]

> ... so as to transfer from our inward
> nature a human interest and a sem-
> blance of truth sufficient to procure
> for these shadows of imagination that
> willing suspension of disbelief for
> the moment, which constitutes poetic
> faith.
>
> SAMUEL TAYLOR COLERIDGE/
> BIOGRAPHIA LITERARIA, BOOK XIV

Postcolonial literature is highly affected by issues of authenticity and the related concepts of authority, credibility, plausibility, ›semblance of truth,‹ and, finally, believability. Authenticity is both evoked and attributed on various levels, three of which will be considered in this article. The first is textual authenticity, meaning the depiction of a particular setting and character in the novel, and the reception thereof by representatives of said context. The second level is authorial authenticity, which refers to the background of the author. In Monica Ali's

---

1   I would like to thank the editors for their review of the first draft, which was a great help in giving this text more focus. I would also like to thank my colleagues at the Interdisciplinary Centre for Gender Studies at the University of Berne for their invaluable comments, especially Carolin Schurr, Melanie Rohner, Dr. Andrea Kofler, Prof. Dr. Brigitte Schnegg, Ruth Ammann, and Michelle Amacker.

case, this is for example the fact that she is BritAsian, but not a Sylheti Bangladeshi like the characters in her first book, or that she is Brit-Asian, but not Portuguese like some characters in her second book. The third level is reader authenticity, centering on the question of who is entitled to voice criticism. I argue that authors of postcolonial background, particularly (young) women, are under considerable pressure to qualify their writing by authenticity. Monica Ali reacts to the violent criticism of her first book *Brick Lane* by framing her subsequent novels in a different way. This article presents a reading of the reception of Monica Ali's novels in the media with the aim of identifying the ways in which the three levels of authenticity are attributed. There are some interesting conclusions to be drawn with regard to evoking ›human interest‹ in the context of a postcolonial particularity situated in contradistinction to Western universality.

›Brick Lane‹ is not only the title of Monica Ali's first novel, but also an example for a real existing place developing into a cultural symbol. It designates a street in London which has become a symbol for the Bangladeshi community in Britain and, for the not particularly fussy majority failing to distinguish between different South Asian cultures, religions, and nations, even for BritAsians in general. Brick Lane is also a restaurant in Manhattan, »Brick Lane Curry House – Home of the *real* curry« (*Brick Lane Curry*; emphasis in the original). From the website of a restaurant called Brick Lane in Dubai, we learn that the real curry is actually BritAsian and, despite the fact that 90% of South Asians living in Banglatown are Bangladeshi from the Sylhet region, it is also Indian: »Indian Take Away – Authentic British Indian Curries Brought to Dubai« (*Brick Lane Curry*). Brick Lane is a label and is being marketed as authentic not for Sylhet but BritAsian culture. Recently, in a crafty move by the council of Tower Hamlets to increase residents' acceptance of London's hosting of the 2012 Olympic Games, Brick Lane and Banglatown have been named »Curry Capital 2012« (»Curry«). The reactions to this endorsement bring to the surface what Brick Lane has become: the epitome of the authentic curry in Britain and a commodified culinary cliché, a stereotypical tourist trap. A product that has to draw the masses will necessarily be a watered-down version or mashed-up conglomerate of original ideas and subsequently be considered inauthentic by purists of the trade.[2] The scope of the term Brick Lane has, however, broadened both culturally and geographically to reach far beyond the culinary or the London tourist attraction. It has evolved to be understood as synonymous with Banglatown, ›little India,‹ or even BritAsian culture.[3] What does this tell us about the perceived authenticity, and by implication, cultural authority over the nature of BritAsianness? The reactions of some Sylheti Bangladeshi to Monica Ali's novel *Brick Lane* – the title invoking all those cultural markers associated with the term – are indicative of an unarguable tetchiness in relation to the issue of representation.

Despite the narrative turn, textual authenticity is very much alive as an indicator of quality in narrative art. An analysis of reviews of Monica Ali's books and other reactions to the novels in the media brings to light quite astonishing results. What is still considered relevant first and foremost are the content and subject matter of the plot as well as the psychological depth and accuracy of characters. The other aesthetic features of novels (e.g. structure, style, mode) are regarded as secondary when experts discuss a novel in the media, just as they seem to be when members of the public react to the literary depiction of a world they feel to be representative (or rather, not representative) of their own.

Authorial authenticity is an especially pronounced expectation for authors considered to be postcolonial or representative of any other minority discourse. So-called postcolonial novels seem to be attributed the function of opening a window into another world, exposing a cer-

---

2 Becoming inauthentic is a necessary result and, echoing Judith Butler's discussion of the non-representativeness of labels, a constitutive feature of political and cultural identity markers taken up by mainstream culture. For an astute discussion linking authenticity with Butler's theories on performed identities including the issue of identity labels and political signifiers as permanent sites of contest and the resulting ephemeral nature of representation, cf. Richter.

3 Another self-proclaimed spokesperson for the inhabitants of Brick Lane writes: »I am a British Bangladeshi; I have lived and worked in and around Brick Lane for most of my life. Brick Lane for Bangladeshis is like Chinatown for the Chinese. It is our cultural home, a place where we gather and share our culture and life with each other and with visitors« (Masroor).

tain educational desire by the reviewer. Publishing houses play on this desire expertly. Using the circumstances of production as a selling point, novels are marketed accordingly, thereby catering to and sustaining escapist and exoticizing expectations. The requirement for authenticity and the moral demands for sincerity due to this based-on-a-true-story effect seem consequential and will be discussed with the help of critical texts linking authenticity and the commodification of literature.

Monica Ali's fictional oeuvre to date consists of the novels *Brick Lane* (2003), *Alentejo Blue* (2006), *In the Kitchen* (2009), and *Untold Story* (2011). I will proceed to give an overview of the media reactions to each of those novels in order to lay out the field for a subsequent examination. I argue that the author as well as publishers are well aware of the processes described above and react by framing her novels accordingly.

Brick Lane is essentially the story of a young Bangladeshi wife newly arrived in London from Dhaka to live with her older husband. Her husband Chanu has been educated in England and has been living and working there for all of his adult life. The marketing of the novel includes a book sleeve with an appealingly colorful typeface including chili, patterned fabric, and food. The author is introduced as being born in Dhaka, Bangladesh, having grown up in England, and living in London with her husband and two small children. The market positioning of the novel by the publisher clearly draws on characteristics of exoticizing postcoloniality. The paratexts include a dedication of the novel to »Abba, with love« and two epigraphs, one by Ivan Turgenev and one by Heraclitus. Whereas the personal dedication of the novel to Monica Ali's father, using the Bengali word, pays tribute to her heritage, the epigraphs by a 19th century Russian novelist and an ancient Greek philosopher as a framing device situate the novel in a cosmopolitan literary tradition. The novel created media controversy both when it was published and again when it was turned into a film.

On publication, feminist writer Natasha Walter wrote a glowing review of the literary merit of Ali's debut novel, entitled in conveniently exoticizing terms »Citrus Scent of Inexorable Desire.« Walter recognizes how the novel's stereotypically fruit-abounding style in the initial Bangladesh chapters (ripening mangoes and coconuts galore) develops with the protagonist's geographical, personal, and cultural translocations and complications – failing perhaps to discover the iron-

ic comment provided by this stylistic feature. Monica Ali, half Bangladeshi and half English herself, evokes the postcolonial stereotypes in
her depiction of Bangladesh to create distance between the narrative
voice and the exotic setting. The novel's success, influenced by its
nomination for the Man Booker Prize, also evoked reactions of a quite
different sort. Fareen Alam, in her article in *The Observer*, summons
the image of the novel as an educational window into a different world
as well as the problem of the fallacy of considering the origins of authors as an obligation to accurately depict circumstances.[4]

Ali's novel has been much praised for its narrative power and for offering a
rare account of the British Bengali diaspora experience. [...] It celebrates the
humanity and complexity of a community which even Bengalis like me know
so little about; a community that has been pushed to the margins of Britain's
ethnic mosaic [...].
Yet the book has angered many. Most Bengalis I spoke to – from the waiter at
my local Indian restaurant to social workers and politicians – have not read the
book, but they have heard that Ali makes insulting remarks about certain segments of the community. Never mind that one of their own is this year's most
celebrated writer [...].
But we would rarely ask other writers the same questions that are asked of
Monica Ali. [...] It seems that only ›ethnic‹ writers carry a burden of ›representation‹ whether they want to or not. [...]
Monica Ali could hardly be expected to capture in a single novel the lives of a
›community‹ of almost 300,000 people.

Fareen Alam takes up several issues in her comment. She sums up the
way *Brick Lane* has been attributed textual authenticity, as well as being criticized for claiming undeserved textual authenticity. Interestingly, she states that the criticism for claiming textual authenticity seems
to come from people who have not read the book, but have been confronted with the attribution of authenticity by the media. She then goes
on to question the way this attribution of textual authenticity seems to
be based on the expectation of authorial authenticity – in this case a

---

4   Fareen Alam is the editor of the Muslim magazine *Q-News*, an independ-
    ent publication with a print-run of 20,000 copies, claiming a distribution of
    60,000 readers on their website.

writer of minority background who is attributed the status of representative.

Almost half a year later, a registered charity called The Greater Sylhet Welfare and Development Council, claiming to represent »many of Britain's 500,000 Bangladeshis« (M. Taylor), wrote an eighteen-page letter of complaint to the publisher as well as *The Guardian*, asking Monica Ali to correct the false depictions of Bangladeshis as pronounced by one of the novel's major characters, Chanu (cf. M. Taylor). Publishers reacted by commenting that »Chanu is a pompous, bigoted man. We should not confuse Monica Ali's views with the views of this character« (Roy). In the *Telegraph* coverage of the matter the next day, Greater Sylhet Welfare and Development Council representative Kalam Mahmud Abu Taher Choudhury was quoted as doubting the ability of a white readership to distinguish between evaluative statements of fictional characters and those of the author (cf. Roy). Granta editor Ian Jack stepped in, also stressing the difference between fictional texts and journalistic representation. However, he could not resist to implicitly accuse the publisher Doubleday for cultural insensitivity by saying that

when the book was published in Britain, Ali's publishers held [a] glorious party in the commodious rooms of an old brewery in Brick Lane. Forgivable then, surely, that the people who live in Brick Lane might think that the book was about them, their beliefs and behaviour, in one way or another.

In the process, ironically, Jack mirrored Choudhury's patronizing assumption of readers' incompetence. Choudhury doubted that white readers would be able to regard *Brick Lane* as a fictional text rather than an ethnographic account; Jack found it understandable that Brick Lane residents would mistake *Brick Lane* as a factual report about themselves.

Meanwhile, U.S. publisher Scribner briefly considered publishing *Brick Lane* under a different title (cf. Smith), but the next uproar did not surge through the media until the filming of *Brick Lane* on location was due. Threats of protest and book burning were issued and distributed in the press. Germaine Greer commented on the affair, leading one to suspect some underlying essentializing ideas of cultural belonging and representation when she said that »[n]one of this would have happened if Ali had not created her own version of Bengaliness. As a

British writer, she is very aware of what will appear odd but plausible to a British audience.« Based on the old feud between Germaine Greer and Salman Rushdie, the latter predictably submitted a letter to *The Guardian* with a scorching comment on Greer's article, saying that »[h]er support of the attack on this film project is philistine, sanctimonious and disgraceful, but [...] not unexpected. As [he] well remember[s], she has done this before« (Rushdie). The battle for Brick Lane seemed in full flow. Finally, and conveniently in time for the release of the movie, Monica Ali herself wrote an article about the *Brick Lane* affair, her reactions to diverse accusations, and her motivations for writing the novel:[5]

The second bit of baggage to unpack comes with the label ›authenticity‹ attached. Who is allowed to write about what? What right does a novelist have to explore any particular subject matter? Who hands out the licences?

It appears that some people object to my having written about a Bangladeshi housewife who speaks hardly any English, when I myself am reasonably fluent in the language. I'm far from being the only writer to be accused of failing the ›authenticity test.‹ Gautam Malkani, author of *Londonstani*, was reprimanded last year for writing about Asian homeboys in Hounslow because he is educated and in full-time employment. (»Outrage«)

Monica Ali's comment combines questions of textual and authorial authenticity, and introduces the third level of authenticity, which I have called readership authenticity. While openly asking the question as to which author is considered suitable to write about what issues, she effectively turns the tables by questioning the authority of readers to determine the ownership of particular subjects. The issue of authority and authenticity in immigrant fiction and immigrant authorship has not only been discussed in the case of Monica Ali. Different motivations might drive these discussions, be they ideological, religious, or commercial. In the famous case of Salman Rushdie's *The Satanic Verses,* the novel was read to misrepresent Islam and therefore considered blasphemous, which led to the issuing of a fatwa. This is a dangerous situation to be in and Monica Ali started to fear for her family.

---

5   For a full discussion, cf. Maxey.

There is, however, another quite cynical side to the coin – market-ability. One online commentator in the affair pointed out how any kind of publicity is desirable in the publishing world and stated that

Monica Ali's interpretation of the inhabitants of Brick Lane has not gone down well. From a Sylheti perspective, she is not from that region and has never visited there, so unless she has good research, her accounts and depictions are likely to be flawed. [...] Sunday's demo, along with the general media attention towards Brick Lane, has increased the popularity of Ali's book, which will fly off shelves once again. The best thing of all is that all this publicity is free. The demonstrators have failed in their aim of sending Ali flying back into oblivion. There is nothing more lucrative than a fatwa, as the saying goes. (Rahman)

However, likening the Brick Lane protests to a fatwa, which would present a threat to the author and her family, implies that a publisher would be prepared to sacrifice an author's safety for an increase in sales. This highly cynical comment might take matters too far, but still the point has been made that publishers are happy to sacrifice literary ambition for marketability if need be.

Graham Huggan, using a theoretical model of authenticity as commodity, takes these aspects of the literary marketplace into account. He pleads for finding ways to reconcile mainstream expectations for authenticity and aesthetically relevant literary evocations and evaluations.

The search for authenticity [...] involves the reaching out to alternative reader-ships, including the people one regards as being one's own. [...] it also involves a reflexive approach to authenticity – one that plays on the expectations of the international ›market reader,‹ as well as on a readership more likely to be acquainted with the text's (inter)cultural nuances and representational codes. (Huggan 176)

Huggan's proposition therefore appeals to the level of conscious readership authenticity, intricately linked with questions of marketability, textual and authorial authenticity. Huggan combines two concepts equally unpopular in literary scholarship. Authenticity as well as marketability cause many literary critics to turn away embarrassed at the terms, or else to dismiss them as invalid analytical categories. This means neglecting the ability of authenticity to function as a deal-maker or deal-breaker in the literary market. Marketing and the label of postcolonial literature are major factors in both the dissemination and the interpretation of works of literature. Commercial market demands and cultural market expectations are weighed against each other in a constant battle for visibility and media platforms. Before I continue to discuss the reception of Monica Ali's subsequent novels, let me briefly expand on what I mean by commercial market demands and cultural market expectations.

The commercial market demands with respect to postcolonial literature are much influenced by the desire for exotic escapism. However, by tapping into exoticizing stereotypes when positioning a novel within a specific genre, its association with postcolonial literature and multicultural Britain results in reader expectations novels seldom manage to keep. This is directly linked to the levels of textual and authorial authenticity mentioned above. If a book like *Brick Lane* succeeds in capturing a mainstream audience, the positioning of the author as multicultural and the resulting referral to authenticity becomes problematic. This happens when the novel is regarded as being representative merely due to the fact of being read by a specifically targeted audience and receiving the respective media attention. A similar point has convincingly been argued by Ursula Kluwick in her discussion of packaging designs of postcolonial books. It is while striving for universal appeal that »any subversive potential [is reduced] in its first contact with readers by marketing the book as ethnic or even exotic« (86). Similarly, Ana María Sánchez-Arce describes a particular use of authenticity serving a »politics of representation that reflects ›reality,‹« which often naïvely claims to describe marginalized situations, thereby constructing their otherness in the process (141). Sánchez-Arce aptly uses the term ›authenticism‹ for this implicit recourse to an original reality. With an understanding of authenticity defined in this way, readers have specific expectations of literary works marketed as products of a different background and referential framework. Which original reality are the books supposed to be representing? As will be elaborated below, I argue that Monica Ali attempts to escape from this market positioning by framing her subsequent novels increasingly as decidedly non-postcolonial.

The cultural expectations in the postcolonial literary market are diverse, incongruent, and contradicting. Ruth Maxey discusses the role of critics in establishing reader expectations by milking exoticizing cultural markers for commercial reasons. This links directly to the level of readership authenticity outlined at the beginning of the chapter. Maxey claims that the opposition to *Brick Lane* based on lack of representativeness is closely linked to the novel's mainstream success as a multicultural text. »Indeed it is perhaps precisely because other critics have proved so intent upon establishing the totemic significance of the novel that its ›authenticity‹ has come under such fire from South Asians« (228). Ruth Maxey's point, placing the expectation of representativeness of Monica Ali's texts on the critics' doorstep, those very critics who establish what she calls »totemic significance,« has an unexpected effect.[6] If the exoticizing expectations of minority representations are indeed due to marketing and publicizing issues as well as subsequent reviews and media coverage, then the expectations should change if the tone of the paratexts as well as the coverage changes. If the causal relation underlying this argument is indeed established, it has to be possible to predict reader expectations from the stance of marketing as well as critical reception. The following overview of the media coverage of Monica Ali's novels after *Brick Lane* might illustrate the accuracy of this point. Additionally, I argue that authors and publishers have certain simple methods at their disposal to influence the positioning of the text. Monica Ali's strategy to use paratexts with *Alentejo Blue*, *In the Kitchen*, and *Untold Story* brings to light how the choice of setting and of protagonist alone can determine to a large extent the perception of the novels.

One might surmise that the reactions to *Brick Lane* and the constant need to defend and justify one's text would lead to a desire to avoid the same hullaballoo with the following novel. Monica Ali was starting to be recognized as well as rejected (but decidedly marketed) as an emerging BritAsian voice, speaking from within. From her public reactions one realizes that she was not entirely happy with the potentially dangerous position she was in. In a commercially daring but aesthetically interesting gesture of experimentation, she chooses to refuse that role by changing both setting and protagonists in *Alentejo Blue*. The place is a small town in Portugal, the protagonists change with every chapter, all featuring distinct narrative voices with stylistic idiosyncrasies. Some of the themes remain – such as the experience of

---

6   For a discussion of this problem, cf. Spivak.

migration, issues of self, society, and identity, the loneliness of love –
but are in themselves not multicultural enough to justify the postcolonial bookshelf. The colorful book sleeve and patterned lettering remain, but the author is now described as the author of one previous
novel shortlisted for the Man Booker Prize and as living in London.[7]
The novel is framed by the acknowledgments which stress that *Alentejo Blue* is neither a history book nor a travel book, but a work of fiction. The dedication, most soberly, is for S.C.T. Besides two epigraphs
by Portuguese Nobel Prize winner José Saramago and Ameri-
can/British poet T.S. Eliot, the novel is preceded by an instruction for
pronouncing »alentejo,« using an example from French. This can be
interpreted as a gesture of pointing towards reader authenticity. Who is
qualified to read this text written in English? The narrative voice
seems to imply a reader who reads English, does not speak Portuguese, but does know how to pronounce French words. On the first
page of the novel, the first character, a Portuguese old man, uses an
untranslated Portuguese word. It is as if Monica Ali turns the tables on
her readers by no longer putting questions of textual or authorial authenticity into the center, but such of reader authenticity.

Natasha Walter »is underwhelmed« by *Alentejo Blue*, and com-
plains that »the further you go in Alentejo Blue the further you seem
to get from Brick Lane. [...] The only thing that holds the book together is its geographical unity« (»Continental Drift«). While, in her
opinion, the young Bangladeshi protagonist in *Brick Lane* marked the
emergence of a writer finding her own voice, she finds that »the most
underwhelming parts occur when she tries to sum up such difficult,
resistant characters as the old peasant in just a few pages, using stock
images and drifting into the picturesque to cover up the absence of the
particular.« Walter observes that »Ali is much better when she gets
closer to home, as with Stanton, the English writer« and sums up that
»you can't help wishing that Monica Ali had chosen to write about
somewhere she knew better, or wanted to know better.« That Walter
herself might not be in a position to judge the accuracy and authenticity of the internal musings of an old Portuguese peasant does not seem
to occur to her, nor does she explain in what particular way the Eng-

---

7   Funnily enough, while in *Brick Lane* the title font featured the postcolonial
     exoticizing markers, now it was the author's name that was set in bold pat-
     terned font.

lish (male) writer should be closer to home to the author Monica Ali. It also does not occur to her that her praise of Ali's exoticizing prose in the Bangladesh chapters in *Brick Lane* illustrated her unquestioned belief in the authenticity of Ali as a South Asian, but apparently not as a writer of fiction. In contradistinction to Walter's review, Alex Clark's article entitled »Escape from Brick Lane« places more value on Ali's exploration of new themes and explains that

> once in the village of Mamarrosa, in a series of vignettes tracking the comings and goings of inhabitants, visitors and assorted ne'er-do-wells, she reprises several of Brick Lane's themes: the nature of a place's integrity, or authenticity, in the face of shifting populations and economic fortunes; the fraught communications between groups of people divided by upbringing; and the possibility, or lack of it, of genuine assimilation.

The effect on the interpretation of this translocation of themes so distinctively marked as BritAsian and postcolonial is only hinted at in the quote. By positioning the issues as transnational, transcultural, and transgendered, Clark recognizes that Ali simultaneously stylizes them as universally human and that the dichotomy between postcolonial particularity and Western universality is questioned.

The next novel, *In the Kitchen,* marks an even more pronounced move away from the stereotypes of exoticism and multicultural postcoloniality and a positioning towards the field of literary fiction without a prefix. The white male protagonist, a chef in central London, presides over a host of international staff while slowly losing first the identification with his own life, then his morals, and finally, his mind. The packaging of the novel is monochrome, clean, with sober lettering and simple design. Monica Ali is introduced as the author of two previous books and as living in London. The novel is dedicated to Kim and there are no epigrams or other paratexts. D.J. Taylor introduces *In the Kitchen* as

> a novel about modern urban tribes, diaspora and mono-cultural smash. In a work environment where »every corner of the earth was represented,« Gabe and fuddled teenage trainee Damian are the kitchen's only home-grown staff. The old folk up in Blantwistle lament the end of ›Britishness‹ and a multiculturalism that sets myriad translations of council leaflets against insufficient library books.

The setting and the protagonist are decidedly distant from the author persona. It becomes clear, however, that Monica Ali stays true to her themes of everyday life, of identity, modes of disconnection, reinvention, and definitions of home. In a similar vein, Christopher Tayler discusses the book on a thematic level:

In the Kitchen works best as a novel about work. Ali has done her homework on restaurant kitchens and weaving, and uses both as sustained metaphors for contrasting visions of society: the cohesive social fabric nostalgically remembered by Gabe's father and his peers, and the melting pot of Gabe's kitchen in the contemporary world of deregulated labour. Perhaps, the New Labour MP suggests, British identity has itself been marketised: »We talk about the multicultural model but it's really nothing more than laissez-faire ... Britishness is or has become essentially about a neutral, value-free identity.«

Tayler acknowledges the amount of research which Ali performed while writing the book, indicating a satisfaction with the textual authenticity of the novel. The MP mentioned in the quote, also white and male, talks about collective values and identity as something that has essentially been erased from society. This can be linked to the distance of the narrative voice, which reports the most disturbing scenes without comment.

Stressing the thematic concerns of the narrative, linking it to the text's ambition to present a voice on national and global politics of identity, labor, trade, and gender, the main concern here is again the issue of credibility, of the quality of research, i.e. of textual authenticity. In an interview with Claude Peck, Ali refers to this almost compulsive attempt at obtaining an authoritative narrative:

Of the current craze for memoirs, reality TV and so-called authenticity, [...] I think it's a misunderstanding of how fiction works. It's a kind of detrimental lowering of the culture, to believe that something is better if it's true, if it's factual. For me, the thing that might be truly illuminating is often made up. (Peck)

It seems that whereas Ali accepts the role of narrative fiction as a source of education, she does not feel that this education is of the sort entailing accurate informative representations of facts. Despite the fact that In the Kitchen presents just as many (if not more) concerns with issues of gender and exploitation on a structural as well as a thematic level, it is the spelled-out instances of comments by the characters on the question of citizenship, multiculturalism, and identity which are in the center of the reviewers' discussions. It might be argued that this is largely due to persisting reader expectations with respect to the post-colonial author of *Brick Lane.*

Monica Ali's most recent novel, *Untold Story*, can be interpreted as an author's move to get even more ground between herself and her subject matter, or, alternatively, as a way of claiming not only her Bangladeshi, but also her English heritage. It is a novel about Princess Diana, who in this story has not been killed in a car accident, but has staged her death in an attempt to escape the public eye and save her mental sanity. As with *In the Kitchen*, the book sleeve is monochrome, sleek, and simple. Again, Monica Ali is introduced as the author of three previous novels and as living in London. The novel is only framed by a dedication to M.M.S., features no epigraphs, and simply acknowledges her resources for her research. The book was again received ambiguously. Joanna Briscoe exclaims in a scandalized tone that

Monica Ali makes some surprising decisions, to say the very least. After her Booker-shortlisted, bestselling debut Brick Lane, she came up with a book of short stories whose setting was inspired by – well, her second home in Portugal. Not every publisher's dream followup, nor, one would hazard, every reader's. Next she chose to write about a hotel kitchen. Now this fine literary author has devoted a novel to the subject of Princess Diana.

Needless to say, Briscoe does not much like the novel, which she puts down to unconvincing characterization, reminiscent of the reactions of some Bengali readers of *Brick Lane.* Briscoe takes issue with breaches of confidence both on the level of textual as well as authorial authenticity. As a reader, she feels forced to suspend her disbelief where she is not prepared to release control. However, Briscoe does not consider readership authenticity. It is Monica Ali's luck to have journalistic champions supporting her attempt to be judged as a literary writer rather than a representative of an ethnic minority. Yasmin Alibhai-Brown reprimands her colleagues most clearly on the topic:

Critics who think that Ali should stick within some ›multicultural‹ enclosure betray their own gated and turgid little minds. They want the author to deliver only intensely flavoured takeaway tales about ›alien‹ Bangladeshis. Yet Brick Lane, the book that made her, was a creative leap too for the half-English, middle-class, Oxbridge writer.

So I fully defend Ali's choice of subject and tone too, populist and accessible: a bold departure for a critically acclaimed writer.

Consequently, Ali's novel has to stand the test as a fully grown literary novel – and fails. Alibhai-Brown is disappointed with the text, surmising that the novel's only merit lies in catering to the Diana-obsessed just for the money, and that being able to sell the movie rights was the key motivation for the choice of protagonist. Clearly, the balance between commercial market demands and cultural market expectations has not been found according to this journalist's opinion. Across the Atlantic, *New York Times* literary critic and Pulitzer-prize winner Michiko Kakutani finds that

[a]t first glance, the novel is quite a departure from the subject matter of Ms. Ali's earlier work; both *Brick Lane* and her second novel, *In the Kitchen*, drew portraits of a gritty, multicultural London, peopled with struggling immigrants and young strivers. Yet by turning Diana (or, as the author has said, »a fictional character, based on Diana«) into a British expat named Lydia, who's hiding out in a small American town, Ms. Ali is able to address some of the same questions of identity and exile that animated her earlier work, while reprising her favorite fish-out-of-water theme.

Literary critics often establish the context for a novel by summoning the same author's previous novels. It makes for readability, possibly reminding readers not particularly adept at remembering names of the identity of the author after having heard the titles of her previous books. Also, I am sure the publishing houses are happy with the references. However, in the next few paragraphs, Kakutani employs vocabulary intricately linked with expectations of verisimilitude, credibility, and authenticity:

But if the narrative machinery expertly grinds out suspense, the details Ms. Ali feeds into that machine are ridiculously contrived. We are asked to believe that [...].

But it's a conclusion, it must be said, that's a lot more satisfying than much of the rest of this implausible and preposterously gimmicky novel.

The reference to the suspension of disbelief illustrates Kakutani's preoccupation with questions of authenticity of the text. This recourse to expectations of believability and plausibility might be considered an instance of a categorical blurring between authentic fact and narrative fiction and as such part of the fallacy of textual and authorial authenticity. Before I expand on this issue, let me introduce novelist Tibor Fischer's evaluation of the situation, which is the most startling of the few reviews currently available on *Untold Story*:

I'm not sure I'm really qualified to review Monica Ali's new novel because I don't know what a French tip manicure is and I'm rather hazy on taffeta. [...] Monica Ali is shaping up to be the Fay Weldon of her generation, producing the publishers' delight, classy commercial fiction – although many male readers like me may find there's a shade too much about dresses and potato salad. [...]
Monica Ali was on one of Granta's best of young British novelists list, in 2003. The Granta lists are regarded as full of Booker fodder, Jamesian exquisites like Alan Hollinghurst or superbrains like Julian Barnes, but they've always been an eclectic mix. Readers of *Untold Story* shouldn't expect that category of literary fiction; this isn't a Dostoevskian exploration of the depths of the human soul or an effort to stretch the remit of the novel. But then it isn't striving to do those things; it's what Graham Greene termed an »entertainment.«

Tibor Fischer, previously Granta Best Young British Novelist himself, seems to refer to the necessity of readership authenticity. Additionally, one cannot shake the feeling that in his case, the question of authenticity and authority pops up again because of the introduction of a different kind of ›minority‹: women writers. Since the author and protagonist belong to the same, namely the other, gender, Fischer feels entitled (authorized) to speak for the »many male readers like« himself and their hesitancy to engage in accounts of such stereotypically female occupations. By stressing the level of readership authority, Fischer is not only unconcerned with the levels of textual and authorial authenticity, but he dismisses the whole novel as unreadable for someone who does not belong to the same group as the protagonist (or writer).

Whereas it seems intuitive that novels should first and foremost be judged according to criteria of aesthetic and cultural value as works of art, it seems that, if the author is not white but South Asian, the products of this artist are expected to be authentic. If the author, for whatever reason, manages to shrug off this label and has the chance to be taken for the artist she is, she better make sure that she chooses not to conjure a female protagonist, since the whole dance might start afresh. It is highly interesting to note that the reactions of parts of the Bengali readership who did not feel themselves adequately represented in *Brick Lane* are closely mirrored by the reactions of parts of the British readership who did not feel themselves adequately represented in the novels set in Britain. Both sides seem to position themselves as performing some sort of gatekeeping function when Monica Ali tackles icons of the Bangladeshi (Brick Lane) and the English (Princess Diana) side of her own heritage.

The creative writing mantra of Write-What-You-Know, famously evoked by Mark Twain, has been going in and out of fashion time and again. Today, it is a popular starting point for beginners, a way to teach the basics of writing. After that, whether this style presents one of the options available to an advanced writer and whether it is employed or not is a matter of taste. Similarly, in literary criticism, failing to be able to distinguish between the author and the authorial voice of a fictional text is considered a classic beginner's mistake. Nevertheless, the public discussion of *Brick Lane* illustrates that both beginners and experienced theoreticians and critics, journalists, readers, and commentators continue to fall prey to an unreflected categorical merging and blurring when it comes to the subject of authenticity. What are authors to do to accomplish suspension of disbelief on the part of their readers? The distinction between expectations of authenticity on the levels of text, author, and readership can help bring light to this intricate network of influences.

The trajectory of reviews and media coverage of Monica Ali's work supports the initially intuitive point that critical reception can be influenced by the very simple circumstantial factors of plot and setting. Taking this knowledge a step further, Monica Ali's example seems to illustrate that authors and publishers have the power to position themselves and their work quite straightforwardly and elegantly in order to be perceived as representative of a specific group. This positioning creates reader expectations and most reviewers and critics in the case of Monica Ali's novels seem to have been tempted to follow the line of least resistance – depending on their background either defending or resisting the literary and fictional representations of her texts.

Discussing one single author's oeuvre and reception is not enough to formulate a general principle with regards to influencing the perception of authorial and textual authority and authenticity. From a critic's perspective, the question of textual authority in the case of literary fiction remains both topical and unsolved. Leaving aside the pervasive and persistent occurrence of readings of novels as sociological texts, literary critics seem to fall prey to the authenticizing fallacy even as they are foregrounding the fictionality of the texts. A plethora of aesthetic, psychological, referential, and receptive authenticities are invoked or rejected in discussing and evaluating the worth of these works of literary fiction. Another strategy to avoid the question of the relevance of authorial or textual authenticity is the labeling of the text as genre literature, thus replacing the demand to disentangle and analyze the meaning of intricate links between style, characterization, plot, and narrative by the simple demand to be entertaining and believable.

Irrespective of the question of literary or commercial success, Monica Ali seems to have managed to write herself out of the postcolonial corner, bursting the shackles of representational responsibilities of a BritAsian author. As a result, she has ceased to be a multicultural writer, but has become a writer with recognizable pet issues – for example the multicultural society.

WORKS CITED

Alam, Fareen. »The Burden of Representation.« *The Observer*. 13 July 2003. Web. 23 June 2011. http://www.guardian.co.uk/books/2003/jul/13/fiction.features

Ali, Monica. *Alentejo Blue*. London: Black Swan, 2006.

——. *Brick Lane*. London: Doubleday, 2003.

——. *In the Kitchen*. London: Doubleday, 2009.

——. »The Outrage Economy.« *The Guardian*. 13 Oct. 2007. Web. 23 June 2011. http://www.guardian.co.uk/books/2007/oct/13/fiction. film

——. *Untold Story*. London: Doubleday, 2011.

Alibhai-Brown, Yasmin. »Untold Story, by Monica Ali.« *The Independent*. 1 Apr. 2011. Web. 23 June 2011. http://www.independent .co.uk/arts-entertainment/books/reviews/untold-story-by-monica-al i-2258479

Brick Lane Curry House Too. 2009. Web. 2 July 2011. http://www. bricklanetoo.com

Briscoe, Joanna. »Untold Story by Monica Ali: Review. Joanna Briscoe Is Bewildered by Monica Ali's Reinvention of the Princess of Wales.« *The Guardian*. 2 Apr. 2011. Web. 23 June 2011. http:// www.guardian.co.uk/books/2011/apr/02/untold-story-monica-ali-review

Clark, Alex. »Escape from Brick Lane.« *The Observer*. 21 May 2006. Web. 23 Jun 2011. http://www.guardian.co.uk/books/2006/may/ 21/fiction.features1

»Curry Capital 2012.« *Tower Hamlets Council*. N.d. Web. 2 July 2011. http://www.towerhamlets.gov.uk/lgsl/800001-800100/80001 7_olympics/curry_capital_2012.aspx

Fischer, Tibor. »Untold Story by Monica Ali: Review. Monica Ali's What-if Novel Based on Princess Di is Classy Commercial Fiction.« *The Observer*. 3 Apr. 2011. Web 23 June 2011. http://www.guardian.co.uk/books/2011/apr/03/monica-ali-princess -diana-untold

Greer, Germaine. »Reality Bites. People in Brick Lane Are in Uproar about a Plan to Film Monica Ali's Novel. Do They Have a Point?« *The Guardian*. 24 July 2006. Web. 23 June 2011. http:// www.guardian.co.uk/film/2006/jul/24/culture.books

Huggan, Graham. *The Postcolonial Exotic: Marketing the Margins*. London: Routledge, 2001.

Jack, Ian. »It's Only a Novel...: Responses to Monica Ali's Brick Lane Testify to the Continuing Power of Fiction.« *The Guardian*. 20 Dec. 2003. Web. 23 June 2011. http://www.guardian.co.uk/ books/2003/dec/20/featuresreviews.guardianreview3

Kakutani, Michiko. »Imagining a Secret Life for Diana.« *New York Times*. 13 June 2011. Web. 23 June 2011. http://www.nytimes.com /2011/06/14/books/untold-story-by-monica-ali-review.html

Kluwick, Ursula. »Postcolonial Literatures on a Global Market: Packaging the ›Mysterious East‹ for Western Consumption.« *Translation of Cultures.* Ed. Petra Rüdiger and Konrad Gross. Amsterdam: Rodopi, 2009. 75-92.

Masroor, Ajmal. »We Want to Be Sensible, Not Censors: We, the People of Brick Lane, Have as Much Right to Feel Offended as Monica Ali Does to Write Her Book.« *The Guardian.* 27 July 2006. Web. 23 June 2011. http://www.guardian.co.uk/commentisfree/2006/jul/27/post260

Maxey, Ruth. »›Representative‹ of British Asian Fiction? The Critical Reception of Monica Ali's *Brick Lane.*« *British Asian Fiction: Framing the Contemporary.* Ed. Neil Murphy and Wai-chew Sim. Amherst, NY: Cambria Press, 2008. 217-36.

Peck, Claude. »›Kitchen‹ Philosopher: Monica Ali.« *Star Tribune.* 23 Mar. 2011. Web. 23 June 2011. http://www.startribune.com/entertainment/books/92463719.html

Rahman, Emdad. »The PR Money Can't Buy: Protests against Plans to Film Monica Ali's Novel Brick Lane Will Ensure that the Book Keeps Flying off the Shelves.« *The Guardian. Comment is free.* 1 Aug. 2006. Web. 23 June 2011. http://www.guardian.co.uk/commentisfree/2006/aug/01/theprmoneycantbuy1

Richter, Virginia. »Authenticity: Why We Still Need It Although It Doesn't Exist.« *Transcultural English Studies: Theories, Fictions, Realities.* Ed. Frank Schulze-Engler and Sissy Helff. Amsterdam: Rodopi, 2009. 59-74.

Roy, Amit. »East End Novel Insults Us, Say Bangladeshis.« *The Telegraph.* 4 Dec. 2003. Web. 23 June 2011. http://www.telegraph.co.uk/news/ukNews/1448414/East-End-novelinsults-us-say-Bangladeshis.html

Rushdie, Salman. »Brickbats fly over Brick Lane« *The Guardian. Letters.* 29 July 2006. Web. 23 June 2011. http://www.guardian.co.uk/books/2006/jul/29/comment.letters

Sánchez-Arce, Ana María. »›Authenticism,‹ or The Authority of Authenticity.« *Mosaic* 40:3 (September 2007): 139–155.

Smith, David. »It's Brick Lane by Any Other Name: Nervous US Publishers Nearly Retitled Booker-listed Novel as ›Seven Seas and Thirteen Rivers.‹« *The Observer.* 14 Sept. 2003. Web. 23 June 2011. http://www.guardian.co.uk/uk/2003/sep/14/bookerprize2003.usa

Spivak, Gayatri Chakravorty. *The Post-Colonial Critic: Interviews, Strategies, Dialogues.* Ed. Sarah Harasym. New York, NY: Routledge, 1990.

Tayler, Christopher. »If You Can't Stand the Heat: Christopher Tayler Samples Monica Ali's Cook's Tale.« *The Guardian.* 18 Apr. 2009. Web. 23 June 2011. http://www.guardian.co.uk/books/2009/apr/18/in-the-kitchen-monica-ali

Taylor, D.J. »Trouble at the Imperial.« *The Spectator.* 9 May 2009. Web. 23 June 2011. http://www.spectator.co.uk/books/3591601/trouble-at-the-imperial.thtml

Taylor, Matthew. »Brickbats Fly as Community Brands Novel ›Despicable.‹« *The Guardian.* 3 Dec. 2003. Web. 23 June 2011. http://www.guardian.co.uk/uk/2003/dec/03/books.arts

Walter, Natasha. »Citrus Scent of Inexorable Desire: Natasha Walter Finds that Monica Ali's Fêted First Novel, Brick Lane, Lives up to Its Hype.« *The Guardian.* 14 June 2003. Web. 12 June 2011. http://www.guardian.co.uk/books/2003/jun/14/featuresreviews.guardianreview20

——. »Continental Drift: Monica Ali leaves Brick Lane for Another Country in Her Second Novel, Alentejo Blue. Natasha Walter is Underwhelmed.« *The Guardian.* 20 May 2006. Web. 13 Jan. 2012. http://www.guardian.co.uk/books/2006/may/20/featuresreviews.guardianreview14

Performances

Poet and the Roots

Authenticity in the Works of Linton Kwesi Johnson and Benjamin Zephaniah

DAVID BOUSQUET

The title of this paper is taken from Linton Kwesi Johnson's first record, published in 1978 by Island Records in London. By bringing attention to the relationship of the poet to his roots, it illustrates the centrality of the question of authenticity in dub poetry, a poetic genre of which Linton Kwesi Johnson and Benjamin Zephaniah are prominent representatives. More generally, authenticity is a crucial concern for artists of the black Atlantic and has been intensely debated by critics over the last decades.[1]

In the Western tradition, authenticity is often perceived as the ascription of a text to an author, particularly in literature and poetry, but also in music. That is the way many historians use the notion of authenticity: an authentic document is a document which can be traced

---

1 The expression ›black Atlantic‹ is associated with thinker and cultural critic Paul Gilroy, who published a seminal book entitled *The Black Atlantic: Modernity and Double Consciousness* in 1993. He uses the phrase to refer to the cultures of the African diaspora, including ›original‹ African cultures, the displaced cultures of African slaves and their descendants in the Americas, and also the cultures of African immigrants in Europe. More precisely, this concept does not indicate fixed cultural entities, but rather the complex and dialectic cultural movements which constitute the African diaspora.

back to an identifiable and reliable source, to an origin which, in the case of a text, is an author.[2] This model of textual authority is often described and criticized through the notion of authorship, which can be defined as follows:

Authorship is a creation of literary culture and the marketplace; it is one of the great markers of ›high‹ as opposed to ›popular‹ culture, and it is invoked to ascribe not just meaning but value – aesthetic or moral as well as monetary – to works and authors identified by literary criticism (and marketing managers) as ›significant.‹ [...] Authorship is, then, a social system imposed on the domain of writing; it is not the act or trade of writing. It is a system for producing hierarchies within that domain. Authors are a product of a social division of labour, and authorship is an ideological notion which functions to privilege not only certain kinds of writing and writers, but also, more importantly, certain ways of thinking about the meaning of texts. [...] It seems to represent a pathological desire for an ultimate origin, a god who will finally limit the infinite potentiality of meaning. (O'Sullivan et al. 21-22)

This type of criticism of the notion of authorship, seen as the literary reflection of political and social modes of authority, is largely inspired by French critics of the 1960s and 1970s like Bourdieu or Foucault.[3] It finds a very potent echo in the context of the neo-oral culture of reggae sound systems within which dub poets operate, where music and poetry are primarily conceived of as oral performances enjoyed by a

---

2   The *OED* states that authenticity is »the quality of being authentic, or entitled to acceptance, [...] as being what it professes in origin or authorship, as being genuine,« while *Webster's Dictionary* defines the word ›authentic‹ thus: »of an origin that cannot be questioned: indisputably proceeding from a given source that is avowed or implied.« As Foucault has shown, history and literature overlap in the tradition of Christian textual analysis, which is obsessively concerned with issues of origin, authorship, and authority; in many ways the concept of author is based on definitions of godly authority (cf. Foucault 297-98).

3   Foucault developed the idea that the ›author‹ is not a real individual, but rather a social function which gives value and authority to a text. Bourdieu has shown how the social field known as literature helps in defining and validating a symbolic language for the ruling classes and the role of the author in this process.

community and not as written texts composed by individual authors. More specifically, cultural artifacts like poems or songs are not essentially linked to the written medium and can very rarely be attributed to a single individual author. Thus, the predominantly textual model of authenticity in the Western tradition has to be criticized in postcolonial contexts like that of Jamaican popular music and poetry, not so much as part of a philosophical enterprise than as a concrete necessity to create theoretical models which can account for hybridized, neo-oral cultural forms of expression.

The aim of this paper is to demonstrate how authenticity is understood by dub poets, which will shed a new light on the concept of cultural authenticity and break away from its essentialist and conservative definitions. In the context of Creole cultures, authenticity cannot be simply reduced to an abstract essence, be it racial, ethnic, social, or cultural. In other words, performances of dub poetry are not authentic because they reinforce a well-established, essentialized sense of identity and community: dub poetry performances do not involve only Caribbean, black, or working-class audiences and poets, and they do not need to be considered authentic in an essentialist sense.

The concept of authenticity that I will put forward here takes a sharp break from the textual models of authorship described above. It emphasizes the relational nature of authenticity, which is seen primarily as a process by which an audience accepts, or does not accept, to relate to one or several performers and thus form a community. In this light, authenticity appears also in its performative nature: it is not a universal value attributed once and for all to a text or any other cultural artifact, but it happens or takes place in the specific time and space of a performance.[4] For each new performance, the audience's adhesion to the process of performance is renegotiated, and so the sense of identity and community (just like authenticity) is not rooted in an abstract

---

4   The study of Jamaican popular music reveals how tempting it is for certain writers and musical analysts to think of songs in terms of texts written by individual authors, to extend the model of authorship to music, while songs are undoubtedly the result of a collective creative process involving musicians, singers, DJs, producers, and sound engineers. If identifying the source of musical compositions can be interesting for historical and documentary purposes, one cannot but wonder at the ideological implications entailed in approaching Jamaican music with alien concepts.

essence, which would stay the same at all times and in all places, but is produced in the contingency of a unique performance and celebrates its very transience and specificity.

I will start by giving a brief historical account of the birth and development of dub poetry. These contextual elements will help to delineate a culture of performance – musical, poetic, or other – where authenticity has to be seen primarily as an endless process of performative (re)creation of imaginary and imagined origins. Finally, I will take a closer look at poems by Johnson and Zephaniah to illustrate in more detail their conception of authenticity.

A BRIEF HISTORY OF DUB POETRY

The term ›dub poetry‹ was coined in the late 1970s by Jamaican poet Oku Onuora to describe the work he and Linton Kwesi Johnson published in these years.[5] The two pioneers were soon followed by a second generation of dub poets like Mikey Smith and Jean Binta Breeze in Jamaica or Benjamin Zephaniah in the UK.[6] Nearly all these poets know each other and each other's work, many of them were trained together at the Jamaican School of Drama, and they generally acknowledge the term ›dub poetry‹ to describe their work. Critics like Mervyn Morris have pointed out a number of common elements in the work of these poets, which can be briefly examined to get a first impression of this genre:

The word ›dub‹ is borrowed from recording technology, where it refers to the activity of adding and/or removing sounds. ›Dub poetry,‹ which is written to be performed, incorporates a music beat, often a reggae beat. Often, but not

---

5 Johnson's first collection of poetry, *Dread Beat and Blood*, was published in 1975 in London and was soon followed by Onuora's *Echo* in 1977. Johnson published another collection in 1980, *Inglan Is a Bitch*, and three records of his poems were performed to a musical accompaniment between 1978 and 1980 (*Poet and the Roots*, *Forces of Victory*, and *Bass Culture*), establishing him as the leading figure of dub poetry.

6 Habekost provides useful biographical information about the most significant dub poets of the 1970s and 1980s. Donnell and Welsh investigate into the third generation of dub poets in the 1990s.

always, the performance is done to the accompaniment of music, recorded or live. Dub poetry is usually, but not always, written in Jamaican language; in Jamaican creole/dialect/vernacular/nation language. [...] Most often it is politically focused, attacking oppression and injustice. (66)

Dub poets write and perform mostly in Creole, and Johnson was one of the first poets ever to publish an entire collection of poetry in this language. Most of the poems deal with the social conditions of the working classes in the West Indies and in West Indian communities in the UK, displaying an explicit political message.[7]

Dub poetry is also a form of performance poetry, which means, in very practical terms, that it is of prime importance for poets to deliver their art on stage to an audience, very often with a musical band. Most of the poets' publications are actually recordings of live or studio performances, with or without music. It entails a conception of poetry which is not primarily textual, but rather oral and thus performance-centered. Yet, the dub poets also publish their poetry as written texts, which is one of the reasons why they call themselves poets, as opposed to other artists of the Jamaican music scene who have very similar practices. This, incidentally, reveals that in Creole cultures poetry and literature are primarily seen as written, which is why certain critics still do not consider the oral poetry of the dub poets as real poetry.[8]

---

7   For that reason, dub poetry has sometimes been reduced to slogan poetry and thus characterized as unpoetic. The political ›message‹ of dub poetry is one of its fundamental and most controversial features which will, however, not be dwelled upon here.

8   Much critical attention has been paid in Creole Studies to orality and literacy as media of cultural expression and the ideological implications they carry. To simplify, Creole cultures are the result of an intense struggle between the imported culture of the white masters, associated with the written medium, and the (re)invented culture of the black slaves, associated with the oral medium. The choice of dub poets to privilege the medium of performance can be seen as a way to take sides with African forms of cultural expression, but the fact that they write and publish their poems also reveals the fundamentally Creole dimension of their work. For more detail about the recognition of dub poetry as ›true‹ literature, cf. Cooper; Donnell and Welsh 22-24, 286-89, 366-68. Cooper interestingly describes dub poetry as ›oraliterature‹ and investigates the strategies of hybridization be-

This emphasis on performance has to be understood in the context mentioned above, that of the neo-oral cultures of slaves who, for a very long time, were denied access to writing. As Paul Gilroy reminds us:

The power and significance of music within the black Atlantic have grown in inverse proportion to the limited expressive power of language. It is important to remember that the slaves' access to literacy was often denied on pain of death and only a few cultural opportunities were offered as a surrogate for the other forms of individual autonomy denied by life on the plantations [...]. Music becomes vital at a point at which linguistic and semantic indeterminacy/polyphony arise amidst the protracted battle between masters, mistresses, and slaves. (74)

These words help to understand the very intimate links between dub poetry and the Jamaican popular music scene. Dub poets perform and record with musicians and claim that their poetry is musical, even when it is recited without musical accompaniment.[9] The term ›dub poetry‹ itself refers to a musical style of the 1970s, while Johnson refers to his work as ›reggae poetry.‹[10] Dub poets openly acknowledge famous Jamaican DJs of the 1970s like U-Roy or Big Yout as one of their main sources of inspiration, like Zephaniah, who clearly compares his work to what Jamaican DJs were doing in the 1970s:

I've been doing poetry since I was seven years old really. First of all with a sound system, just chatting to music. Then one day there was a power cut and I just went on talking – without music. That's how I started doing poetry, with-

---

tween oral and scribal modes of meaning production in the texts and performances of dub poets (cf. 68-86).

9   Johnson has worked throughout his career with bass player Dennis Bovell, also known as a major producer on the British reggae scene (as Blackbeard) and founder of Matumbi, one of the most influential British reggae bands of the 1970s.

10   »When people have asked me to categorise what I do I say, well, if it's true that I write poetry within the reggae tradition (which I do) then I suppose that you could call some of my works as [sic] Reggae poems« (Johnson in Habekost 13).

out knowing someone who told me you have to do it this or that way. (Johnson in Habekost 30)

In Jamaica, DJs do not only play records, they ›chat‹ or ›toast‹ to the music and have come to be recognized as vocal artists in their own rights, just like singers, and even as poets:

The toaster tradition [...] in Jamaica involved the DJ talking smart, slick and often silly jingles into the microphone, either in introduction of a tune or in the spaces between the music. This was happening with Ska in the early sixties, and developed further with Rock Steady, a music with wider spaces. Techno-logical change in the mixing of music, the advent of the 16-track tape and easy over-dubbing, the development of the synthesiser, intensified the DJ's role as manipulator of sound, juggler of gimmicks, controller of rhythm and pace, ex-horter of the audience, who would be soldiered into jumping, prancing, raising their hands in the air, wining, grinding, and jamming, getting up or getting down to it. The DJ became high priest in the cathedral of canned sound, frag-mented discotheque image projections, broken lights, and youth seeking lost rituals amid the smoke of amnesia. (Brown, Morris, and Rohlehr 9)[11]

Next to the expansion of the role of the DJ, the 1970s saw another ma-jor innovation in the reggae music scene. The musical practices known as dub are extremely interesting for my point here: dubbing is an oper-ation which consists in rearranging a song from its constitutive ele-ments. Each vocal and instrumental track is first isolated before the sound engineer reorganizes them in a new combination, very often

---

11 The multiple roles of the DJ (singer, commentator of social or political events, ghetto journalist, dancer, actor) echo the significance of music in the cultures of the black Atlantic. The DJ is often seen as a modern version of the African griot, as Habekost suggests (cf. 31-33). He is also very often compared to Ananse, the West African spider-god who survives through his ability to change and disguise himself (cf. in particular Cooper 47-48). In the language of sound systems, an authentic performance is often de-scribed as mystic or mystical, it is conceived of in religious or spiritual terms especially by Rastafarians, who see musical or poetic performances as instances of meditation. On a more theoretical level, dub poetry perfor-mances can fruitfully be described as experiences of trance, magic, or ec-stasy which affect the body and the soul of the participants.

quite different from the original. The engineer adds personal elements like sound effects, gimmicks, or jingles, but also new vocal and/or instrumental tracks:

Each single instrument, the lead vocals and harmonies were recorded on at least one, frequently more tracks which could be re-arranged and remixed one by one. Together with this new process of mixing or ›over-dubbing,‹ new ideas were incorporated: sound effects with echo machines, reverberation, distortion. While the voice track disappeared completely most of the time in this ›dub version,‹ the remaining tracks were mixed in and out, confusingly sometimes. (Habekost 26)

Another key element in the world of Jamaican popular music is the sound system, a term which describes the privileged mode of diffusion and consumption of reggae music and related styles. Originally, the expression ›sound system‹ is used to refer to a set of machines used to play music in public places, namely a record player, an amplifier, and loudspeakers. By extension, the phrase came to designate the various people involved in the operation of the sound system: the soundman (owner of the equipment), the operator (who puts the records on the player), the selector (who chooses the records and gives them to the operator), and the DJ. But in Jamaican popular culture, a sound system is much more than a concert or a mere party, it is an opportunity to create and transmit meaning autonomously. A sound system involves music but also dancing and a great number of other social activities in a country where the expression of the lower classes was regularly banned.[12] Here is how Lloyd Bradley describes the functions of sound systems in Jamaican society:

---

12 Sound systems are very often illegal or clandestine parties in the sense that they are not authorized by the state or city councils. Organizing a sound system implies a reappropriation of public spaces for cultural expression, which results in sometimes violent conflicts with the authorities. This type of cultural resistance to the colonial order has deep roots in Jamaican history, particularly in the heritage of the Maroon communities (i.e. escaped slaves who formed autonomous communities in the Blue Hills and resisted the colonial state for centuries) later taken up by Rastafarians. It is also very much present in many Western subcultures like free parties, which

Outdoor dances [...] evolved from merely one more form of urban entertainment into the hub around which Kingston's various inner cities turned. For the crowds that flocked to wherever the big beat boomed out, it was a lively dating agency, a fashion show, an information exchange, a street status parade ground, a political forum, a centre for commerce, and, once the deejays began to chat on the mic about more than their sound systems, their records, their women or their selves, it was the ghetto's newspaper. (5)

All the books and documentary films dealing with the history of reggae and contemporary Jamaican popular music emphasize the centrality of the sound system not only as a form of ghetto entertainment and distraction from the hardships of (post)colonial life, but as a time and a space where cultural significations are produced, diffused, and consumed collectively. It is also interesting to note that, in a truly diasporic fashion, the »bass culture« of sound systems has moved away from the inner cities of Kingston and can now be found in all the different places around the world where West Indian communities live.[13] This is most notable in the UK and in the U.S. where the Jamaican practices linked to dub and sound systems laid the foundation for the emerging hip hop culture in the 1970s.

AUTHENTICITY IN THE BASS CULTURE OF SOUND SYSTEMS

Dub, DJs, and sound systems can give us a first idea of how the question of authenticity is perceived in Creole cultures. The popularity of a sound system derives from its collection of ›dubplates,‹ that is to say versions of songs that are produced specifically for a sound system: the vocalist records a new vocal track, includes the mention of the name of a specific sound system, and praises its quality. As musical analyst Lloyd Bradley has pointed out in his book *Bass Culture*, these practices imply a shift in the modes of consumption of cultural pro-

---

borrow not only the term ›sound system‹ but also part of this tradition of resistance.

13 »Bass Culture« is the title of one of Johnson's most famous records, published in 1980.

ductions, which are not valued so much for their originality but for their exclusivity: the important thing for a sound system is not to play new songs, but to offer a new and exclusive configuration of previously recorded material. Using Jamaican music as an example, Paul Gilroy explains that in the cultures of the African diaspora »the right to borrow, reconstruct, and redeploy cultural fragments drawn from other black settings was not thought to be a problem by those who produced and used the music« (94).

The example that springs to mind immediately when discussing the question of originality and borrowing in Jamaican popular music is certainly the work of Bob Marley. His songs have become a kind of subtext or intertext for much contemporary Jamaican music: Marley's lyrics are constantly quoted (more or less explicitly) and put to new musical accompaniments, while his music (his ›riddims‹) are unceasingly re-recorded and used by singers and DJs who deliver their own lyrics to it.[14] But Marley's popularity is not limited to Jamaica; as Gilroy indicates, the tendency to borrow and rearrange pre-existing material is a characteristic of black Atlantic cultures in general: the same phenomena could be identified in African American musical styles like blues, jazz, soul, or hip hop.

The practices of reggae DJs are another example of this tendency to rearrange or recycle cultural material which already exists, thus displacing the criteria for authenticity from originality (the ability to create something that never existed) to exclusivity (the ability to reconfigure existing material in a unique performance). In a sound system, DJs do not respect any order between the songs, nor do they play the songs from beginning to end. They very often interrupt a tune to play it again a few seconds later or to move on to the next one. They reinterpret or even rewrite entirely the lyrics of the original songs and are praised for their versatility, their ability to improvise ›lyrically‹

---

14 The word ›riddim,‹ a Creole deformation of the English ›rhythm,‹ is used by musicians to refer to the rhythm track of a song. With the advent of sound systems, instrumental versions of songs became more and more popular, notably because the DJs could use them to deliver their own lyrics. This tendency later developed into dub and today most reggae songs are produced first as riddims on which several singers and DJs record their voices.

and to constantly satisfy the requests of the audience for an exclusive experience.[15]

More generally, the concept of intellectual property cannot apply to the Jamaican music industry where cultural material is constantly borrowed and recreated: lyrics are quoted and reappropriated, songs are rewritten and rearranged, music is extensively copied and played in public spaces with no authorization from the artist or the producer. Sound systems, dub, and DJs all contradict the notion of authorship presented at the beginning of this paper. More precisely, they imply a resistance to authority both in political and cultural terms: art and culture are seen as fundamentally collective experiences where the implication and reaction of the audience is not just incidental but constitutes the ultimate criterion for establishing an artistic performance as authentic. The example of the DJ is quite telling in that respect: his or her versatility precisely means his or her ability to at the same time anticipate, react to, and satisfy the expectations of the audience. More generally, the participation of the audience is a key element of the sound system, which makes it quite different from otherwise similar public manifestations: people speak, shout, sing, dance, and use various devices like whistles, horns, flags, or lighters to show their appreciation or their displeasure.[16]

Dub poets relate to the culture of sound systems by using similar practices in their performances: they widely resort to borrowed material both in the script of the poems (nursery rhymes, myths, legends, or proverbs from the West Indian oral tradition) and in the musical accompaniment. The authenticity of the poems does not derive from their being ascribed to a unique and stable point of origin (an author); it is a process which may (or may not) take place within the specific

---

15 The term ›lyrically‹ belongs to the language of reggae DJs and musicians and refers to the words or lyrics of a song. It does not have anything to do with lyricism or the Western tradition of lyrical poetry.

16 Many critics see audience participation as a defining element of cultures of the African diaspora. It is manifest in music in what is called the ›call/response pattern,‹ which structures much music of the black Atlantic from blues to reggae or hip hop: a call is made by an individual voice and is answered by a chorus. As Gilroy successfully shows, this principle (which he calls antiphony) has been transferred to literature; it is also central to dub poetry performances (cf. 78-79).

time and space of each new performance. In other words, cultural productions are not given value once and for all, but are seen as authentic if, and only if, they can be reappropriated collectively in a specific performance. This is exactly what Cooper suggests about dub poetry:

It is this interweaving of disparate elements from oral and scribal literary sources that characterises the neo-oral performance poetry of both Breeze and Smith. Poems such as these will inevitably become part of the communal repertoire just as Louise Bennett's poems have been appropriated and performed by other actors. This process of communal appropriation raises the paradoxical issue of originality: that which already existed or that which is newly made. Old-fashioned Western, scribal definitions of the poet as maker – a lonely individual talent – collapse into broader oral notions of the poet as transmitter of ›pre-packaged‹ cultural forms and values which are realisable only in specific contexts of production and reception. (84)

Once again, the emphasis on performance, which entails the idea that art is transient and its value has to be constantly renegotiated, has to be put in the general context of the African diaspora: Caribbean cultures quite literally originated in a displacement of various populations, notably millions of Africans. For the slaves and their descendants, the African origin of their culture is irremediably and forever lost; it can never be accessed directly, but has to be constantly recreated through acts of the imagination. Although this statement might be qualified according to specific historical and geographical circumstances, the idea of an utter and complete loss of the African origins of the slaves has been identified as a characteristic of black Atlantic cultures by critics like Martiniquan intellectual Edouard Glissant, who uses the concept of dispossession to describe the situation of the slaves and their descendants in the Caribbean. It is worth noting here that in the colonies, slaves were denied access to virtually all elements of their cultures of origin: using African languages was strictly forbidden, sometimes on pain of death, just like worshipping African deities; slaves were also christened and renamed to erase all traces of their African origin.

In this context, music appears as an exception as it was the only form of autonomous cultural expression tolerated by the masters. Musical performances in the African diaspora have thus come to combine a number of expressive functions that are generally dissociated in other cultures. On a conceptual level, musical and poetic performances can be defined as constantly new occasions to imagine, or re-imagine, lost origins. Because the origins are always already lost, they can only be accessed through the imagination, they can only be recreated imaginatively and performances of music and/or poetry are a privileged medium to do so. Gilroy puts it this way: »the premium which all these black diaspora styles place on the process of performance is emphasized by their radically unfinished forms – a characteristic which marks them indelibly as the products of slavery« (105). Similar ideas are developed by Glissant, who characterizes artistic productions of the African diaspora as parts of what he calls »the thought of trace« (in French »*la pensée de la trace*«), a process through which African origins have to be constantly re-imagined from latent traces in the memory of slaves and their descendants (cf. 227, 401-19).

According to Glissant, the return to the origins (*le retour*) is always a detour (*le détour*) through a creative process of the imagination, notably the process of musical performance. Other critics use different terms to refer to the same idea: Dabydeen speaks of »de/reconstruction« (qtd. in Donnell and Welsh 410), Cooper of »an alter/native aesthetics« (40), Ashcroft, Griffiths, and Tiffin use the terms »abrogation and appropriation« (37-39), while I personally resort to the notional couples ›displacement/replacement‹ or ›dislocation/relocation.‹ Whatever the vocabulary employed, what is referred to here is simply the fact that the African origins of the slaves were only accessible through the language and the culture of the masters: any form of return to the origins first implies a subversion, a displacement, or a deconstruction of this imposed medium.[17]

In this context, authenticity cannot be seen as the strict adherence to essentialized origins. Rather, it is primarily a process (one could speak of identification or authentication) in which musical and poetic performances play a crucial role. In that respect, authenticity can be said to be of a performative nature:

---

17 Interestingly, linguistic studies show that Creole languages follow the same historical process of development as Caribbean or black Atlantic cultures in general: although they are based on European languages, they are deformed to the point of becoming impossible to understand for the masters themselves. On this point, cf. Ashcroft, Griffiths, and Tiffin (38-77).

Apart from anything else, the globalisation of vernacular forms means that our understanding of antiphony will have to change. The calls and responses no longer converge in the tidy patterns of secret, ethnically encoded dialogue. The original call is becoming harder to locate. If we privilege it over the subsequent sounds that compete with one another to make the most appropriate reply, we will have to remember that *these communicative gestures are not expressive of an essence that exists outside of the acts which perform them* and thereby transmit the structures of racial feeling to wider, as yet uncharted, worlds. (Gilroy 110; emphasis added)

AUTHENTICITY IN THE POEMS

In a further step I will now look at examples of how the question of authenticity is treated by dub poets. In the poem called »If I Woz a Tap Natch Poet,« Johnson ironically defines his place in literary culture by quoting a number of famous or less famous poets. These include other West Indian poets (Kamau Brathwaite, Derek Walcott, or Lorna Goodison) but also more generally poets from the black Atlantic (Jayne Cortez or Amiri Baraka) and from Africa (Chris Okigbo or Tchikaya U'tamsi). This shows that, even though the poem is concerned with issues of ancestry and tradition, black identity is seen as diasporic and cannot be reduced to a direct link to an African origin. In this poem, Johnson alludes directly to the question of authenticity:

still
mi naw goh bow an scrape
an gwan like a ape
peddlin noh puerile parchment af etnicity
wid ongle a vaig fleetin hint af hawtenticity
like a black Lance Percival in reverse
ar even worse
a babbling bafoon whe looze im tongue (l. 72-79)

The reference to Lance Percival is quite telling; Percival was a white British comedian who performed and recorded his version of the calypso classic »Shame and Scandal in the Family« in 1965. With the ironic line »black Lance Percival in reverse« it seems the idea of authenticity as the strict adherence to an essentialized African identity is discarded in favor of an anti-essentialist stance reflecting the endless displacements which constitute the African diaspora.

Unsurprisingly, the poetic work of Johnson is frequently quoted to characterize the Black British identity of Caribbean immigrants to the UK, who carry with them a sense of their (displaced) roots and come into contact with other immigrant communities.[18] As Johnson expresses in a famous poem called »It Dread inna Inglan,« these communities, which are historically and culturally distinct, are all victims of the same institutional racism and this fact can help to develop a new sense of identity, which would be open and inclusive:

Maggi Tatcha on di go

wid a racist show

but a she haffi go

kaw,

rite now,

African

Asian

West Indian

an Black British

stan firm inna Inglan

inna disya time yah

far noh mattah wat dey say,

come wat may,

we are here to stay

inna Inglan,

inna disya time yah... (l. 9-24)

The same idea is expressed in one of Johnson's earlier poems, »Yout Rebels«:

a bran new breed of blacks

have now emerged,

---

18 Johnson is not only a poet, but also a cultural and political activist involved in the struggles of ›his‹ community as well as more generally in antifascist and antiracist struggles of the 1970s and 1980s in the UK. His views on immigration, racism, and Black British identity are often taken up both in the press and in critical writings.

leadin on the rough scene,

breakin away

takin the day,

sayin to capital nevah

movin fahwod evah.

[...]

young blood

yout rebels:

new shapes

shapin

new patterns

creatin new links

linkin

blood risin surely

carvin a new path,

movin fahwod to freedom. (l. 1-7, 18-27)

It is interesting to notice in these lines that identity and authenticity are described as performative processes rather than abstract categories, a shift emphasized by the use of present participles and by various expressions indicating that identity is not to be found in a mythified past but has to be constantly redefined according to new circumstances (repetition of the word ›new,‹ ›movin fahwod evah,‹ ›blood risin surely‹). Quite typically, identity is defined in this poem in a Deleuzian fashion: we are presented here with a rhizomatic vision of identity, where authenticity is seen as the ability to create new and surprising connections, to connect to always new people in always new contexts.[19]

Several poems by Benjamin Zephaniah deal with the notion of authenticity in a similar way. In »Back to What,« a poem ironically dedicated to former British Prime Minister John Major, Zephaniah rejects,

---

19 Glissant takes up the model established by Deleuze and Guattari in *Mille Plateaux* and adapts it to the context of Creole cultures, which to him illustrate perfectly the shift from an essentialized definition of identity (as the conformity to an abstract and absolute essence) to a rhizomatic definition of the concept (where identity becomes a performative process of identification, an ability to relate to others and to situate oneself in ever-changing networks of relationships) (cf. 30-31, 59-60).

like Johnson, essentialist and conservative notions of identity by simultaneously stating the impossibility and the necessity of a return to his
African roots:

Back to basics
Back to the creator
Back to Africa
Back to what

Back to basics
Back to back
Back to Black
Back to what (l. 17-24)

The first element worth noticing here is the utter lack of originality of
the poem, at least in formal terms. The poem presents itself as a nursery rhyme or a children's singsong and does not offer any original metaphors or metrical experiments. It is an instance of a poem almost
entirely based on borrowed material, the only element of change being
the last and third word of each line. Yet, the poem is quite successful
in rejecting essentialized definitions of identity: despite the rigid structure which echoes the imperative of a return to the origins, this return
is always a detour or a displacement and identity can never be tracked
down to a well-defined point of origin.

The same thing happens in a poem entitled »Knowing Me« which
is structured around the line »I don't have an identity crisis.« Zephaniah refuses to let himself be entrapped in a reductive and essentialized
definition of his identity. As a black West Indian living in Birmingham, he states:

Being black somewhere else
Is just being black everywhere,
I don't have an identity crisis.
At least once a week I watch television
With my Jamaican hand on my Ethiopian heart
The African heart deep in my Brummie chest,
And I chant, Aston Villa, Aston Villa, Aston Villa,
Believe me I know my stuff. (l.30-37)

These lines underscore once again the idea that identity is a matter of performance, it is a feeling renewed on each occasion when it is performed and not an abstract rule written in stone. Identity and authenticity are also seen as rhizomatic: the African roots connect to Caribbean culture, which itself is connected to British culture. These various displacements, which mirror the displacements of African and Caribbean populations, imply that Black British identity is a mix of heterogeneous elements: being authentic does not consist in denying the hybrid character of identity but rather in acknowledging and celebrating it.[20] Once again, it is interesting to notice that this process of acknowledgment and celebration is associated with a performance. In other words, identity, just like authenticity, is a performative process as the last lines of the poem underline:

I am not half a poet shivering in the cold
Waiting for a culture shock to warm my long lost drum rhythm,
I am here and now, I am all that Britain is about
I'm happening as we speak.
Honestly,
I don't have an identity crisis. (l. 70-75)

CONCLUSION

To the dub poets, an authentic performance does not have anything to do with the audience being a homogeneous community defined by an essentialized identity (black, West Indian, or working class). Rather, the authenticity of performances depends on the ability for the poet or performer to relate to always new audiences in always new places. As Gilroy explains, critical discussion of these diasporic forms of cultural expression must reject any form of essentialism:

---

20 In other passages of the poem, stereotypical markers of Caribbean identity are discarded to show that they do not have anything to do with authenticity: »I don't wonder what will become of me / If I don't eat reggae food or dance to mango tunes, / Or think of myself as a victim of circumstance« (l. 23-25). On the contrary, these markers are used by the authorities to perpetuate the colonial order and maintain an inferior black essence.

Original, folk, or local expressions of black culture have been identified as authentic and positively evaluated for that reason, while subsequent hemispheric or global manifestations of the same cultural forms have been dismissed as inauthentic and therefore lacking in cultural or aesthetic value precisely because of their distance (supposed or actual) from a readily identifiable point of origin. (96)

This type of critical discourse is fundamentally conservative and therefore inadequate to discuss cultural forms of expression like dub poetry. It reproduces a vision of identity and authenticity based on the nation/state, which is becoming more and more irrelevant to approach the displacements and migrations characteristic of the contemporary world. In that sense, we can only subscribe to Gilroy's conclusions on the meaning of authenticity in the context of the black Atlantic and the critical challenges it raises:

It bears repetition that even where African-American forms are borrowed and set to work in new locations they have often been deliberately reconstructed in novel patterns that do not respect their originators' proprietary claims or the boundaries of discrete nation states and the supposedly natural political communities they express or simply contain. My point here is that the unashamedly hybrid character of these black Atlantic cultures continually confounds any simplistic (essentialist or anti-essentialist) understanding of the relationship between racial identity and racial non-identity, between folk cultural authenticity and pop cultural betrayal. (99)

WORKS CITED

Ashcroft, Bill, Gareth Griffiths, and Helen Tiffin, eds. *The Empire Writes Back. Theory and Practice in Post-Colonial Literatures.* London: Routledge, 1989.

»Authenticity« *The Oxford English Dictionary.* Prep. by J.A. Simpson and E.S.C. Weiner. 2nd ed. Oxford: Clarendon Press, 1989.

»Authenticity« *Webster's New Encyclopedic Dictionary.* New rev. ed. Paris: Éditions Le Prat, 1995.

Bourdieu, Pierre. *Les Règles de l'Art: Genèse et Structure du Champ Littéraire.* Paris: Seuil, 1992.

Bradley, Lloyd. *Bass Culture: When Reggae Was King*. London: Penguin, 2000.

Brown, Stewart, Mervyn Morris, and Gordon Rohlehr, eds. »Introduction.« *Voiceprint: An Anthology of Oral and Related Poetry from the Caribbean*. Harlow: Longman, 1989.

Cooper, Carolyn. *Noises in the Blood: Orality, Gender and the ›Vulgar‹ Body of Jamaican Popular Culture*. London: Macmillan Caribbean, 1993.

Donnell, Alison, and Sarah Lawson Welsh, eds. *The Routledge Reader in Caribbean Literature*. London: Routledge, 1996.

Foucault, Michel. *Philosophie: Anthologie*. Paris: Gallimard, 2004.

Gilroy, Paul. *The Black Atlantic: Modernity and Double Consciousness*. Cambridge, MA: Harvard UP, 1993.

Glissant, Edouard. *Le Discours Antillais*. Paris: Gallimard, 1997.

Habekost, Christian. *Dub Poetry: 19 Poets from England and Jamaica*. Mannheim: Michael Schwinn, 1986.

Johnson, Linton Kwesi. »If I Woz a Tap Natch Poet.« Johnson, *Revalueshanary* 94-97.

——. »It Dread inna Ingland.« Johnson, *Revalueshanary* 25-26.

——. *Mi Revalueshanary Fren: Selected Poems*. London: Penguin, 2002.

——. »Yout Rebels.« Johnson, *Revalueshanary* 22.

Morris, Mervyn. »A Note on ›Dub Poetry.‹« *Wasafiri* 26 (1997): 66-69.

O'Sullivan, Tim, et al. *Key Concepts in Communication and Cultural Studies*. London: Routledge, 1994.

Zephaniah, Benjamin. »Back to What.« *Propa Propaganda*. Newcastle-upon-Tyne: Bloodaxe Books, 1996. 34.

——. »Knowing Me.« *Too Black, Too Strong*. High Green: Bloodaxe Books, 2001. 62-64.

The Dilettantish Construction of the Extraordinary or the Authenticity of the Artificial

Tracing Strategies for Success in German Popular Entertainment Shows[1]

ANTONIUS WEIXLER

In this day and age, there is a great demand for everything to be authentic: food, clothing, politicians, works of art. Authenticity is the desire for the natural, the real, the original (cf. Lethen 229). The very opposite of authenticity is the extremely artificial. This paper will examine two episodes of one of Germany's most successful popular entertainment shows, the *Fest der Volksmusik* (›festival of folk music‹) hosted by Florian Silbereisen.[2] This example is interesting because, in

---

1 Combining aspects of authenticity and popular culture with the example of *Herbstfest der Volksmusik* has been the subject of discussion of a postgraduate seminar led by Prof. Matías Martínez in Summer 2010 at the Bergische University Wuppertal. The author is very grateful to the participants of the seminar. Further special thanks go to Tara Windsor and Lukas Werner.

2 Each broadcast of this show has its particular name related to the season in which it is aired. There is a *Frühlingsfest* (spring festival), a *Sommerfest* (summer festival), a *Herbstfest* (autumn festival), and a *Winterfest der Volksmusik* (winter festival of folkmusic). In some years, there are additional broadcasts like an *Adventsfest der Volksmusik* (Advent festival of

contrast to similar broadcasts, this folk music show appears, at first sight, to be anything but authentic. It will be argued, however, that the show's amazing success can be explained by its generation of an aesthetics of authenticity. This article examines how the production of the artificial and kitschy can appear to be authentic to a particular target group. It will be shown that the producers of the show use certain strategies in order to cater for the visual preferences and habits of the target group. I contend that there are structural similarities in the concepts of authenticity, popular culture, and dilettantism. These three concepts are not identical, but, as all three overlap with each other, they form a web of meanings and concepts. Dilettantism, popular culture, and authenticity provide the audience with strategies of identification. Authenticity and popular culture seem to compensate for a reality that is perceived as being unreal and artificial. Furthermore, both are accorded particular significance in postmodern discourse. Reference to the history and the notion of the concept ›dilettantism‹ will provide further insights into how authenticity is evoked in popular culture. In order to illuminate specific and distinct similarities within this web of meanings and concepts, I shall use the concepts of personalization, exaggeration, redundancy, consistency, and extraordinariness along with the notion of the desire to be a genuine, natural, and authentic person, i.e. the notion of a ›unified person.‹[3]

---

folk music). In this article, there are two episodes of the show under scrutiny, the *Herbstfest der Volksmusik* and the *Frühlingsfest der Volkmusik*, aired by national TV-broadcaster ARD on 16 October 2010 and 9 April 2011, respectively.

3   Historically, the development of the concept of authenticity is closely related to developments and changes in the concepts of subjectivity and individuality. For a thorough examination on this link, cf. Susanne Knaller's *Ein Wort aus der Fremde*. Jean-Jacques Rousseau's philosophy can be seen as the paradigm for the concept of a genuine, natural, and authentic person (›unified person‹). Jean Starobinski has argued that in Rousseau's concept (and in his texts), a direct and ontological reference between the writer and the work of art can be applied. From this point of view, a work of art is a direct, immediate, and authentic personalization of the personality of the artist (cf. Starobinski 295-98). This notion ceases to be valid in modern discourse when identity and the ›I‹ comes under question and a literary text is no longer perceived as the emanation of a writer's person-

Christian Huck and Carsten Zorn have argued that pop or popular culture is a provocation against Niklas Luhmann's system theory, arguing that it appears to be the only system of communication that goes beyond the ›social systems‹ as Luhmann understands them, insofar as the popular is a structure that transcends the functional differentiation of society. Luhmann describes the structure of modern society as functionally differentiated, i.e. the systems of society consist of autonomously functioning subsystems such as economy, science, justice, religion, politics, education, love, and arts (cf. Luhmann *Gesellschaft*). Each system is defined by its mode of operation within which it employs a binary code in order to be able to decide whether an event or a piece of information is of importance for the subsystem or not (cf. Jahraus 285-87). Economy, for instance, works strictly within the binary code of money/no money, politics with power/no power. Our everyday experience, however, does not follow this strict binary division since, for example, politicians are elected because of appearance and character (e.g. when they are perceived as being very authentic), women are less well paid in the economy than men, and people consume and buy things just for fun instead of for purely economic purposes (cf. Huck and Zorn 7). In Huck and Zorn's argumentation, the popular is characterized by personalization, by bringing together various distinguished discourses and by transcending all differentiated social systems. It is one of the very few phenomena that does not obey the requirements of the functional differentiation of (post)modern society, but focuses on the »inadequate functioning and blurring of codes, media, forms, and system's logic« (Huck and Zorn 10; my translation).[4] Popular modes of communication can be described as a blurring of codes through the semantics of personalization (cf. 10-12).

In my opinion, the transcendence of social systems is something that popular culture and authenticity have in common. Both provide the audience with strategies of identification, for example through personalization: stars, politicians, investment bankers become popular,

---

ality. In art, an ontological, referencial authenticity between the artist and a work of art cannot be assumed any more. Rousseau's concept, however, is still in use when applying the label ›authentic‹ to ›primitive‹ cultures, in contrast to modern society (cf. Lethen 210).

4 »Fehlfunktionen und Überlagerungen von Codes, Medien, Formen und Systemlogiken.«

trustworthy, and authentic people by portraying themselves as private individuals. Hence, the codes are blurred and the differentiated social system is transcended as the politician becomes a powerful and trustworthy person in the political social system precisely by being presented and staged as authentic and genuine. These aspects are alien to the code of the political social system and therefore, theoretically, to be ignored (cf. Huck and Zorn 7).

If we define authenticity as an aesthetic phenomenon that the spectator ascribes to objects, there is a striking similarity to Huck and Zorn's effect of personalization: both authenticity and the popular challenge the functional differentiation of society. As Roland Barthes has shown, the *effet de réel* is caused by dysfunctionality. But as this dysfunctionality results in an *effet de réel,* it can be said, taking this idea further, that it then becomes a functional element (cf. Martínez and Scheffel 117). The paradoxical phenomenon of a functional dysfunctionality can therefore be described as a core aspect of the concept of authenticity.[5] Let us take one step back for a moment: what causes the blurring of the codes and leads to this process I have called personalization? This is one point at which dilettantism and authenticity come together. Dilettantes tend to exaggeration and subjectivism, and it is their non-professional approach that undermines the functional differentiation of the social system, that blurs the codes and that is therefore, on a first level, dysfunctional within the social system. But on a second level the dilettantes' dysfunctionality results in authenticity as a functional effect.

Hence, by analyzing authenticity using the concepts of dilettantism and popular culture, I shall discern three layers:

---

5 It has been argued that authenticity can best be explained »by a paradoxical definition« (»in einer paradoxen Begriffsbestimmung« Knaller and Müller, »Einleitung« 11; cf. Müller 62-63). In *Aesthetic Theory*, Theodor Adorno has produced a whole range of paradoxes in order to describe the multidimensional aspects of authenticity, e.g. »expression of the expressionless« (154), »the realization of the unrealizable« (140), »determination of the indeterminate« (165). Finally: »But the function of art in the totally functional world is its functionlessness« (404; »Aber die Funktion der Kunst in der gänzlich funktionalen Welt ihre Funktionslosigkeit« Adorno, *Ästhetische Theorie* 475).

- Authenticity and dilettantism: the desire to be an authentic person, which is a core aspect of both dilettantism and authenticity. It is important to underline here that this is a *desire*, as the dilettante has been divided from being an authentic person (›unified person‹), i.e. from his or her genuine nature, by culture. Historically, ›culture‹ and ›civilization‹ have been used in contrast to nature and barbarism (cf. Hejl 357), an antagonism that will be explained in more detail later. With reference to authenticity, this is an aspect of authenticity of the subject.[6]

- Dilettantism and popular culture: the genuine and authentic person, in the quest and the desire for authenticity, and the dilettante, in order to deal with reality and/or nature, tend to exaggeration by focusing on the self, as well as to the production of the extremely artificial, personal, campy, and kitschy. Within the social systems this results in a dysfunctionality which blurs the codes of the differentiated social systems; this is a phenomenon that corresponds with the above description of popular culture.

- Popular culture, the artificial, and authenticity: if the dysfunctional becomes functional, on another level, even the most artificial can be described as authentic.

AUTHENTICITY – DILETTANTISM

The history of the term and concept of authenticity goes back to the Greek origin of *authentikos*, which refers to an author and creator as

---

6   Susanne Knaller has proposed a heuristic differentiation of authenticity of the subject and authenticity of the object on one level, and a differentiation of authenticity of reference, art, and subject on a second level (*Wort* 21-25; »Genealogie« 17-35). Besides this, she also gives a broad discussion and overview of the intertwined development of authenticity and the concept of subjectivity (*Wort* 141-53). In addition, it has been argued that there is a strong connection between authenticity, subjectivity, and the genre of *Bildungsroman* (if not the genre of the novel in general) (cf. Wieler 7-8) and autobiography (cf. Kramer).

well as an agent or perpetrator.[7] Nowadays, the concept of authenticity implies the notion of being natural, real, genuine, original as well as being immediate or presented in an immediate manner. This paper understands authenticity not as an ontological category but a phenomenon or an aesthetics that is ascribed to objects or people by spectators (cf. Weixler). Therefore, it is argued that authenticity is generated by certain narrative strategies in order to meet the viewers' expectations of what constitutes the authentic. Two different notions of authenticity will be used in the following. On the one hand, one traditional meaning of authenticity is connected to the subject.[8] Luhmann argues that the concept of individuality developed alongside the evolution of social differentiation: whereas in former modes of social differentiation, i.e. in segmentation and stratification, the individual was defined by inclusion, in the current functional differentiation of modern society, the individual is determined by exclusion (cf. *Gesellschaft* 618-34). In a segmented, i.e. a primitive and archaic society, the individual is defined by belonging to a family. In the hierarchical differentiation between nobility and common people of a stratificated society, e.g. the medieval estates of the realm or the Indian caste system, the individual is defined by its status (cf. 613). In a functionally differentiated society, however, the individual is taking part in each subsystem by, for instance, consuming within the economic subsystem, voting in the political system, appealing to a court in the judicial system, and by choosing to believe in a certain religion or not (cf. 625). As Luhmann states, »the individual cannot live in a functional system alone« (*Gesellschaftsstruktur* 158; my translation).[9] The individual is functionally differentiated, hence the originally authentic person (›unified person‹) is divided. On the other hand, the second understanding of authenticity

---

7   For comprehensive overviews of the history of the concept of authenticity, cf. Kalisch 31-44; Knaller, *Wort* 10-21; Knaller, »Genealogie« 17-35; Martínez 9-10.

8   An aspect Susanne Knaller refers to as subject authenticity (»Subjektauthentizität« Knaller, »Genealogie« 21); cf. Knaller, *Wort* 22.

9   »Die Einzelperson kann nicht in einem Funktionssystem allein leben.« Cf. also: »The individual cannot be defined by inclusion any longer but only by exclusion.« (»Das Individuum kann nicht mehr durch Inklusion, sondern nur durch Exklusion definiert werden.« *Gesellschaftsstruktur* 158; my translation).

used in this article is related to how Luhmann describes authenticity as a synonym for reality from the position of a »first-order observer« (*Mass Media* 4; »Beobachter erster Ordnung« *Massenmedien* 13; cf. Knaller and Müller 9): »However, we can speak of the reality of the mass media in another sense, that is, in the sense of what *appears to them*, or *through them to others*, to be reality« (Luhmann *Mass Media* 4; emphases in the original).[10] Hence, a product of mass media needs to meet the expectations and visual habits of the target group in order to appear to be as real and as original as their everyday life. Authenticity in this sense has the connotation of consistency with the normal and the genuine. Again, the narrative strategies analyzed with reference to popular entertainment shows deliberately generate an amateurish, normal, average or, as will be explained in more detail below, dilettantish aesthetics.

Apart from its colloquial use, the concept of dilettantism is often overlooked and has not been a major part of art or theory discourse since World War I.[11] The current meaning and significance of dilettantism has been reduced to a minimum and is mostly used in a pejorative sense. Today we perceive dilettantes to be amateurs, dabblers, laypersons, triflers, as the unaccomplished, shallow, ungifted, and uninitiated. Historically, both the scope and the valency of the concept have varied considerably over the centuries. Therefore, most scholars agree that the extensiveness of the different and diverse concepts of dilettantism throughout the decades makes it nearly impossible to catch and define this phrase (cf. Vaget 18; Wieler 14-15). Generally, dilettantism has been the subject of broad discussions at times when the concept of art was under question and about to be redefined (cf. Vaget 131; Wirth 25). In light of this observation, dilettantism can be seen as a core feature of aesthetic discourse, and different aspects of dilettantism are still relevant in the concept of the autonomy of art, the concept of the artwork, the concept of art, and the social stance of the artist. In Germany, discussions about dilettantism have usually mediated between

---

10 »Man kann aber noch in einem zweiten Sinne von der Realität der Massenmedien sprechen, nämlich im Sinne dessen, was *für sie* oder *durch sie für andere* als Realität *erscheint*.« (*Massenmedien* 12; emphases in the original).

11 Wieler is able to show that Heinrich Mann replaces ›dilettantism‹ with synonyms when he revised his 1894 text *In einer Familie* in 1914 (cf. 30).

ideals of individualism and debates solely focusing on the work of art. Above all, and contrary to the current notion of dilettantism as a formal insufficiency, the historical concept of dilettantism was rather an aspect of existence, even though insecure, weak, and unnatural (cf. Wieler 30). In general, it has been suggested that dilettantism should be defined as an attempt to become a genuine, natural, and authentic person through the practice of art (cf. Wieler 30-31). This broad definition of dilettantism is appealing in its similarity with one basic notion of authenticity.

In the German language, the term and concept *Dilettantismus* was given distinction by Johann Wolfgang von Goethe and Friedrich Schiller. Schiller first dealt with the concept in his 1784 work »Ueber das Gegenwärtige Teutsche Theater,« stating that in acting the dilettante is to be preferred to the professional actor, as the former is not only acting and pretending to have certain feelings, but *is* actually having them (cf. 85). This changed around 1800, most markedly with Schiller's move to a negative notion of dilettantism, when the concept came to differentiate between the high and low, the good and the bad practice of art. In May 1799, Schiller and Goethe began to work together on a broad and categorical theory of arts for the journal *Propyläen* called »Über den Dilettantismus,« a project that they both failed to finish and that, if it had been completed, would have become, as Hans Rudolf Vaget argues, the main document of Weimar Classicism (cf. 10).

Schiller and Goethe wanted to draft a categorical and polemic statement on what they perceived as being wrong and dangerous developments in the arts (which therefore jeopardized their perception of art). »Über den Dilettantismus« was, therefore, intended not only to reject any forms of dilettantism in various manifestations or in media, but also to point to their theory of arts. With the growth of the bourgeoisie and middle class, and with the emancipation of the artist from his or her dependency on the higher nobility, church, and academia, art lost its former context as well as its practical and theoretical grounds. Therefore, Schiller and Goethe put a great deal of effort into filling this theoretical vacuum with the concept of the aesthetics of genius (*Genieästhetik*) and the autonomy of art (*Kunstautonomie*) (cf. Vaget 214). Both concepts are a defense against the spreading and contemporary development of what they called dilettantism.

As in Schiller's thoughts on the actor, the dominant differentiation prevails between the professional as artist versus the dilettante as the non-professional and thus non-artist. The dilettante is »an enthusiast of the arts, who does not only want to watch and enjoy but also to take part in its execution« (Goethe and Schiller, »Dilettantismus« 780-81; my translation).[12] The dilettante is not an artist (*Künstler*), he or she is an enthusiast (*Liebhaber*). Furthermore, the dilettante takes his or her passive, but thoroughly sensitive reception (*rezeptive Empfindungs-fähigkeit*) as a sign for his or her capability for production (*produktive Bildungskraft*).

Because the dilettante's urge to create derives solely from the effect which works of art have on him, he confuses this effect with objective causes and motives. And so he now believes it possible to use the emotional state into which he has been transported as a means of being productive – which is tantamount to trying to produce flowers by means of its fragrance. (Goethe and Schiller, »On Dilettantism« 214)[13]

The dilettante and the enthusiast ignore the gap between reception and production. The artist and the genius, however, exercise their talent through hard courses of study and hence develop the capability of converting the reception of emotions and impressions into the production of a piece of art. Uwe Wirth concludes in his analysis of the dilettante: »[T]oo much feeling, too little opus« (»zu viel Gefühl, zu wenig Werk« 30; my translation). While in the Italian Renaissance dilettantism was a core of an ideal of education, Goethe and Schiller made clear that exercising art is only for artists, and that the bourgeois would never be able to reach an ideal of education (*Bildung*) and would persist in being dilettantish in art and in life (cf. Wieler 31).

Further ideas about dilettantism, although hardly explicit, can be traced in Schiller's aesthetic writings. In »Ueber Naive und Sentimentalische Dichtung« Schiller develops his theory of art by discussing

---

12 »ein[...] Liebhaber der Künste, der nicht allein betrachten und genießen, sondern auch an ihrer Ausübung Teil nehmen will.«

13 »Weil der Dilettant seinen Beruf zum Selbstproduzieren erst aus den Wirkungen der Kunstwerke auf sich empfängt, so verwechselt er diese Wirkungen mit den objektiven Ursachen und Motiven, und meint nun den Empfindungszustand, in den er versetzt ist, auch produktiv und praktisch zu machen, wie wenn man mit dem Geruch einer Blume die Blume selbst hervorzubringen gedächte« (Goethe and Schiller, »Dilettantismus« 778).

the relationship between nature and culture, and between reality and art. Hence, the modern human being has been divided from nature by culture: »It is because with us nature has disappeared among men« (Schiller, »On Naive« 555).[14] Naïve in this sense means that in former precultural times thinking, sensing, and reflecting as well as the moral, the intellect (*das Geistige*), and the physical body formed an unconscious – that is a naïve – entity/unity.[15] Within the contemporary human being, however, feeling and perception form an antagonistic dichotomy (cf. Wieler 107).

The sentimental (*das Sentimentalische*), from Schiller's point of view, is the desire to be naïve, i.e. to be a genuine, authentic person (›unified person‹). What the sentimental and the dilettantish have in common, according to Wieler, is the discrepancy between the natural, naturally unconscious (i.e. naïve) way of life and the perception of reality. He describes Schiller's notion of dilettantism as one, admittedly extreme, example of the sentimental (cf. 106). The sentimental dilettante, Schiller continues, thinks that one might reach and realize the ideal – i.e. to be naïve or an authentic person (›unified person‹) – through making art. In this respect the dilettante is mistaken: the creation of art cannot be the means to reach this ideal. In fact, it cannot be attained at all, only the initiated genius is capable of producing ideal art in a naïve way. Furthermore, dilettantes feel the need to let their imagination, which they often misleadingly perceive as being ideal, become reality in a work of art. But again, in creating a piece of art, the dilettante is not able to carry out this realization according to the

---

14 »weil die Natur bey uns aus der Menschheit verschwunden ist« (Schiller, »Dichtung« 430).

15 »If man enters upon the path of civilization, if art begins to mould him, the harmony *of the senses* ceases, and he can only aspire at *moral* unity, and manifest himself as such. The agreement between his sensations and thoughts which was a reality during his sensual state, now only exists *in idea*« (Schiller, »On Naive« 557; emphases in the original) (»Ist der Mensch in den Stand der Kultur getreten, und hat die Kunst ihre Hand an ihn gelegt, so ist jene sinnliche Harmonie in ihm aufgehoben, und er kann nur noch als moralische Einheit, d.h. nach Einheit strebend, sich äußern. Die Übereinstimmung zwischen seinem Empfinden und Denken, die in dem ersten Zustande wirklich statt fand, existirt jetzt bloß idealisch« Schiller, »Dichtung« 437).

natural, real, or once again, naïve circumstances. The sentimental is dilettantish in perception and production. And because dilettantes want to fulfill their ideal by transforming their imagination into a piece of art/reality, they also devalue trivial reality (cf. Wieler 105-11). As a result, in failing to produce a naïve and authentic aesthetics or work of art respectively, the dilettante leans towards exaggeration, sentimentalism, and subjectivism.

DILETTANTISM – POPULAR CULTURE

The discourse of dilettantism arose again a hundred years later, around 1900. Again, the discussion was intertwined with negotiations about the relationship between reality and art, which was challenged by what has been described as major changes in perception during that time: the dilettante was an alternative way of perceiving, sensing, and thinking.[16] Therefore, a shift to a more positive conception of dilettantism can be identified. Alongside the *décadent*, the dandy, and the snob – which all served as synonyms at that time – the dilettante became a possible prototype for the artist of the *fin de siècle* and the avantgarde. The exaggeration of reflection and selfishness of the *décadent* leads to new connotations within the concept of dilettantism: too much reflection entails a lack of will and indecisiveness (cf. Leistner 81). In addition, one specificity of this indecisiveness results in an obsession with bringing together the unrelated (*Sammlerwut*), an aspect Goethe and Schiller criticized quite profoundly about their contemporaries (cf. Leistner 65-69).[17] The fusion of the dilettante and the dandy, however,

---

16 It is agreed that Albert Einstein's theory of relativity, Max Planck's quantum physics, and Sigmund Freud's psychoanalysis along with increased urbanization all paved the way for a major change in perception of the individual and the world. This is a phenomenon Georg Simmel examines in »Die Großstädte und das Geistesleben« and Walter Benjamin in *Das Kunstwerk im Zeitalter seiner Technischen Reproduzierbarkeit*. Silvio Vietta most notably refers to all these developments as resulting in a »Ichdissoziierung« (»Dissociation of the I« 30; my translation). Cf. also Stahl 30.

17 »Many dilettantes have large collections. We might even say that all large collections owe their existence to dilettantism.« (Goethe and Schiller, »On

is often described as a certain way of transcending reality by means of the completely artificial (cf. Leistner 86).

The concept of and discourse on dilettantism was abandoned around the time of the First World War, and largely replaced, according to Michael Wieler, by the evolving concept of kitsch. Yet dilettantism has always been not only an aspect of aesthetics, but a state of mind and an idea of existence, whereas kitsch is a rather concrete aspect of style and form (cf. 30). What kitsch and dilettantism have in common is, once again, the exaggeration of subjectivity and the desire for stronger impressions and stimuli. Wieler concludes that the dilettante *produces* kitsch, whereas the kitsch-consumer *perceives* in a dilettantish way (cf. 32). Generally, the labeling of something as kitsch devalues a piece of work, seeing it not as true art but as excessive, flamboyant, and artificial. In this view of kitsch as flippant work made by ungifted, uninitiated dabblers, or laypersons, some elements of today's understanding of dilettantism can be traced. Kitsch is appealing through overstated emotions or an exaggerated display of harmony, e.g. idyllic ambiences. Critics state that kitsch is a mass production of false emotions and false feelings of security and that this falsity cannot be observed by the target group (cf. Volkmann 318-19).

In my opinion, a consistent development can be seen from the dandy and dilettante of the 1900s through the kitsch-discourse and finally to what Susan Sontag called the aesthetics of ›camp‹ in the 1960s. Sontag describes the essence of camp as a sensibility and »its love of the unnatural: of artifice and exaggeration. […] Many examples of camp are things which, from a ›serious‹ point of view, are either bad art or kitsch. […] Nothing in nature can be campy« (Sontag 105-8). Several aspects of this depiction of camp are of interest for the following examination of a popular entertainment show.[18] With »Notes on Camp,« Sontag not only presents one of the first examples of a non-elitist perception of popular culture – camp is about »a good taste of bad taste« (118) – but also combines this perspective with the

---

Dilettantismus« 213; »Man trifft viele Dilettanten mit großen Sammlungen an, ja man könnte behaupten, alle großen Sammlungen sind vom Dilettantism entstanden.« »Dilettantismus« 747).

18 It must be noted here that Sontag's notion of camp is usually described as an urban phenomenon but is being extended here and applied to the rather rural aesthetics of the German *Volksmusik* popular entertainment shows.

aforementioned aspects of dilettantism.[19] It can be seen as resuming Schiller's thoughts on the dilettante when Sontag argues: »One must distinguish between naïve and deliberate Camp. Pure Camp is always naïve« (110). Deliberate camp, therefore, is a dilettantish camp. But camp, as Sontag describes it, is quite the opposite of what is usually described as being ›authentic‹: it is the love of the unnatural and the artificial. »In naïve, or pure, camp, the essential element is serious-ness, a seriousness that fails« (112). An authentic aesthetics is the product of a genuine artist who wants to express something in a seri-ous manner. Here, again, Sontag continues Schiller and Goethe's thoughts, as seriousness that fails is the dilettante's way of producing art. But contrary to dilettantism as Schiller and Goethe saw it, pure camp is perceived as being a positive aesthetics and style.

POPULAR CULTURE/THE ARTIFICIAL – AUTHENTICITY

In order not to prejudge the popular entertainment show to be exam-ined here, we must take the taste of a particular target group into ac-count. A Cultural Studies perspective is applied in analyzing *Herbstfest* and *Frühlingsfest der Volksmusik* so as to avoid describing these shows in an elitist manner, which would only result in dis-missive bemusement. Such a condescending perspective would identi-fy Florian Silbereisen's show as kitschy and the very opposite of authentic. This article aims, however, to explore the authenticity of the

---

19 Generally and historically, privileging high culture meant that popular, low culture was not perceived as being part of culture at all. In fact, Schiller's »Ueber Naive und Sentimentalische Dichtung,« as well as Goethe and Schiller's »Über Dilettantismus,« are an elaborate framework for dividing good/high culture from what they thought were wrong and dangerous de-velopments and bad/low art. The Birmingham School of Cultural Studies with, amongst others, Raymond Williams tried to overcome the elitist un-derstanding of culture by developing a neutral perception of popular cul-ture (cf. Sommer 27-42). Adorno in his aesthetic theory – which has been described by Harro Müller as a theory of authenticity (cf. 55-67) – denies that popular culture is authentic at all.

extremely artificial, arguing that the show's success can be explained through its creation of an aesthetics of authenticity for its target group.

In his theory of a hermeneutical visual sociology of knowledge, Jürgen Raab generates the concept of »visual community« (»Sehgemeinschaft« 196; my translation). Within our visual culture, Raab differentiates between aesthetic fields of perception and action that are relatively stable, lasting, and separate (cf. 306-16). Thus, visual communities are formed, stabilized, affirmed, and closed (to the inside and outside) by visual regimes and aesthetic rules. Referring to Georg Simmel, Raab analyzes the mediation of the visual as an aspect of society, concluding that there are distinct visual communities as social sub-groups generating exclusion and inclusion via aesthetic artifacts. This is why – taking the socio-structural differentiation of visual communities into account – a popular entertainment show needs to be produced according to the visual habits and expectations of the anticipated spectators, an aspect Raab calls »recipient design« (242). According to Raab, such recipient design needs to aim for an easy intersubjective understanding by using a narrow repertoire of styles, only standardized and traditional cutting, and by applying concepts of repetition, redundancy, and affirmation (cf. 199-206, 243, 306-27). One of Raab's subsequent conclusions is that such visual patterns can even be described as what Émile Durkheim has called ›elementary forms‹ (*formes élémentaires*), i.e. the basic and most primitive forms that constitute a culture (or respectively a religion in the context of Durkheim's research) (cf. Raab 320).

Although Jürgen Raab explores patterns in editing and visual (recipient) design used by amateurs in producing amateur films, some of his findings can be applied to the analysis of professionally produced popular entertainment shows.[20] Most specifically, Raab's examination of the production of transparency via consistency and redundancy (cf. 202-03) as well as the production of transcendence by extraordinariness (cf. 240-45) will be considered.

---

20 Raab argues that in one of his examined examples, wedding movies, the visual community could be described as low and lower middle class with a medium or low level of education, a milieu that Gerhard Schulze has also referred to as the harmony milieu and the entertainment milieu (cf. Raab 242).

With this in mind, I shall differentiate three structural layers and – by applying Raab's concepts – three conceptional patterns. The action happening on stage will be analyzed as an aspect of the a) ›event.‹ The different events are combined and contextualized to a b) ›story,‹ while the ways in which a) and b) are combined will be considered as the aspect of c) ›discourse.‹[21] The ›event‹ layer will provide a closer insight into *what* is actually presented in our example of a popular entertainment show. The aspect of story is somewhat surprising for a TV show that is supposedly about *showing* not *telling*, which therefore distinguishes it from other shows. The aspect of discourse will investigate *how* the story and events are presented.[22] The first two conceptional patterns, event and story, ensure that the show can be easily understood and consumed by the target group: in order to avoid fraction, fragmentation, or postmodern aggravations such as contingency, a great deal of effort is made to produce A) ›consistency.‹ This conceptional layer is intertwined with the story-aspect, whereas the following phenomena are aspects of the discourse. In watching Florian Silbereisen's show, a pronounced B) ›redundancy‹ can be observed. Last but not least, four aspects of the phenomenon of C) ›extraordinariness‹ shall be considered. I) There is a quest for exceptionality in constantly presenting the songs and actions on the show as special and unique. II) This show endeavors to be more extraordinary than others by being even more emotional. III) Extraordinariness in the sense of a contrast to everyday life is achieved by presenting special events and celebrations. IV) Aspects of a ritual can be traced in the show. Aspects II) to IV) also refer to the title of the show. The show that Florian Silbereisen presents is, first and foremost, a *Fest*, i.e. a celebration and festivity. This is in distinction to other German folkloric, popular entertainment programs in which the festival character is evident but not central as they are presented more like stage shows and do not aim to

---

21 ›Event,‹ ›story,‹ and ›discourse‹ are used according to Seymour Chatman (cf. Martínez and Scheffel 26).

22 In his study *The Craft of Fiction* Percy Lubbock has introduced the concepts of telling and showing in order to distinguish a narrative (telling) from a dramatic (showing) mode (cf. 62).

create an aesthetics of extraordinariness.[23] In the following examination of two episodes of *Fest der Volksmusik*, it will be shown that the aesthetics of the show can be explained along the central aspects of dilettantism as sketched above. The dilettante narrative strategies of the show will then be analyzed using Raab's concepts of consistency, redundancy, and extraordinariness. Whereas consistency and redundancy succeed in creating a natural, genuine, and naïve atmosphere, extraordinariness creates a special and intense experience. These aspects combined result in an aesthetics the spectators perceive as being more authentic than any other popular entertainment show.

THE NAÏVE QUEST FOR THE NAÏVE

The two German popular entertainment shows under examination here are two episodes of the *Fest der Volksmusik*, in particular the *Herbstfest der Volksmusik* and the *Frühlingsfest der Volksmusik*, aired by national TV-broadcaster ARD on the prestigious Saturday night prime-time slots on 16 October 2010 and 9 April 2011, respectively. The first show was watched by 6.07 million spectators in total, which amounted to 19.4 % market share; the second show had 6.41 million viewers in total and 22.4 % share. The show is therefore one of the most successful in German television.[24] It has been on air since 1994 and was given a further boost when Florian Silbereisen took over the show as host in 2004.

Firstly, a closer look at the ›events‹ presented on the show reveals that each edition presents up to twenty bands and/or songs and five to nine show acts in a total broadcast of approximately three hours. What is striking at first sight is the diversity of a broadcast that is called a music show. In fact, every *Fest der Volksmusik* ends with a stunt act

---

23 A comparison with other German popular entertainment shows like *Carmen Nebel* or *Musikantenstadl* will be presented in more detail later in this article.

24 The author was able to interview a member of the production team of this show. While reluctant to reveal concrete figures, it was said that the show is produced by a staff of 150 in total, making it probably not only one of the most successful but also one of the most costly entertainment shows on German TV.

by the host Florian Silbereisen, making an action show act the climax of the program. This aspect is highlighted further by the fact that every show begins with a sequence summarizing all the final stunt acts of the previous shows. Therefore, music, although filling a lion's share of the total show time, seems not to be the only important part of this so-called festival of music. All entertainment shows, in order to be successful and to attract spectators from various sub-groups of society, are obliged to present a vast diversity of acts and elements, but the breadth seen here is beyond comparison: we are shown, for example, folding napkins, ironing, gun shooting, magic tricks, walking over burning coal, stunt acts with monster trucks, as well as classical pieces of art. Such an exaggerated bringing together of the unrelated as a result of indecisiveness is one example of the show's dilettantish character.

Furthermore, the two shows present an astonishingly high number of children and animals on stage. Contrary to W.C. Fields's famous warning never to work with animals or children, having both on stage seems to guarantee success in the context of such popular entertainment shows. The reason for this can also be traced in what has been explained as the relationship between authenticity and dilettantism. Children and animals are perceived as being the epitome of the authentic, because they are both genuinely dilettantish and non-dilettantish. On the one hand, in contrast to the professional adults, children and animals are *per se* dilettantish, natural, and therefore authentic; they simply do not have the ability and experience to be professional. In fact, children and animals are a perfect symbol for the authentic non-professional. On the other hand, with Schiller's division of the naïve and the sentimental it has been argued that the dilettante is separated from the naïve unity with nature by culture. Therefore, children and animals symbolize a pre-dilettantish status where the naïve unity with oneself and nature still prevails. It is in this very aspect that children and animals are ascribed a notion of ›innocence.‹ To be more precise, children and animals symbolize the desire of the dilettante for such a pre-dilettantish status that has been described as the desire to be a genuine, authentic, and unified person. Scanning the two shows reveals that 35 to 45 % of the show acts are accompanied by children and/or animals. The *Herbstfest* of October 2010 was co-hosted by a little boy, while the co-host in the *Frühlingsfest* of April 2011 was a small dog. Employing two different denotations of the concept dilettante, it can be explained why children and animals are perceived as being highly authentic. It becomes clear, however, that this itself is a dilettantish perspective on the naïve nature of children and animals. In other words: it is a naïve – in today's meaning of the word – way of producing Schiller's unity with nature (*das Naive*).

The ›story‹ that is told by the events of the show and, more explicitly, by the lyrics of the songs is that of a harmonious life and world, of love, friendship, family, and mastered strokes of fate. However, it is fairly surprising for a program that is branded as a folk music show that, firstly, folk music does not play a major role. In fact, most of the music acts are examples of a German popular music genre called *Schlager*. Secondly, and in contrast to other comparable folk music shows, home (the German concept of *Heimat*), the Alps,[25] and Christian beliefs only play a minor role in the songs in the *Feste der Volksmusik*.[26] Instead, what the singers constantly include in their lyrics are more secular forms of the metaphysical: angels, fairies, and other magical phenomenons.

It is remarkable that storytelling should be an important facet of this show at all. Whereas the narratological aspect ›story‹ is defined by the concept of *telling*, one would expect a TV-show to be rather about *showing*. The show examined here, however, is doing both, *telling* and *showing*. Moreover, this is a pivotal aspect in distinction to all other comparable popular entertainment shows. In the *Feste der Volksmusik* episodes, not one single act is presented with the sole purpose to play music, but is integrated into a narrative in order to produce consistency. Before any singer or band mounts the stage, the host explains exactly why they are on the show tonight. In contrast to other music shows, where such explanations usually introduce a new album, new tour, or new movie, Florian Silbereisen's explanations always con-

---

25 This genre of shows presenting folk popular music is one of the very few examples of TV broadcasts in which all the German-speaking European countries take part.

26 The show is produced by the Mitteldeutscher Rundfunk (MDR) for the German national TV broadcaster ARD. The MDR is the TV station for Saxony-Anhalt, Saxony, and Thuringia, hence three federal states in eastern Germany. As the GDR was a secular state, Christianity and religion still only play a minor role in people's lives in the five eastern federal states today.

struct some kind of story.[27] Most of the lyrics are part of that narrative, thus most of the songs are specially written for that particular show.[28] In the few cases when the lyrics are not part of the constructed narrative, the singers do still take part in a further show act after the song. The storytelling succeeds in producing a consistency making the shows easy to understand, hence avoiding fractions, fragmentations, and contingency.

Last but not least, consistency is not only produced within the successive acts of the broadcast, but also in relation to other programs aired on the channel. For example, in the *Herbstfest der Volksmusik* of October 2010, ARD news-anchorman Tom Buhrow appeared on the show asking the audience for help choosing new glasses. In every show, there is a switch to the news show *Tagesthemen* presented in a frame-within-frame style. This not only produces consistency in order to keep the audience watching the next TV program, which is quite common in today's television, but consistency is also constructed here so that one may value this popular entertainment show as equally valuable and useful as other programs broadcast on television. When ARD executive Volker Herres visited the *Herbstfest* show, he did not take part in the show, but sat in the middle of the audience, suggesting that he, too, is an average spectator. Throughout the 180-minutes broadcast, he was shown six times. Hence, in a show presenting a harmonious premodern world, hierarchy is still in power. On the *Frühlingsfest* show, Empress Sissy's great-grandson was introduced with all his aristocratic titles. All these examples are evidence for a strategy that is deliberately producing consistency with the outside world. It is a strategy of adding a certain value to the show in order to make it

---

27 Roger Whittaker's birthday, for example, which is celebrated on the *Frühlingsfest 2011*, provides the context for several acts. His wife is introduced before Whittaker's performance, his daughter and grandchild afterwards. A children's dancing group presents a birthday cake. In between all of this, the Dorfrocker's performance of a song that has nothing to do with the context of Whittaker's birthday, is integrated by stating that they will sing their song only for this occasion. Hence consistency is constructed through context, even when the actual song has nothing directly to do with the story.

28 In the *Frühlingsfest* it is explicitly announced that Marianne & Michael will present a song specially composed for that very show.

count as normal and ›real‹ TV as much as other broadcasts. Moreover, in a show presenting a harmonious world of love and friendship, the strategy of consistency, most notably with the news show, succeeds in producing an *effet de réel* making the show (seemingly) belong to the non-fictional part of the TV schedule. The non-fragmented world of harmony, the naïve – in today's meaning of the word – desire for a genuine, real, and authentic life is not only a sentimental and dilettantish quest, but a consistent part of the spectrum of TV programs beyond this specific show.

THE DILETTANTISH PRODUCTION OF DILETTANTISM

Let us now have a closer look at how the show is presented and produced, the aspect I have referred to as ›discourse.‹ The shots, camera angles, and editing are – just like the range of tunes and rhythms of the songs – conventional and even more explicitly non-experimental. The camera focus, for example, is never too wide nor too close, mostly presenting the images in a so-called ›American shot,‹ the most conventional shot angle of Hollywood movies (cf. Kandorfer 78). Most TV entertainment shows use a rather similar set of shots and editing, making the few variations that do occur even more significant. Whereas other popular entertainment shows sometimes use fast cutting and panning in order to match the aesthetics of the show with contemporary state-of-the-art movies, the *Feste der Volksmusik* diverge from the conventional style less often. Too much variation would jeopardize the show's consistency and therefore its authenticity.[29] If the image does depart from the conventional style, it is not in an attempt to be experimental, but only to produce an image even more amateurish than the common style. The show begins with letters flying into the screen similar to a rather dilettantish Powerpoint presentation or to amateur home videos. In one song about Polaroid picture taking, the image is occasionally frozen as a still image, generating rather dilettantish snapshots of the band. In addition, the focus of the cameras is constantly on spaces beyond the stage – in many scenes you can see the backstage

---

29 Lethen discusses consistency as an aspect of authenticity (cf. 229).

area, the lights, or the ceiling of the arena. Concerning this point, it is important to keep in mind that these shows are produced with a large amount of money and professional equipment and effort. The constant failure to produce professional and perfect images suggests that this show aims to generate authenticity with a ›discourse‹ strategy that produces an aesthetics of dilettantism. What can be observed is a very professionally produced aesthetics of non-professional and dilettan- tish-looking images. This might be something quite specific to this very entertainment show, *Fest der Volksmusik*, whereas American en- tertainment shows in general, as well as other German examples, e.g. *Willkommen bei Carmen Nebel* or *Musikantenstadl*, are perfectly made and staged. In my opinion, this indicates that the shows *Herbstfest* and *Frühlingsfest der Volksmusik* are produced in order to meet the expec- tations and everyday visual habits of its specific visual community. What is unique about this very show is that it successfully meets Raab's idea of recipient design by generating a dilettantish and campy aesthetics, an aesthetics that the target group perceives as being au- thentic.

The next aspect under examination, redundancy, is also something that contributes to the consistency of the show, making it easy to watch and understand. In almost every music act, the lyrics are also displayed on stage by background actors.[30] What is sung and can be heard is also shown and can be seen. Redundancy here is generated by the doubling of sound and image. Most of the time, the sound is not only doubling the image or vice versa, but the host even explicitly ex- plains what can be seen at that moment. This aspect is also very unique to this particular show and cannot be perceived in comparable German entertainment shows. Moreover, redundancy is also produced through repetition. For example, in the *Frühlingsfest der Volksmusik* the host begins the show by announcing that the popular band Die Flippers will end their career on this very show. This announcement is repeated several times throughout the broadcast. Finally, the very last performance is announced by stating that this will be the band's last appearance on stage, followed by the host asking the band members,

---

30 Even a song that does not consist of real words and can hardly be dis- played on the stage is doubled in a redundant way. The Dorfrocker's song in the *Frühlingsfest* consisting of the lyrics »jiha jiha jiha ho, jiha jiha jiha ho« is accompanied by girls showing posters displaying this text.

for rhetorical emphasis, if it will *really* be their last appearance. This strategy of redundancy by repetition can even be traced throughout the different editions of the show. In the *Herbstfest der Volksmusik*, the host Florian Silbereisen asked the band Brunner & Brunner, who were also ending their career on that very show, the same question in exactly the same manner and wording. Moreover, Die Flippers performed the very same song with the very same background show in both broadcasts under examination here. Repetition and redundancy, therefore, not only add to the consistency of the show, but also generate a sphere of recognition, so that one feels at home and at ease.

Completing my examination of Florian Silbereisen's popular entertainment show, I shall now analyze four different aspects of deliberately staged extraordinariness. Firstly, the host presents the singers, bands, and show acts as being something rather exceptional. Throughout the whole show a great deal of effort is put into portraying the participants as stars. ›Star‹ is probably the word used most frequently throughout the whole show, although, in using a popular scale for valuing stars, these singers would hardly be categorized as higher than C-list stars. But this effort has two effects: on the one hand, since high-profile international stars or celebrities appear on the show only very rarely, these shows have to create stars of their own. Hence, this sub-genre of popular music consists of stars known only to a specific social sub-group, i.e. the target group of the show. Thus, as there is nothing exceptional about them, the exceptionality has to be constructed by the context and the storytelling surrounding the performances. In fact, not a single music or show act is announced and presented without the use of exaggeration and superlatives (e.g. ›the most successful,‹ ›the best-selling,‹ ›the first appearance since,‹ ›the very last show of their career‹). As most of the performances are not unique since they are repeated (redundancy) on almost every single edition of the show, exceptionality has to be created by the discourse of the presentation.

At the same time, the presentation of the singers and bands as exceptional stars is done precisely in order to be able to demonstrate how normal, average, natural, and authentic they have remained. Therefore their dilettantism is quite helpful and a necessity on the show. These performers are not necessarily good musicians, and they by no means reach the standards of professional musicians whether of the opera, classical, or the international pop music sphere. Instead, they appear like the boy or girl next door, making music as an enthusiast, not an artist. Yet the participants are very professional in what they are doing: in deliberately appearing not professional but dilettantish.[31] I have shown above that dilettantism was considered a pejorative by Schiller and Goethe because of its high degree of subjectivity, whereas culture and true works of art were considered to be objective. In this entertainment show, subjectivity and the personality of the singers and participants are more important than their actual performances. For this reason the audience does not really care that the singers perform with recorded backing tracks or that some of them even fail to move their lips at the right time to the backing music. The subject as a person is more important than art. Hence the performers on such entertainment shows must refrain from having private lives, indeed they must reveal far more about their personal lives than high-profile ›stars‹ usually do. In the majority of the music acts, the narrated context, the performed songs, and the subsequent interview are about aspects of the artists' private lives, such as a new love, a planned wedding, birthday celebrations, illnesses overcome. In fact, it often appears as if the reason for a singer or band to perform on that very edition was in order to reveal something private. There are four conclusions to be drawn here. Firstly, the show is exceptional because it presents many stars. Secondly, the exceptionality of a star appearing on the show is enhanced by revealing something private and personal, which the stars would only reveal on this kind of show. Thirdly, because the stars can reveal both the public side of their personality (being a star) and their personal side, they – in contrast to the untouchable stars of international pop music – appear to be genuine, natural, and authentic people. This very aspect of personalization relates to how the popular has been described above and displays how both the popular and authenticity blur the codes of distinct social systems. Fourthly, since these stars can only appear in their ostensibly authentic and genuine nature on this show, the show itself is, in fact, more original, genuine, and more authentic than other shows.

---

31 On the *Frühlingsfest*-episode there is one musical singer performing a song. She is professional and stands out from the other performances. Most notably, this very music act is presented with a completely different aesthetics, i.e. without any form of redundancy, storytelling, or extraordinariness, which in turn underlines the relevance of my examination of the dilettantish performances.

Some of the aforementioned facets also play a role in the next layer of producing extraordinariness whereby the show is made more emotional than others. The *Feste der Volksmusik* are more emotional because the stars constantly reveal very personal feelings and news – sometimes this is presented in such a kitschy way that it might be hard for somebody outside the target group to relate to. Michael Hirte, winner of *Das Supertalent* in 2008,[32] is introduced in the following highly emotive way: he was once a lorry driver, who was blinded in his right eye by an awful accident, spent two months in a coma, lost his job, had to work on the streets. Then he found Jesus and became a Christian, became a superstar, has now found his love and written a love song for his beloved, and today is the first time his beloved girl is presented to the public and the first time this love song is performed.[33] A similar effect of emphasizing the emotional aspect of the show is linked to the use of exaggeration and superlatives (e.g. ›the first appearance on stage after a long illness,‹ ›the very last show in their career,‹ etc.), a strategy which appeals to the audience and often results in standing ovations. Overstated emotion and exaggerated displays of love, harmony, and idyllic ambiences – all aspects of kitsch as explained above – are further illustrations of the show's dilettantism.

All the aforementioned findings culminate in the performance of an extraordinariness that contrasts with everyday life. The *Herbstfest* and *Frühlingsfest der Volksmusik* are branded as genuine festivals and celebrations not regular TV-shows that can be watched on a daily basis. The festival is something distinct from everyday life, it is special and extraordinary. This aspect not only appears by chance in the title of the show, but is something that is constantly referred to within the broadcast and the setting. One might question whether the artificial and unnatural scenery of the show can generate authenticity at all. However, the amateurish look of the setting evokes a village hall set up for a celebration, a place where friends come together. At the same time, the scenery corresponds perfectly with the above depiction of kitsch and camp. It is intriguing, however, that the scenery of both

---

32 The German version of *Britain's Got Talent*.

33 Michael Hirte's girlfriend Jenny was sitting in the audience when she was surprised with this love song. In the way it was presented it could have been anyone of the spectators of the target group having a ›star‹ singing a song only for them.

shows – in the *Herbstfest* autumn leaves, in the *Frühlingsfest* blooming plants – displays campy and kitschy motifs of nature. »Nothing in nature can be campy,« but in its dilettantish exaggeration of idyllic ambiences, nature is in fact presented here as kitschy and campy. Both shows examined here present several different celebrations: as part of the usage of superlatives in generating exceptionality, there are jubilees and anniversaries to be celebrated on stage, e.g. a 15-year-long career, a celebration to mark the end of a band's career, and, on each episode, the celebration of a star's birthday. The extraordinariness of these birthday celebrations, in both cases, is even enhanced by personalization, showing private pictures and presenting family and friends. Hence, these celebrations combine the aforementioned performative aspects of exceptionality and emotionality to an even more exceptional and emotional highlight of the show.

Finally, one aspect of the performed extraordinariness can be seen in the fact that just like religious or family celebrations, this show-festival is staged rather like a ritual act. One of the very first shots of each show establishing the scenery and the stage is shot from over one spectator's shoulder. Such a ›subjective camera shot,‹ from the very beginning crosses the line of the imaginary axis of the classical ›180-degree rule‹ of movie-making. What is of interest here is that just like in a ritual act, in which everybody is part of the (religious) community and participates in the action, the audience does not only play a passive role watching the show. This broadcast is presented in a way that pretends that the audience is actively taking part. In fact, a wide range of possible audience participation is used in the two episodes: call-ins, interviewing spectators, viewers interviewing the stars, votings, etc. This aspect may apply to many popular entertainment shows, but it is adopted more frequently, more explicitly and, in my opinion, more deliberately in the *Feste der Volksmusik* than in similar shows. Likewise, by presenting the stars in the aforementioned way, with striking similarities to the classical concept of dilettantism, they are more equal to the spectators than high-profile stars would be.

In conclusion, all the explored facets of extraordinariness contribute to an effect of transcendence of the everyday to the extraordinary. The celebration of a festival as something special and extraordinary is enhanced by presenting the show in a more emotional and more exceptional way. At the same time, the ritual aspect gives the show an inclusive element. As we saw at the beginning of this article, Luhmann argues that everyday life in modern society is functionally differentiated. Since celebrations like the ones seen in the show are extraordinary and distinct from the everyday, they are therefore also distinct from Luhmann's functional differentiation. The show generates a strategy of how a modern individual can gain comprehensive inclusion, thereby challenging Luhmann's idea of functional differentiation. Such inclusion makes it possible for the modern spectator to become a genuine, natural, and authentic person, something which Luhmann says is only possible for the premodern individual of stratified society. In producing this extraordinariness by using aspects and facets of dilettantism, as has been shown in this article, the show succeeds in presenting extraordinariness through the everyday aesthetics of an amateur or dilettante. As a result, the dilettantish, ordinary everyday life of the spectator is in turn transcended to extraordinariness. In meeting the expectations and dilettantish visual habits of the visual community, the two shows under examination here succeed in generating an aesthetics of authenticity precisely through their presentation of the extremely kitschy, camp, and artificial.

WORKS CITED

Frühlingsfest der Volksmusik. ARD (MDR). 9 Apr. 2011.

Herbstfest der Volksmusik. ARD (MDR). 16 Oct. 2010.

Adorno, Theodor W. *Aesthetic Theory*. Ed. Gretel Adorno and Rolf Tiedemann. Transl. Robert Hullot-Kentor. Minneapolis, MN: U of Minnesota P, 1997.

——. *Ästhetische Theorie*. Ed. Gretel Adorno and Rolf Tiedemann. Frankfurt am Main: Suhrkamp, 1970.

Barthes, Roland. »L'Effet de Réel.« *Œuvres completes: Tome 2: 1966-1973*. Ed. Éric Marty. Paris: Seuil, 1994. 479-84.

Benjamin, Walter. *Das Kunstwerk im Zeitalter seiner Technischen Reproduzierbarkeit*, Frankfurt am Main: Suhrkamp, 2006.

Goethe, Johann Wolfgang, and Friedrich Schiller. »On Dilettantism.« *Goethe: The Collected Works*. Ed. John Gearey. Princeton, NJ: Princeton UP, 1994. 213-16.

——. »Über den Dilettantismus.« *Johann Wolfgang Goethe. Sämtliche Werke. Bd. I.18 Ästhetische Schriften 1771-1805*. Ed. Friedmar

Apel. Frankfurt am Main: Deutscher Klassiker Verlag, 1998. 739-85.

Hejl, Peter M. »Kultur.« *Metzler Lexikon Literatur- und Kulturtheorie: Ansätze – Personen – Grundbegriffe*. Ed. Ansgar Nünning. Stuttgart, Weimar: J.B. Metzler, 2004. 357-58.

Huck, Christian, and Carsten Zorn. »Das Populäre der Gesellschaft. Zur Einleitung.« *Das Populäre der Gesellschaft: Systemtheorie und Populärkultur*. Ed. Christian Huck and Carsten Zorn. Wiesbaden: VS Verlag für Sozialwissenschaften, 2007. 7-42.

Jahraus, Oliver. »Niklas Luhmann (1927-1998).« *Klassiker der modernen Literaturtheorie*. Ed. Matías Martínez and Michael Scheffel. Munich: Beck, 2010. 280-300.

Kalisch, Eleonore. »Aspekte einer Begriffs- und Problemgeschichte von Authentizität und Darstellung.« *Inszenierung von Authentizität*. Ed. Erika Fischer-Lichte. Tübingen: Francke, 2000. 31-44.

Kandorfer, Pierre. *Lehrbuch der Filmgestaltung: Theoretisch-technische Grundlagen der Filmkunde*. Gau-Heppenheim: Mediabook, 2003.

Knaller, Susanne. *Ein Wort aus der Fremde: Theorie und Geschichte des Begriffs Authentizität*. Heidelberg: Winter, 2007.

——. »Genealogie des ästhetischen Authentizitätsbegriffs.« Knaller and Müller, *Authentizität* 17-35.

Knaller, Susanne, and Harro Müller, eds. *Authentizität: Diskussion eines Ästhetischen Begriffs*. Munich: Fink, 2006.

——. »Einleitung.« Knaller and Müller, *Authentizität* 7-16.

Kramer, Christine. *Lebensgeschichte, Authentizität und Zeit: Zur Hermeneutik der Person*. Frankfurt am Main: Peter Lang, 2001.

Leistner, Simone. »Dilettantismus.« *Ästhetische Grundbegriffe*. Ed. Karlheinz Barck et al. Stuttgart: Metzler, 2001. 63-87.

Lethen, Helmut. »Versionen des Authentischen: sechs Gemeinplätze.« *Literatur- und Kulturwissenschaften: Positionen, Theorien, Modelle*. Ed. Hartmut Böhme and Klaus R. Scherpe. Reinbek: Rowohlt, 1996. 205-31.

Lubbock, Percy. *The Craft of Fiction*. London: Cape, 1972.

Luhmann, Niklas. *Gesellschaftsstruktur und Semantik: Studien zur Wissenssoziologie der Modernen Gesellschaft*. Vol. 1. Frankfurt am Main: Suhrkamp, 1993.

——. *Die Gesellschaft der Gesellschaft*. Vol. 2. Frankfurt am Main: Suhrkamp, 1998.

——. *Die Realität der Massenmedien*. Wiesbaden: VS Verlag für Sozialwissenschaften, 2009.

——. *The Reality of the Mass Media*. Cambridge: Polity, 2000.

Martínez, Matías. »Zur Einführung: Authentizität und Medialität in Künstlerischen Darstellungen des Holocaust.« *Der Holocaust und die Künste: Medialität und Authentizität von Holocaust-Darstellungen in Literatur, Film, Video, Malerei, Denkmälern, Comic und Musik*. Ed. Matías Martínez. Bielefeld: Aisthesis, 2004. 7-21.

Martínez, Matías, and Michael Scheffel. *Einführung in die Erzähltheorie*. Munich: Beck, 2005.

Müller, Harro. »Theodor W. Adornos Theorie des Authentischen Kunstwerks: Rekonstruktion und Diskussion des Authentizitätsbegriffs.« Knaller and Müller, *Authentizität* 55-67.

Raab, Jürgen. *Visuelle Wissenssoziologie: Theoretische Konzeption und Materiale Analysen*. Constance: UVK, 2008.

Schiller, Friedrich. »On Naive and Sentimental Poetry.« *Schiller's Complete Works. Vol. II*. Ed. Charles J. Hempel. Philadelphia, PA: Kohler, 1861. 549-79.

——. »Ueber das Gegenwärtige Teutsche Theater.« *Schillers Werke. Bd. 20 Philosophische Schriften*. Ed. Benno von Wiese. Weimar: Böhlau, 1962. 79-86.

——. »Ueber Naive und Sentimentalische Dichtung.« *Schillers Werke. Bd. 20 Philosophische Schriften*. Ed. Benno von Wiese. Weimar: Böhlau, 1962. 413-503.

Simmel, Georg. »Die Großstädte und das Geistesleben.« *Georg Simmel. Gesamtausgabe. Bd. I*. Ed. Otthein Rammstedt. Frankfurt am Main: Suhrkamp, 1995. 116-31.

Sommer, Roy. *Grundkurs Cultural Studies/Kulturwissenschaft Großbritannien*. Stuttgart: Klett, 2003.

Sontag, Susan. »Notes on Camp.« *A Susan Sontag Reader*. Ed. Elizabeth Hardwick. New York, NY: Farrar, Straus & Giroux, 1982. 105-19.

Stahl, Enno. *Anti-Kunst und Abstraktion in der Literarischen Moderne (1909-1933): Vom Italienischen Futurismus bis zum Französischen Surrealismus*. Frankfurt am Main: Lang, 1997.

Starobinski, Jean. *Rousseau. Eine Welt von Widerständen*. Munich: Hanser 1988.

Vaget, Hans Rudolf. *Dilettantismus und Meisterschaft. Zum Problem des Dilettantismus bei Goethe: Praxis, Theorie, Zeitkritik.* Munich: Winkler, 1971.

Vietta, Silvio. »Teil II: Probleme – Zusammenhänge – Methodische Fragen.« *Expressionismus.* Ed. Silvio Vietta and Hans Georg Kemper. Munich: UTB, 1997. 21–213.

Volkmann, Laurenz. »Kitsch.« *Metzler Lexikon Literatur- und Kulturtheorie. Ansätze - Personen - Grundbegriffe.* Ed. Ansgar Nünning. Stuttgart: Metzler, 2004. 318-19.

Weixler, Antonius. »Authentisches erzählen – authentisches Erzählen: Über Authentizität als Zuschreibungsphänomen und Pakt.« *Authentisches Erzählen. Produktion, Narration und Rezeption eines Zuschreibungsphänomens.* Ed. Antonius Weixler, forthcoming.

Wieler, Michael. *Dilettantismus: Wesen und Geschichte; Am Beispiel von Heinrich und Thomas Mann.* Würzburg: Königshausen und Neumann, 1996.

Wirth, Uwe. »Der Dilettantismus-Begriff um 1800 im Spannungsfeld psychologischer und prozeduraler Argumentation.« *Dilettantismus um 1800.* Ed. Stefan Blechschmidt and Andrea Heinz. Heidelberg: Winter, 2007. 25-33.

»Brooklyn Zack Is Real«

Irony and Sincere Authenticity in *30 Rock*

FLORIAN GROSS[1]

Seeking authenticity in its numerous inflections has become nothing short of a fashion, and there can be little doubt that authenticity has turned into a commodity. In fact, according to Knaller and Müller, there is now an »authenticity industry« (»Authentizitätsindustrie« 8; my translation) which constantly attempts to »stage effects of authenticity,« and »authenticity, with its aura of realness, veracity, nativeness, immediacy, *Eigentlichkeit* has become a successful brand item and logo« since the second half of the 20th century (7; my translation).[2] Knaller and Müller's timeframe and the concomitant rise of postmodernism is of course indicative here, especially if we consider Haselstein, Gross, and Snyder-Körber's observation: »In Trilling's view, the counter-cultural movement of the 1960s was heir to both the Romantic and the modernist version of authenticity, combining ideo-

---

1 I want to thank my co-editors, Irmtraud Huber and Wolfgang Funk, for immensely helpful comments on the first drafts of this article. Furthermore, I am indebted to Andreas Höschele's unpublished master's thesis »»It's Not Product Placement, I Just Like It.‹: Postmodern Advertising in *30 Rock*« and its thorough account of metafictional advertising in the series.

2 »Authentizität mit seiner Aura von Echtheit, Wahrhaftigkeit, Ursprünglichkeit, Unmittelbarkeit, Eigentlichkeit ist zu einem erfolgreich eingesetzten Markenartikel und Emblem geworden. [...] In allen Sparten der öffentlichen Medienarbeit müht man sich darum, Authentizitätseffekte zu inszenieren.«

logical iconoclasm with subjective experiences of deprivation and marginalization as the sources of individual and collective resistance to the status quo« (12). Nevertheless, postmodernism, especially in its philosophical inflections, was often seen as authenticity's other (cf. Haselstein, Gross, and Snyder-Körber 14), and postmodern culture as a culture of irony and the simulacrum that is fundamentally incommensurable with existential understandings of authenticity. And yet, in recent years, the quintessentially postmodern practice of ironically appropriating mass cultural products has nevertheless become a staple means of establishing authenticity, albeit of a different kind. In its »Fake Authenticity Issue« (1999), the philosophical magazine *Hermenaut* addresses a certain group of »Authentic Ones,« those who are both »obsessed with authenticity« and vintage consumer goods and yet keep it at arm's length by seeking ironic distance and a position somewhere between nostalgia and camp: »Undoubtedly you will recognize many of the names and places in these pages, though it will all seem *off* to you somehow, like maybe we take this stuff *too seriously*, instead of ›ironically‹ like you do« (Glenn, »Editor's Note« 8-9; emphases in the original). The fact that *Hermenaut* editor Joshua Glenn recently republished his introduction may hint at more than Glenn's attempt to keep his publications in circulation. It might speak volumes about the continued necessity to negotiate certain contemporary attempts at regaining authenticity, and the role that irony plays in this.

For Glenn, »[t]he misdirected quest for authenticity is an ugly thing,« with predominantly white, middle class people seeking the authentic in pre-aged furniture and clothing, exotic locales, nostalgic restaurants, organic food, or idiosyncratic art (»Introduction« 11). Consequently, these attempts pertain to the realm of »fake authenticity [...] that which is false, in the sense of ›counterfeited‹« (11). Opposed to the »fake,« which insufficiently tries to emulate an authentic original and thus retains the fundamental relationship between the two, the »fake authentic« does not even care any longer about an original and constructs an authentic artifact without any connection to reality, thus getting rid of any existential notion of authenticity in favor of commercialism (11-12; cf. Potter).[3] While the former is harmless »kitsch«

---

3 Potter's book *The Authenticity Hoax* is a case in point here, as he also outlines the fundamental problematic of seeking authenticity, but puts all responsibility on those seeking it, and not those selling it. Between Glenn

that can be made camp »by the lovingly ironic person,« the latter, with its attempt to construct the as-if real, is a disturbing simulacrum (12; cf. Baudrillard). Glenn ends on a by now familiar note:

> Irony, the engaged kind of irony which does not preclude real emotion, nor even seriousness, is still possible in a world of fakeness; but in a world where fake authenticity has triumphed, nothing remains but *sincerity* on the one hand, and a glib, mocking version of irony – *cheese* – on the other. (12; emphases in the original)

This dialogue between authenticity and irony is also a central aspect of the comedy show *30 Rock* (NBC, 2006-), which both draws on the fake authentic and, in contrast to Glenn's assumptions, attempts to salvage authenticity by a reconciliation of its close sibling sincerity and the trope of irony. To understand this aesthetic strategy, it makes sense to recap an instance where the show directly engages with the blatantly fake authentic: In the beginning of the episode »Brooklyn Without Limits,« we see the show's protagonist, television writer Elizabeth »Liz« Lemon, in a young, hip boutique in Brooklyn. With her pretentious friend and colleague Jenna Maroney, she shops for jeans in the intentionally run-down store that still has strait-jackets on display because supposedly the building used to belong to a mental institution. Lemon's objection that the hipster store is »trying way too hard« is quickly diffused after she settles for a pair that is exceptionally flattering to her figure. Back at work, she tells her colleagues about the additional perk that it is made by the house brand of a Brooklyn-based company which offers pants that were »hand-made in USA« and has stores in the hip neighborhoods of »Gaytown, White Harlem and the Van Beardswick section of Brooklyn.« Brooklyn Without Limits is a store all about »fair trade, local artisans, and staying green« and thus fits well into her politically liberal and consumer-critical stance. When her boss Jack Donaghy later confronts her and tells her that she, as a writer for NBC, is an employee of the international corporation GE and therefore part of the capitalist system, Lemon claims that, technically, she is a freelancer who makes a difference by buying »quality, locally-made jeans.« However, Lemon gradually has to learn

---

and Potter, I think that there is a third way of dealing with the nexus between the impossibility of and a continued strive for authenticity.

that the pants were manufactured by juvenile wage slaves in Vietnam. Even more, although she wants to believe that »Brooklyn Zack is real,« the cute and hip, supposedly owner-managed store is in fact owned by no other corporation than Halliburton, who needed an outlet for a surplus of waterboarding hoods. In a narrative of increasing satire, the episode thus debunks a pattern of consumption that attempts to signify authenticity by expressing criticism of consumerism and the demands of a capitalist consumer society. In »Brooklyn Without Limits,« 30 Rock's engagement with this form of authenticity is one of pure negation, exposing it as noble but naïve at best, and as a mere capitalist illusion along the lines of fake authenticity at worst. And it is of course directed at a particular social set of people: the contemporary hipster, the young, white, urban persona that aesthetically defies society's mores and yet is often perceived to be at the center of the commodification of life, and also at the heart of Glenn's »Authentic Ones.«[4]

30 Rock addresses the predicament of being unable to arrive at any form of existential authenticity as well as the danger for irony amounting to no more than jaded cynicism. In fact, what Glenn describes as »existential ›authenticity‹« comes very close to what I think is central to 30 Rock's engagement with authenticity: »that mode of existence in which one becomes ironically and radically suspicious of all received forms and norms, and in which one strives to lucidly affirm and creatively live the tension of human reality in all its contingency, ambiguity, and absurdity« (15). Yet, in the particular case of 30 Rock, I think it makes more sense to conceptualize the show's engagement with authenticity as ›sincere authenticity,‹ as it develops a mode of authenticity radically at odds with those existential inflections traditionally related to authenticity. Opposed to existential notions of immediacy and primordial reality, it is a heavily constructed form of authenticity that highlights this construction as a conscious aesthetic strategy. Through its self-consciously ironic narrative as well as a complex and at times paradoxical negotiation with various layers of authenticity, the series constructs a figuration of authenticity as sincere authenticity,

---

4   In the following, when I refer to the hipster, I do not mean the historical hipster as coined most famously by Norman Mailer in »The White Negro« (1957), but rather its specifically contemporary inflection as defined for instance by Mark Greif.

laying claim to the desirability of authenticity at the same time that it renders existential authenticity impossible. In what follows, I will read *30 Rock*'s debunking of its own and others' fake authenticity in close relation to its simultaneous construction of sincere authenticity through an ironic take on visual style, biographical content, and meta-fictional illusion-shattering. *30 Rock*'s irony is part of a paradoxical aesthetics of authenticity that (at least at times) moves beyond the purely ironic, towards meta-ironic aesthetics that precariously negoti-ate with and thereby attempt to construct what seems to be essentially non-constructible: authenticity.

30 ROCK AND AUTHENTICITY

But why *30 Rock*, when there are many other, seemingly infinitely bet-ter examples to be found in the contemporary television landscape when it comes to authenticity? Most prominently, there is the gritty realism of *The Wire* (HBO, 2002-08), which has been praised for its authentic depiction of social struggle in Baltimore, and by extension the United States. Set and filmed in Baltimore, created and written by a former police reporter, and cast with actual actors from that area, it draws on several registers of authenticity. In slightly different terms, we have the historical realism of *Mad Men* (AMC, 2007-), which is celebrated for its authentic depiction of the 1960s. In effect, we are dealing here with two different though related modes of televisual au-thenticity through verisimilitude. *The Wire* presents us with a case of social naturalism and, for the lack of the better term, contemporary primitivism which rings true for a largely well-educated and affluent audience by showing how the other half lives (or rather, survives). In the case of *Mad Men*, it is a discourse of accuracy, be it historiograph-ic, style-related, or in terms of its depiction of the decade's structures of feeling. This, however, is not without problems of its own. Both the socio-economic authenticity of *The Wire* as well as the historical au-thenticity of *Mad Men* need to resonate with certain assumptions, speculations, feelings, and memories, whose own accuracy is inherent-ly precarious. As such, televisual authenticity along the lines of real-ism emerges as a linguistic convention that depends as much on its receivers as does the trope of irony, whose realization ultimately de-pends entirely on the interpreter (cf. Hutcheon, *Irony* 4, 116-40). Even though authenticity is centrally concerned with immanence, individuality, and independence, it is also essentially in the eye of the beholder. Moreover, *The Wire* and *Mad Men* may be said to employ rather insincere forms of authenticity, because both present a highly stylized product as unadorned. In the framework of fake authenticity, it might be even more problematic for its relatively straightforward location of authenticity in the socio-economic, spatial, and/or temporal Other. In Thomas Frank's words:

Perhaps the most offensive aspect of our craving for authenticity is our never-ceasing conviction that authenticity is enjoyed effortlessly and unproblematically by the Other: the class, race, nationality, religious group, or even gender who we are not. Under the guise of authenticity we tolerate all manner of essentializing and even racist entertainments without ever seeming to wonder about it. (»Green Hills« 79)

Compared to the *The Wire* and *Mad Men*, *30 Rock* is hardly ever mentioned in relation to authenticity, save with regards to its visual style, and this may speak volumes about its specific aesthetics of authenticity. *30 Rock* is a half-hour comedy which, together with a number of other recent workplace comedies, from *Scrubs* (NBC/ABC, 2001-10) to *The Office* (U.S.: NBC, 2005-) and *Parks and Recreation* (NBC, 2009-), eschews the sitcom's traditional multi-camera setup and laugh track for a single-camera setup without canned laughter. This choice for documentary rather than theatrical visuals is further emphasized by a visual style that veers between cinematic and documentary aesthetics. The show's mobile camera work and frequent location shots distinguish it markedly from a conventional sitcom like *Two And A Half Men* (CBS, 2003-). Yet, in its embrace of a less artificial »comedy vérité,« *30 Rock* does not adopt the mockumentary format of *The Office*, but rather depicts its characters as being unaware that they are being filmed, akin to similar shows set in the world of entertainment production like *Curb Your Enthusiasm* (HBO, 2000-) and *The Larry Sanders Show* (HBO, 1992-98) (Mills 91). In a recent *Variety*-piece, Steve Heisler claimed fittingly that the recent upsurge in single-camera comedies is partially due to the fact that »[s]ingle-camera lends itself to authenticity. It's less like theater and more like film, employing closeups and sometimes documentary-style interviews to convey comedy at an intimate level. Actors play to the camera, not the studio audience.« He also quotes *Modern Family*-producer Steve Levitan with the following words: »Audiences – maybe because of reality TV, maybe because of YouTube and the Internet – are longing for things that feel more authentic and real.« Out of this emerges the perception that *30 Rock*'s visual style conveys authenticity through aesthetic realism, by a strong endeavor to establish the illusion of objective, non-mediated viewing as well as a more direct audience address – and more freedom for the individual viewer who is not told any longer when to laugh. And yet, the fact that it uses a (by now) well-worn, conventionalized visual style and that audiences need to ›feel‹ the emerging authenticity brings us back to the question whether something can be authentic if it is adopted from something else and dependent on other people's attribution. Furthermore, *30 Rock*'s construction of authenticity through visual style seems to be at odds with its critique of the kind of corporate manufacturing of authenticity behind the fake authentic clothing store Brooklyn Without Limits. Enter self-conscious irony.

At the same time that the show rejects visual aesthetics that have become conventionalized and are increasingly deemed artificial, it uses another highly artificial set of aesthetics to signify authenticity – and makes us aware of it: One instance of this is evident in »Live Show,« *30 Rock*'s fifth-season episode that takes a bow to live comedy aesthetics by using a multi-camera setup, a laugh track, and cheap props for its live broadcast.[5] In the opening scene, Jack Donaghy recognizes that there is something different, and asks Liz: »Does it seem weird in here to you? [...] Everything looks like a Mexican soap opera,« which is accompanied by clearly artificial laughter. And in the end of the episode, when the camera filter changes to the usual one, he says: »That's more like it.«[6] I claim that this foregrounding of visual aesthetics typical for different approaches to televisual comedy goes beyond pure play for two reasons: First, it engages with and reflects on its own visual aesthetics of authenticity, and second, it mixes its meta-

---

5   This episode was shot and broadcast live; therefore, two slightly different versions exist, one for the East Coast and one for the West Coast.

6   Similarly, scenes like the one in which Lemon fails to crawl out of Donaghy's office and says that »this would work on *Ugly Betty*« further drives home the show's attempt at emphasizing narrative artifice (»Up All Night«).

fictional digressions with several autobiographical markers, thus furthering its paradoxical, multilayered play with authenticity.[7] *30 Rock* is a comedy show broadcast by NBC about the production of the NBC live-action comedy show *TGS With Tracy Jordan*; it is the simulation of a television show, a second degree imitation (cf. Wisnewski, »Introduction« 2). At the same time, it includes its own creator, co-writer, and executive producer Tina Fey, former star and head writer of *Saturday Night Live* (NBC, 1975-), in the role of Liz Lemon. Lemon has to juggle her private and professional live(s), conciliate the creative team she supervises and the economically driven corporation she works for, and all the while emerges more and more as a slightly skewed autobiographical version of Fey herself. Apart from general semblances, Liz Lemon's claim that »every Tina I've known is a real judgmental bitch« (»Gentleman's Intermission«) is just as blatantly self-referential as the show's frequent references to *Star Wars*, of which Fey herself is a very articulate fan.[8] Beyond the Lemon/Fey-nexus, we have the writer John D. Lutz appearing as none other than a television writer called John D. Lutz.[9] Furthermore, the entire aspect of a fictional NBC show at the center of an actual NBC program is, of course, also such a marker, while the fact that *30 Rock* is filmed in New York instead of Los Angeles, and thus practically on location, drives home this point.[10] On the more playful end of the spectrum, it is furthermore possible to read Alec Baldwin's character Jack Donaghy as a version of Baldwin's character Blake in *Glengarry Glen Ross* (1992), thus linking intertextual play with biographical content (cf. Shaw 203).[11]

---

7   For more on the sitcom genre's increasing digressiveness, cf. Simonini.

8   Cf. for instance her television interviews on *The Late Late Show with Craig Ferguson* and *Late Night with Conan O'Brien*.

9   This is of course also reminiscent of the postmodern literary practice of fictionalizing authors, most prominently done by Paul Auster.

10   Concerning the last aspect, *Scrubs* as a medical show filmed in a former hospital is another case in point.

11   Baldwin's career is also addressed in »100,« when (among many other allusions to his past) Jack tells Tracy about the hazards of walking away from a successful movie franchise, thus mirroring Baldwin's own exit from the successful Jack Ryan-franchise after *The Hunt for Red October* (1990).

This kind of metafictional twist is also present in »Brooklyn Without Limits«: When Lemon puts on the jeans for the first time and inspects her figure, she cannot but ask: »Is that really me?« Apart from expressing incredulity about her new great looks, this statement also hints at something else. As will become gradually clearer during the episode, we actually do not see Tina Fey's body in the mirror, but a body-double's. And when she speaks of »staying green,« she performs a hand gesture similar to her famous Sarah Palin impersonation, again conflating actress with character.[12] All of these instances go beyond the show's diegesis and self-consciously mirror and disrupt *30 Rock*'s own creation of a fictional illusion. Through this, the series ›confesses‹ its inauthenticity at the same time as it attempts to remain authentic through this confession. In this respect, the metafictional aesthetics of the television program *30 Rock* function similar to Patricia Waugh's conceptualization of metafictional literature's function of »laying bare« the illusion at the basis of fiction writing, thus merging creation and criticism (6). And yet, *30 Rock* does more than shatter the illusion of transparent fiction – it shatters the illusion that this illusion-shattering might bring you closer to reality. The fiction created and commented on in *30 Rock* is not only the obvious fiction of a fictive story, but also the ›fiction‹ of authenticity. This is meta-metafiction, both for its self-conscious adaptation of literary metafiction as well as its transfer to another medium, with its very own implications. As we will see, metafiction and self-consciousness in television pose problems of their own, especially when it comes to aspects of authenticity.

SINCERE METATELEVISION

By 2012, metafiction, self-reflexivity, intertextuality, and ironic self-consciousness have become established parts of television, a medium that for many critics has always been postmodern, but was for a long time denied to be part of the wider philosophical and aesthetic phenomenon indicated by the suffix ›-ism.‹ The apparent postmodernization of television has been analyzed by critics since the mid-1980s (cf.

---

12 During the 2008 presidential election, Fey became internationally famous for her numerous impersonations of then vice-presidential candidate Sarah Palin on *Saturday Night Live*.

Feuer, Kerr, and Vahimagi 44-56; Marc 129-66; Miller; Olson; O'Day). Early reactions to this range from Feuer, Kerr, and Vahimagi's celebration of self-reflexivity as a crucial characteristic of the very ›Quality TV‹-style they identify in MTM programs to utter despair in the work of Mark Crispin Miller, who identifies »preemptive irony« in self-reflexive programs through which »TV preempts derision by itself evincing endless irony« (14). He assumes that self-denigrating irony on television serves the function of preempting any criticism leveled against it. Its ultimate function is that of concealing consumption and commerce through mock-Enlightenment. Even more: in the hands of commercial programs and networks, it disinvents the formerly subversive tool of irony from all its liberating power, making it yet another means to enthrall the mass audiences of today's popular culture. David Foster Wallace, heavily influenced by this kind of reasoning, claims in his influential essay »E Unibus Pluram: Television and U.S. Fiction« that preemptive irony not only corrupts the possibility of criticizing television from the outside, but also the critical potential of (postmodern) literature. For him, the fact that self-conscious irony has become part and parcel of contemporary TV programming shows how this formerly liberating and enlightening rhetorical strategy has been co-opted and thus rendered ineffective by the culture industry. In its binary opposition of authentic literature and co-opting television, Wallace's logic neatly follows what Thomas Frank calls polemically

> the co-optation theory: faith in the revolutionary potential of ›authentic‹ counterculture combined with the notion that business mimics and mass-produces fake counterculture in order to cash in on a particular demographic and to subvert the great threat that ›real‹ counterculture represents. (*Conquest* 7)

Even Frank himself, although he disagrees with the basic assumptions behind this theory of co-optation, directly connects cultural irony and the ironic quotation of cultural material across the spectrum as a jaded, ubiquitous, and ultimately fake strategy in order to conceal uncritical consumption of facile and commodified rebellion (cf. *Conquest* 230-33).

As these examples show, it is no exaggeration to claim that irony has become »a problematic mode of expression at the end of the twentieth century« (Hutcheon, *Irony* 1). Supposedly, this got even worse in the 21st century: In a post-9/11 piece Roger Rosenblatt famously claimed that »the age of irony comes to an end,« that the intellectuals' ironic detachment which was a hallmark of the postmodern era was shattered in its defiance of reality by the very reality they were so fond of denying in their language games that took nothing seriously. Even though most people witnessed the atrocious attacks via exactly those televisual pictures that informed much of postmodernism's skepticism vis-a-vis real experiences, the apparent literalness of them supposedly put an end to postmodernism's »ironic inauthenticity« (Grossberg qtd. in Mayer 165). With his detraction of irony, Rosenblatt chimes into a critical stance on irony that had already suffused the 1990s and spanned from the leftist critics cited above to the conservative pundit Jedediah Purdy, who outlines irony and authenticity as antithetical concepts and reads irony as nothing but »a defensive response to a culture of inauthenticity« (O'Brien 157). It seems fitting in this regard when Wallace ends his famous pre-9/11 diatribe against postmodern irony with the following tentative prediction:

The next real literary ›rebels‹ in this country might well emerge as some weird bunch of anti-rebels, born oglers who dare somehow to back away from ironic watching, who have the childish gall actually to endorse and instantiate single-entendre principles. Who treat of plain old untrendy human troubles and emotions in U.S. life with reverence and conviction. Who eschew self-consciousness and hip fatigue. These anti-rebels would be outdated, of course, before they even started. Dead on the page. Too sincere. Clearly repressed. Backward, quaint, naive, anachronistic. Maybe that'll be the point. Maybe that's why they'll be the next real rebels. Real rebels, as far as I can see, risk disapproval. The old postmodern insurgents risked the gasp and squeal: shock, disgust, outrage, censorship, accusations of socialism, anarchism, nihilism. Today's risks are different. The new rebels might be artists willing to risk the yawn, the rolled eyes, the cool smile, the nudged ribs, the parody of gifted ironists, the ›Oh how banal.‹ To risk accusations of sentimentality, melodrama. Of overcredulity. Of softness. Of willingness to be suckered by a world of lurkers and starers who fear gaze and ridicule above imprisonment without law. Who knows. (82)

Of course, as the numerous levels of irony at the heart of his novel *Infinite Jest* (1996) testify, Wallace himself never followed his own prediction verbatim; and neither did most of his literary peers that began around the same time to work themselves out of the postmodern literary paradigm. Instead of opting for aesthetics that abolished postmodernism in a way Purdy would have approved of, authors such as Jonathan Franzen, Richard Powers, or Jonathan Lethem never claimed the possibility of returning »to a state of pre-postmodern innocence regarding language and the processes of representation« (McLaughlin 65, cf. Mayer 166). Even if they reinstated mimetic modes of writing, they always connected this with postmodern insights into the ultimate impossibility of stable signification. And Wallace himself tried to expose irony's end(s) through an exacerbating use of and negotiation with irony – meta-irony – and thus attempted to move beyond cynicism and towards sincerity (cf. Schneck; Boswell; Velmeulen and van den Akker).

Ironically enough, *30 Rock* uses a strikingly similar aesthetic strategy of generating sincerity and thus redeems Wallace's goal – even though it is seemingly the exact cultural phenomenon against which he developed his plea for naïve irony. At first glance, with the co-optation theory in mind, self-conscious irony on television is indeed everything but authentic: it is second-hand, copied, nothing more than a mass marketed version of the supposedly subversive self-consciousness at the heart of postmodern literature. Furthermore, considering post-Romantic notions of authenticity as being self-reliant and rebellious, television as a fully integrated part of the culture industry seems to be fundamentally incommensurable with this kind of authenticity as well. On the other hand, *30 Rock*'s self-conscious highlighting of artificiality and construction sublates one of the most central paradoxes of any aesthetics of authenticity: the moment you represent authenticity, you are already one step removed from it. Moreover, the series also metafictionally highlights its own capitalist incorporation, something which many authors in the postmodern canon never did, as well as its own metafictional treatment of postmodern self-consciousness. And while *30 Rock* features a dedicated mediation between creative and commercial, between individual and societal demands, it most blatantly presents itself as a highly commercial product that integrates narrative with commercials in ways even the most pessimistic cultural critic might not have dreamed of. In the very first episode, Jack Donaghy presents the (actually existing) GE Trivection Oven, the characters use Apple computers throughout, they eat at McDonald's, and they drink Snapple. However, while this kind of product placement is hardly original, the show's treatment of it certainly is, as for instance in scenes when Liz Lemon, after talking at length about Verizon, asks into the camera »can we have our money now?« (»Somebody to Love«), or when Jerry Seinfeld promotes his *Bee Movie* (2007) by appearing as himself and telling the audience, again by breaching the fourth wall, that the movie is »opening November 2nd,« three weeks after the original broadcast (»SeinfeldVision«).[13] While these scenes combine product placement with the outright acknowledgment that the show does that, the following example goes even further. In the first season episode »Jack-Tor,« the integration of Snapple is addressed by the show in three scenes, in which the writers negotiate with Donaghy about the integration of products in their show. During the initial discussion, Liz strongly opposes product integration because it would mean »compromising the integrity of the show to sell« at which point she is interrupted by a succession of shots during which her colleagues (and eventually she herself) explicitly praise the beverage. Later in the episode, her refusal to be GE's »shills« is further ridiculed when Liz and her producer Pete Hornberger encounter a man in a giant Snapple costume, just as Liz claims that *TGS* is not a »commercial.« Eventually, the episode's A-plot explicitly addresses *30 Rock*'s self-consciousness:

Jack: What can I do for you?
Liz: So we wrote a product integration sketch, but we wanted to run it by you first because it's about how GE is making us do this. And we were kind of hoping that the GE executive in the sketch could be played by you.
Jack: Oh I get it. The whole self-referential thing. Letterman hates the suits, Stern yells at his boss, Nixon says »sock it to me« on *Laugh In*. Yeah. Hippie humor.

In this plot, *30 Rock* self-consciously addresses its own integration with capitalism and concludes it with a self-conscious comment on its own self-consciousness. Initially, this was celebrated by critics and

---

13 Jerry Seinfeld is of course also instructive concerning the actual originality of *30 Rock*'s product placement. With its blatant inclusion and metafictional treatment of Snapple beverages, his sitcom *Seinfeld* (NBC, 1989-98) has to be considered as a forerunner to *30 Rock*'s aesthetics. However, both concerning the frequency as well as the connection to authenticity, *30 Rock* emerges as a much more pronounced example for this.

often taken as evidence of the series' good writing, but by the third season, it also became subject to criticism (cf. Nussbaum). In the case of criticism on the series' explicit allusions to McDonald's (later called »McFlurryGate«) in »St. Valentine's Day,« Fey even responded herself:

It gives me great pleasure to inform you that the references to McDonald's in last night's episode of *30 Rock* were in no way product placement. (Nor were they an attempt at product placement that fell through.) We received no money from the McDonald's Corporation. We were actually a little worried they might sue us. That's just the kind of revenue-generating masterminds we are. Also, the upcoming story line where Liz Lemon starts dating Grimace is just based on a recurring dream I have. Seriously, though, it's not product placement. Also, whoever is writing my Twitter account is pretty funny, but it's not me. (Graham)[14]

Over and beyond Fey's half-mocking response, *30 Rock* addressed this particular controversy also within its diegesis. In »The Ones,« an episode that aired two months after »St. Valentine's Day,« Liz is prominently wearing the branded blanket Slanket in her office. When Tracy walks in on her working in this domestic apparel, she responds in best fake authentic fashion that she is just »wearing it as a joke.« Later, when Donaghy sees her dressed like this, she claims that »it's not product placement, I just like it,« thereby taking yet another position on the inclusion of products. The series once more stresses the claim for an honest appreciation of this consumer item through the last scene featuring the Slanket. Lemon, now at home, is sitting on her couch in her Slanket and eating her »night cheese,« thus combining the Slanket with the most passionate habit of hers: food. In sum, this episode provides us with a number of possible reasons for the inclusion of branded products. And if we take *30 Rock*'s aesthetics seriously, it does not matter what the actual motive is – for this indeterminacy is the whole point, for better or worse. Here, TV critic Alan Sepinwall's question

---

14 Here, things get really complicated, for as Gillan has shown, Fey is probably not entirely honest here. While it seems to be true that the producers of *30 Rock* received no direct money for the integration, McDonald's nevertheless spent a considerable amount of money for commercials during the original broadcast of this episode (cf. 188-93).

about the motive behind the Verizon-scene is indicative: »Was the above [›Can we have our money now‹] just a dig at product placement, or was it a coded message from the WGA? You decide.« Even with commercial irony, we have to acknowledge its fundamentally unstable meaning, and therefore acknowledge that the Verizon-product placement might have been the vehicle for *30 Rock*'s statement on the 2007-08 WGA strike just as much as it was a blatant commercial.

FAKING IT BEYOND THE FAKE AUTHENTIC

30 Rock's aesthetics are based on a dialectics between fake authenticity and what I call sincere authenticity; for me, these two options represent two different ways of constructing the as-if real. Despite the choice of words, I do not believe that it is possible to ethically judge them per se; rather, it is striking how much the fake authentic foregrounds sincerity and how much the sincere authentic foregrounds fakery. Neither of the two assumes the existence of some sort of primordial authenticity it strives for. Rather, in both, authenticity emerges as an effect that sends up semblances of reality and truth. They both insist on the necessity to aesthetically construct it, and yet differ in their aesthetic means of arriving at this, and in their view on the ultimate desirability of authenticity.

Beyond its visual style, autobiographical content, and metafictional antics, *30 Rock*'s negotiation of (fake) authenticity also negotiates authenticity on the level of narrative and character. In the 100th episode, the current fetish of authenticity is shown to be an illusion when African American actor Tracy Jordan is interviewed on *The Today Show* by Matt Lauer about his trip to Africa to rediscover his roots. Lauer asserts in a stereotypical fashion: »It's because you didn't feel like your authentic self that you walked away from success. That's actually very brave, don't you think? [...] You fly free. I'm a bird in a cage [...] a true artist. He feels things we don't.« Before his appearance on *The Today Show*, Tracy already tried to wreck his reputation – for reasons too comically exaggerated to be covered here – by erratic behavior on *The Rachael Ray Show* and *Live with Regis and Kelly*. In the latter show, he even confessed that his trip to Africa was nothing but a ruse, only to be celebrated by Kelly Ripa for his »honesty.« These three scenes ridicule the craving for authenticity on lifestyle television, but they do so with the help of those very television hosts that are caricatured in this episode of *30 Rock*. As a consequence, the television hosts also rise above their own diurnal fabrication of fake authenticity and lay claim to a more sincere approach to the authentic – through faking it and partaking in fabricated versions of their own shows. However, contrary to *30 Rock*, Matt Lauer, Rachael Ray, Regis Philbin, and Kelly Ripa's attempts are less grounded in a full-fledged narrative of (in)authenticity and therefore hardly reverberate beyond these isolated instances. With *30 Rock*'s weekly seriality, it is possible to reinforce the message time and again – but as we have seen with respect to product placement, this might also lead to conventionalized structures that have become inherently problematic with regards to their credibility.

Seriality is also a good transition to *30 Rock*'s (to date) latest interrogation of the hipster's ironic stance on authenticity. When Tracy Jordan was first introduced to *30 Rock*, we saw news footage of him running down a highway, shouting »I am a Jedi« (»Pilot«). In his attempt to damage his reputation, he does this again in the episode »100,« thus restaging something from the series' memory, the effect of which clearly points beyond the show's diegesis. More significantly still is the reaction of the (heavily stereotyped) hipster who sees Tracy's act: »Hey look, Tracy Jordan is ironically reappropriating his bad past behavior as a commentary on Fitzgerald's dictum that ›there are no second acts in American live.‹ I wanna make a picture of him with my old-fashioned camera« (»100«). This hipster's reaction thus again evokes the hybrid attempt to evoke authenticity through nostalgia and camp epitomized by Glenn's »Authentic Ones.« In this scene, *30 Rock* once more reaffirms the close proximity between irony and the fake authentic, and distances itself from it without claiming to exist beyond it.

The same episode includes a subplot in which Jenna admits to being »not that good at playing *la realité*.« And indeed, she is right. In »Brooklyn Without Limits,« she admits that, contrary to mentally unstable Tracy, she is »more aware« of what she is doing and should therefore be held responsible for her (egocentric, scheming, narcissistic) behavior – which is indeed what has already happened: In an earlier episode, staff writer Frank, a cliché hipster complete with logo trucker hats, nerd glasses, and general jadedness, calls Jenna a »phony« and a »fake,« and accuses her of having never done anything »real or genuine« (»Up All Night«). In turn, she accuses him of the same, of being a fake, of trying to act cool with his »thrift store T-shirts« and »big weird glasses« and motto trucker hats, spending »just as much time and energy trying to look weird as I do trying to look beautiful.« While both are clearly right, they can only arrive at a moment of authenticity when Jenna inadvertently flatulates, which is commented on by Frank as »the first time you've ever done something like a real person,« and which becomes a cathartic moment over which the two bond, as both usually work hard at upholding their respective acts. Apart from that, the characters display different ways of failing at being authentic: If Jenna is the endpoint of excessive artificiality, and Frank is the endpoint of hipsterdom's fake authenticity, the »literal-minded« (Dohnimm 8), anti-ironic Kenneth, the NBC page from Stone Mountain, Georgia – a character somewhere between idiotic »mouth-breathing« hillbilly and moral compass – clearly is the endpoint of naïve sincerity. He is so literal-minded as to be ridiculous. In-between these options, we find the equally paradox, but more affirmatively rendered Liz and Jack. It is their relationship that, amidst the comic exaggerations of their co-workers, comes closest to a ›realistic‹ one. Starting off as a relationship in which Donaghy soon assumes the role of mentor to his subordinate, this is among the only aspects of the show that indicate some depth and development. It is also the relationship that most clearly combines the two supposed binary oppositions of creative and corporate.

With respect to its paradoxical relationship towards capitalism and consumerism, *30 Rock*'s narrative representation of the conflictual relationship between creative and corporate factions is indicative. Between the GE executive Jack Donaghy on the one and Liz's team of writers on the other hand, a binary opposition is constructed that highlights aspects like hip creativity vs. square commercialism or working ethic vs. hedonistic pleasure.[15] Yet again, this connects the show to its more complex dialogue with authenticity. The program represents and – to a certain extent – promotes the countercultural defiance of corporate mainstream, yet all the while also ridiculing it (cf. »Brooklyn Without Limits«). Most crucially, it does so from a position simulta-

---

15 An aspect of the show I have analyzed in more detail elsewhere (cf. »Transnational Cool«).

neously within and without. Its irony is constantly veering between the jaded form of irony that is actually inoculating (perceived) capitalist mores, but also bespeaks the ironic stance of someone »who faces up to the historical contingency of his or her own most central beliefs and desires, and recognizes that these beliefs and desires don't refer back to anything transcendent« (Glenn, »Introduction« 15). At the heart of *30 Rock*'s sincere authenticity is a high degree of self-consciousness, and with it a high degree of self-conscious irony; and this may also explain *30 Rock*'s ire towards hipsters: First, because it recognizes itself to be not too different from them. But second, and even more crucial, it criticizes the hipster's ironic stance towards everything but him- or herself. This ironic stance toward its own ideological position is probably the most central aspect of the show, and with it the most interesting element of *30 Rock* to construct an aesthetics of authenticity. From the position of *30 Rock*'s aesthetics of authenticity, which is inherently removed from any existential authenticity, the show highlights its own artificiality as well as its awareness of it. It thus moves beyond pure metafiction and recursively harks back to an authenticity that has little to do with originality. *30 Rock*'s aesthetics of authenticity depend on the show's narrative negotiations with contemporary consumer culture just as much as on its interweaving of autobiographical and visually ›authentic‹ elements with anti-illusionist metafiction, which mimetically represents the impossibility of any unfiltered representation (cf. Funk in this volume).

Of course, this authenticity, as much as it is yearned for, can never be the primordial »unthinking« that an artist like e.e. cummings was rooting for as a crucial prerequisite of authentic art (cf. Haselstein, Gross, and Snyder-Körber 9). It will always be a carefully crafted, fully conscious endeavor and therefore attempt to attain that which it can never reach with its specific means. Adding this to the fact that the show presents the individual's relationship to society more in a dialectical and less in a necessarily antagonistic relationship, the show replaces existential authenticity with sincerity (cf. Haselstein, Gross, and Snyder-Körber 18). The contemporary reconfiguration of authenticity along the lines of sincerity was already noted by Haselstein, Gross, and Snyder-Körber, who, following Trilling, claimed that »[s]incerity is the convincing personal expression of a social or cultural convention« (11). Compared to the Romantic defiance of society, contemporary attempts at autonomous self-expression have become much more a means than an end, given that they are performed in a culture in which the individual moves back and forth between the assertion of independence and the adherence to rules. Accordingly, the show evokes moments and desires of Romantic authenticity the very moment it thwarts them by convention, imitation, and incorporation. Vis-a-vis the dichotomy between authenticity and commercialism, *30 Rock* derives its authenticity precisely from its open acknowledgment of its involvement with corporate structures. This frankness is connected to the fact that the show is, after all, marked as highly self-conscious and, as we have seen above, autobiographical. Even though its specific aesthetic strategy, irony, per definition runs blatantly counter to Trilling's famous conceptualization of sincerity as »a congruence between avowal and actual feeling« (2), it continues something that Kelly has already identified in Wallace, who urges his readers to find a way of dealing with contemporary culture from within. Says Kelly, »One must begin by recognizing the lack of any transcendent, absolute, Archimedean point from which to judge the authentic from the inauthentic, the sincere from the manipulative, truth from ideology, and so on« (137-38). It is exactly this position taken by *30 Rock* – which is, considering Wallace's take on irony, quite ironic. In his essay, Wallace claims that through self-conscious irony, »[t]elevision's managed to become its own most profitable analyst« (30). For Wallace, television's self-conscious irony makes criticism from the outside (for instance by literary authors) impossible due to television's closed system. And yet, with *30 Rock*'s constant self-diagnosis, the exact opposite is the case: It opens up the text to its (perceived) inauthenticity, albeit on its own terms.

The show stands in line with the kind of aestheticized postmodernism that nevertheless asserts its political edge, as Linda Hutcheon already noted in her *Politics of Postmodernism*. For Hutcheon, postmodern aesthetics' »complicitous critique« (*Politics* 1), »a strange kind of critique, one bound up, too, with its own complicity with power and domination, one that acknowledges that it cannot escape implication in that which it nevertheless wants to analyze and maybe undermine« (4), was at the center of its aesthetics of »denaturalizing,« which, among others, depended on irony, intertextuality, and appropriation (2). Now, the next turn of the screw on display in *30 Rock* is certainly not its general »complicitous critique,« but rather its specific use of irony. Irony in *30 Rock* functions less as a tool of de-naturalization but rather as a tool of authentication. Thus, it debunks the detaching power of irony and opts for a use that effects the exact opposite: further highlighting complicity. This however, is not necessarily the postmodernization of (parts of) a medium that Hutcheon herself still characterized as follows: »Most television, in its *unproblematized* reliance on realist narrative and transparent representational conventions, is pure commodified complicity, without the critique needed to define the postmodern paradox« (*Politics* 10; emphasis in the original). While Hutcheon ignores any self-conscious television, Wallace is uneasy with television's turn towards self-consciousness, because it is so clearly at odds with his conceptualization of television as mass cultural medium. But both inadvertently hint at a paradox in and of itself when it comes to contemporary television, parts of which work themselves out of the postmodern paradigm just like literature does.

CONCLUSION

30 Rock presents a multi-faceted, inherently contradictory engagement with authenticity. It is in fact the ironic, metafictional aspect of *30 Rock* that, in paradoxical combination with certain ›conventional‹ markers of authenticity like visual realism, autobiography, and a sustained negotiation with fake-authentic behavior, serve as the basis for its specific aesthetics of sincere authenticity. Instead of relating irony and authenticity in a mutually exclusive *or* inherently connected way, *30 Rock* puts these two concepts in a dialectical relationship that alternates between paradox, contradiction, and mutual dependency. To a certain degree, *30 Rock*'s conspicuously constructed, always obviously mediated aesthetics can be seen as a paradoxical, maybe even perverted approach to authenticity. It uses conventionalized aesthetics of authenticity at the same time as it debunks them as mere (inauthentic) convention. *30 Rock*'s sincere authenticity wears its thinking, its limitations, its incorporation, on its sleeve – and yet does not engage in cynicism or pure play, nor does it necessarily evade the fake. This does not, however, mean that this is ethically unproblematic; it may well serve as a potent vehicle for the commodification of dissent (cf. Frank and Weiland). However, opposed to much consumer-critical literature, it does not imagine its own narrative as being outside or beyond commodification. Another authentic option beside the longing for the primordial, direct, unfettered experience, it is the only option left when all experience has become represented, mediated, and commodified over and over again. Simultaneously using and moving beyond the postmodern arsenal, sincere authenticity highlights its incorporation in contemporary capitalist structures, while at the same time keeping a critical and non-identical position.

WORKS CITED

»100.« *30 Rock*. NBC. 21 Apr. 2011.

30 Rock. By Tina Fey. Perf. Tina Fey, Alex Baldwin, Tracy Morgan. NBC, 2006-.

Baudrillard, Jean. *Simulations*. Trans. Paul Foss, Paul Patton, and Philip Beitchman. Los Angeles, CA: Semiotext[e], 1983.

Boswell, Marshall. *Understanding David Foster Wallace*. Columbia, SC: U of South Carolina P, 2003.

»Brooklyn Without Limits.« *30 Rock*. NBC. 11 Nov. 2010.

Dohnimm, P. Sue. »Being Kenneth: Some Moral Lessons.« Wisnewski, *Philosophy* 7-15.

Fey, Tina. Interview. *Late Night With Conan O'Brien*. 4 Oct. 2007. NBC.

——. Interview. *The Late Late Show with Craig Ferguson*. 18 Apr. 2011. CBS.

Feuer, Jane, Paul Kerr, and Tise Vahimagi, eds. *MTM ›Quality Television.‹* London: BFI, 1984.

Frank, Thomas. *The Conquest of Cool: Business Culture, Counterculture, and the Rise of Hip Consumerism*. Chicago, IL: The U of Chicago P, 1997.

——. »The Green Hills of Elsewhere.« *Hermenaut* 15 (1999): 76-80.

Frank, Thomas, and Matt Weiland, eds. *Commodify Your Dissent: Salvos from* The Baffler. New York, NY: Norton, 1997.

»Gentleman's Intermission.« *30 Rock*. NBC. 4 Nov. 2010.

Gillan, Jennifer. *Television and New Media: Must-Click TV*. New York, NY: Routledge, 2010.

Glenn, Joshua. »Editor's Note.« *Hermenaut* 15 (1999): 8-9.

——. »Fake Authenticity: An Introduction.« *Hermenaut* 15 (1999): 10-25. (republished as: Glenn, Joshua. »Fake Authenticity.«

HiLobrow 6 Jan. 2010. Web. 25 Oct. 2011. http://hilobrow.com/20
10/06/01/fake-authenticity/

Graham, Mark. »Breaking: Tina Fey Responds to McFlurrygate; Also:
That's Not Her on Twitter.« *Vulture* 13 Feb. 2009. Web. 2 Nov.
2011. http://nymag.com/daily/entertainment/2009/02/vulture_exc
lusive_tina_fey_res.html

Greif, Mark. »Epitaph for the White Hipster.« *What Was the Hipster?
A Sociological Investigation.* Ed. Mark Greif, Kathleen Ross, and
Dayna Tortorici. New York, NY: n+1, 2010. 136-67.

Groß, Florian. »A Kinder, Gentler Americanization? Transnational
Cool and the TV Series *30 Rock.« Transnational American Studies: Proceedings of the 58th Annual Conference of the German Association for American Studies.* Ed. Udo Hebel. Heidelberg:
Winter, forthcoming 2012.

Heisler, Steve. »Laughed Behind: Single-Cam's Ascendancy Continues.« *variety.com* 12 Aug. 2011. Web. 02 Oct. 2011. http://
www.variety.com/article/VR1118041034/

Haselstein, Ulla, Andrew S. Gross, and MaryAnn Snyder-Körber. »Introduction: Returns of the Real.« Haselstein, Gross, and Snyder-
Körber, *Pathos* 9-31.

——, eds. *The Pathos of Authenticity: American Passions of the Real.*
Heidelberg: Winter, 2010.

Hutcheon, Linda. *Irony's Edge: The Theory and Politics of Irony.*
London: Routledge, 1995.

——. *The Politics of Postmodernism.* 1989. London: Routledge, 2002.

»Jack-Tor.« *30 Rock.* NBC. 16 Nov. 2006.

Kelly, Adam. »David Foster Wallace and the New Sincerity in American Fiction.« *Consider David Foster Wallace: Critical Essays.* Ed.
David Hering. Los Angeles, CA: Sideshow Media Group, 2010.
131-46.

Knaller, Susanne, and Harro Müller. »Einleitung: Authentizität und
kein Ende.« *Authentizität: Diskussion eines ästhetischen Begriffs.*
Ed. Susanne Knaller and Harro Müller. Munich: Fink, 2006. 7-16.

»Live Show.« *30 Rock.* NBC. 14 Oct. 2010.

Marc, David. *Demographic Vistas. Television in American Culture.*
1984. Rev. ed. Philadelphia, PA: U of Pennsylvania P, 1996.

Mayer, Ruth. »A Rage for Authenticity: Richard Power's *The Time of
Our Singing,* Jonathan Lethem's *The Fortress of Solitude,* and the

Quest for Pure Hybridity.« Haselstein, Gross, and Snyder-Körber, *Pathos* 163-78.

McLaughlin, Robert L. »Post-Postmodern Discontent: Contemporary Fiction and the Social World.« *symploke* 12.1-2 (2004): 53-68.

Miller, Mark Crispin. *Boxed In: The Culture of TV.* Evanston, IL: Northwestern UP, 1988.

Mills, Brett. »Contemporary Sitcom (›Comedy Vérité‹).« *The Television Genre Book.* 2nd ed. Ed. Glen Creeber. London: BFI, 2008. 88-91.

Nussbaum, Emily. »What Tina Fey Would Do for a SoyJoy: Product Integration, *30 Rock*, and the Trouble With Using Brands to Write TV.« *New York Magazine.* 5 Oct. 2008. Web. 13 Nov. 2011. http://nymag.com/news/features/51014/

O'Brien, Susie. »On Death and Donuts: Irony and Ecology after September 11.« *Cultural Critique* 58 (Autumn 2004): 148-67.

O'Day, Marc. »Postmodernism and Television.« *The Routledge Companion to Postmodernism.* Ed. Stuart Sim: London: Routledge, 2005. 103-10.

Olson, Scott R. »Meta-television: Popular Postmodernism.« *Critical Studies in Mass Communication* 4 (1987): 284-300.

»Pilot.« *30 Rock*. NBC. 11 Oct. 2006.

Potter, Andrew. *The Authenticity Hoax: Why the ›Real‹ Things We Seek Don't Make Us Happy.* New York, NY: Harper, 2010.

Rosenblatt, Roger. »The Age of Irony Comes to an End.« *Time* 16 Sept. 2001. Web. 7 Oct. 2007. http://www.time.com/time/covers/1101010924/esroger.html

Schneck, Peter. »Image Fictions: Literature, Television, and the End(s) of Irony.« *Amerikastudien/American Studies* 46.2 (2001): 409-28.

»SeinfeldVision.« *30 Rock*. NBC. 4 Oct. 2007.

Sepinwall, Alan. »30 Rock: Can We Have Our Money Now?« *What's Alan Watching?* 16 Nov. 2007. Web. 8 Oct. 2011. http://sepinwall.blogspot.com/2007/11/30-rock-can-we-have-our-money-now.html

Shaw, Marc E. »Performing at *30 Rock* (and Everywhere Else).« Wisnewski, *Philosophy* 195-207.

Simonini, Ross. »The Sitcom Digresses.« *The New York Times.* 23 Nov. 2008. Web. 7 Sept. 2011. http://www.nytimes.com/2008/11/23/magazine/ 23wwln-comedy-t.html

»Somebody to Love.« *30 Rock*. NBC. 15 Nov. 2007.

»St. Valentine's Day.« *30 Rock*. NBC. 12 Feb. 2009.

»The Ones.« *30 Rock*. NBC. 23 Apr. 2009.

Trilling, Lionel. *Sincerity and Authenticity*. Cambridge, MA: Harvard UP, 1971.

»Up All Night.« *30 Rock*. NBC. 8 Feb. 2007.

Vermeulen, Timotheus, and Robin van den Akker. »Notes on Metamodernism.« *Journal of Aesthetics and Culture* 2 (2010): n.p.

Wallace, David Foster. »E Unibus Pluram: Television and U.S. Fiction.« 1990. *A Supposedly Fun Thing I'll Never Do Again*. New York, NY: Little, Brown, 1997. 21-82.

Waugh, Patricia. *Metafiction: The Theory and Practice of Self-Conscious Fiction*. London: Methuen, 1984.

Wisnewski, J. Jeremy, ed. 30 Rock *and Philosophy: We Want to Go to There*. Hoboken, NJ: Wiley, 2010.

——. »Introduction.« Wisnewski, *Philosophy* 1-3.

Authentic Simulacra or The Aura of Repetition

Experiencing Authenticity in

Tom McCarthy's *Remainder*

IRMTRAUD HUBER AND SOPHIE SEITA[1]

AUTHENTICITY AS IDEAL

He flows into his movements, even the most basic ones. Opening fridge doors, lighting cigarettes. He doesn't have to think about them, or understand them first. He doesn't have to think about them because he and they are one. Perfect. Real. My movements are all fake. Second-hand. (McCarthy, *Remainder* 23)

These words, with which the nameless protagonist of Tom McCarthy's *Remainder* comments on the acting of Robert De Niro, aptly summarize the obsession that lies at the heart of the novel: authenticity. It is the elusive ideal, the unobtainable object of desire which drives the plot to its radical culmination. At the outset of the novel, this desperate, even pathological, yearning originates in the traumatic experience of the narrator-protagonist, who has partly lost his memories and control over one side of his body after an almost fatal acci-

---

1   We would like to thank all members of the seminar »The Soul is the Size of Elsewhere« at the summer academy of the German National Academic Foundation at Görlitz in 2010, led by Dr. Eben Wood for the fruitful discussions out of which the ideas for this article have developed. We would also like to thank Christina Rickli for valuable feedback and input.

dent, the nature of which is never clearly specified. This set-up sounds familiar: the traumatized and amnesiac protagonist who attempts to recover his or her life-story, his or her true identity, has been of interest as a literary topic to more than one author.[2] However, in its depiction of a quest for ultimate authentic being, *Remainder* progresses beyond a mere recovery of personal history and identity. From the very start, the authenticity the protagonist lacks is characterized as peculiarly physical. In a slow and strenuous process he has to regain his physical mobility by becoming conscious of and successively executing every single muscle movement. As a result of this, he feels once-removed from reality: »No Doing without Understanding: the accident bequeathed me that for ever, an eternal detour« (22). What he believes he has lost is the authenticity of an immediate access to experience, an access that is intuitive, natural, and not incessantly reflected upon.

Although his situation is, as such, quite unique, he soon recognizes his detachment from reality as a paradigm of contemporary, alienated existence:

I'd always been inauthentic. Even before the accident, if I'd been walking down the street just like De Niro, smoking a cigarette like him, and even if it had lit first try, I'd still be thinking: *Here I am, walking down the street, smoking a cigarette, like someone in a film.* See? Second-hand. The people in the films aren't thinking that. They're just doing their thing, real, not thinking anything. Recovering from the accident, learning to move and walk, understanding before I could act – all this just made me become even more what I'd always been anyway, added another layer of distance between me and things I did. (24; emphasis in the original)

In this manner, the novel begins with the recognizable postmodern lamentation of mediated existence: the protagonist's experience of detachment is a frequent malaise in a society that is ›hyperreal‹ in the Baudrillardian sense. But instead of being blamed for its inauthenticity, the artificial reality produced by the film industry is in this instance turned into the authentic ideal. Authenticity, as presented here, turns out to be entirely artificial, constructed by media images that profit from a desire for the real which they themselves create, but can never

---

2   Vintage published an anthology on the subject in 2000, edited by Jonathan Lethem.

satisfy. The real seems to be irretrievably lost in the plethora of simulacra. Authentic experience, that is, the experience of a direct connection to reality, becomes, for the protagonist, a paradigmatic Lacanian *objet petit a*, an object of desire that is inherently elusive and that creates and perpetuates desire precisely by staying always beyond reach. In the novel, authenticity is idealized as a perfect state of existence. Intriguingly, it is the resistance of unaccommodating matter in its irreducible and undeniable presence, its inane *reality*, that resists this ideal. Following a Platonic logic, insensible matter corrupts the ideal: »the lighter doesn't spark [...], the fridge door catches and then rattles, milk slops over« (24). For the protagonist of *Remainder*, the desire for ideal authenticity therefore leads to an increasingly ruthless and fanatic attempt to establish total control over matter in order to achieve states of authentic perfection. Tracing the gradual moral and psychological detachment of its protagonist, the novel offers an almost clinical dissection and thoughtful critique of the possible consequences of an idealization of authenticity as it increasingly seems to acquire cultural currency in today's mediated society.

In this article we will argue that the novel accomplishes this critique by presenting authenticity as a quality of experience. As Susanne Knaller explains in her contribution to this publication, »[a]uthenticity always presumes a dynamics of subject and object; it persists in ever-renovated mises en scène« (36). While authenticity is conventionally attributed to either the subject or the object, *Remainder* situates it in the very moment of the mise en scène itself, thereby emphasizing its producibility (as opposed to authenticity as an inherent quality), its transitoriness (as opposed to being a stable value category), and its detachment from content and context (as opposed to denoting mimetic fidelity). Drawing on Baudrillard's notion of the simulacrum and Benjamin's theory of the aura of the artwork, we will outline how *Remainder* produces authenticity as an ideal with cult value, turning it into the object of fanatic quasi-religious worship that is deeply asocial, amoral, and, in more than one sense, fatal.

TOWARDS ESSENTIAL AUTHENTICITY

The novel progresses towards this essentialized authenticity of experience gradually. In his obsessive search, McCarthy's protagonist experiments with a number of actions and venues to produce authentic experiences. His first attempt to rediscover an authentic state evokes a conventional stereotype of alterity as a guarantor for authentic experience. While sitting in a café, the protagonist watches a group of homeless people: »After a while I started thinking that *these* people, finally, were genuine. That they weren't interlopers. That they really did possess the street, themselves, the moment they were in« (52; emphasis in the original). Since the homeless are outsiders of society and, ostensibly, escape the logic of capital and thus the tyranny of simulation, they seem to offer an alternative existence – one that is less circumscribed by social regulations, less burdened by commodities, and thus more immediately connected to an elusive ideal of authentic existence. Here, the novel seems to indulge in a nostalgic romanticization of the dropout and a tawdry celebration of an authenticity of the less privileged. As the protagonist establishes contact with the homeless, the Other is turned into the promise of a rediscovery of the lost self. However, the novel ridicules its own move into trite stereotype immediately. The narrator debunks this encounter as mere invention. Even the homeless people's attitude itself turns out to be as artificial as the fantasy he constructed around it:

They had a point to prove: that they were one with the street; that they really owned the space around them. Crap: total crap. They didn't even come from London. [...] And then their swaggering, their arrogance: a cover. Usurpers. Frauds. (56)

After the failure of this first attempt to access authenticity, the protagonist discovers a different route. In a moment of epiphany he experiences an intense déjà vu, vividly remembering an apartment house, its various inhabitants, and their occupations. He is, however, unable to place this memory. Suffering from severe brain damage as the result of the traumatic accident, the moment of déjà vu promises the recovery of his memory, his past, and, in a next step, of a more authentic knowledge of himself. Consequently, the protagonist devotes all his energy and the immense sum of compensation money he received after the accident to re-enact this particular memory. He buys and redesigns an apartment building, creating his personal ›stage‹ and hires scores of people as staff. He is absolutely uncompromising in this project and slavishly reconstructs even the smallest details of his vision, obsessed with what at first appears to be an authentic representation, the perfect equivalence and reproduction of an original memory. But this turns out to be not the point at all. Increasingly the narration reveals that such an original might never have existed, that all those performances are nothing more than »re-enactments of events that hadn't happened but which, nonetheless [...], were on the verge of being repeated« (126).

Jean Baudrillard's concept of the simulacrum, the copy without an original, immediately springs to mind. What *Remainder*'s protagonist seems to pursue here recalls the »[p]anic-stricken production of the real and of the referential« (7) which Baudrillard diagnoses for the era of simulation, in which the real is substituted by the signs of the real (cf. 2). Initially the protagonist's adamant demands for accuracy pay homage to the idea of the perfect reproduction, but the re-enactments are anything but a perfect copy which could no longer be distinguished from the original.[3] The individual scenes the protagonist focuses on are often minuscule, without any narrative charge that would give them comprehensible significance; he repeatedly changes the scenes and manipulates the actors and when he cannot remember (or imagine?) the face of the concierge of his memory-house he simply has her wear a blank face mask. The authenticity of the re-enactment lies no longer in the accuracy of an original's reproduction, but rather in the simulation of authenticity: in the meticulousness of the re-enactment's execution, in its performative stance, creating the real to which it only pretends to refer. In what seems to be a paradox, the re-enactment's authenticity lies precisely in its status as simulacrum.

It becomes evident that the manic re-enactment does not aim to recover the past at all. Since there is no original memory, there is no original authentic self to which the protagonist could return. Even though the story is told from his perspective, the protagonist seems largely to lack interiority and the novel reveals surprisingly little about his feelings, his psychological state, or even the reasons for his ac-

---

3   Charlie Kaufman's movie *Synecdoche, New York* (2008) presents an interesting object for comparison here. Starting from a similar premise, the reconstructions of the past the central character in the movie constructs *do* turn into perfect copies, into multiple versions of reality until no one (and least of all the audience) knows what is real and what is fiction. In *Remainder*, such a confusion is neither the aim nor the point.

tions, which are never interrogated or doubted. Indeed, he even lacks the most basic marker of individuality: a personal name. Clearly, the protagonist's objective is not to follow the credo of authentic subjectivity, Polonius's advice »To thine own self be true.« Instead, the sole reason for all these careful constructions is to evoke a specific *sensation* in the protagonist, a bodily feeling of tingling in which he loses himself completely and can *feel* authentic, even though the memory he presumably restages might be entirely imaginary. These moments of intense bodily experience are the essence of the authenticity the protagonist is after; moments in which his »body seemed to glide fluently and effortlessly through the atmosphere around it – gracefully, slowly, like a dancer through water« (135). Authenticity is here entirely detached from content, it is pure form and, as such, purely aesthetic.

AESTHETIC AUTHENTICITY

The exactingness with which the protagonist pursues his re-enactments is a formal concern – a procedural aesthetics of detachment – and yet the actions' very artificiality leads to this intense physicality. He experiences the first re-enactment as a moment of heightened aesthetic perception, in which every detail is given attention and significance:

Moving across the landing and down the staircase I felt like an astronaut taking his first steps – humanity's first steps – across the surface of a previously untouched planet. I'd walked over this stretch a hundred times before, of course – but it had been different then, just a floor: now it was fired up, silently zinging with significance. Held beneath a light coat of sandy dust within a solid gel of tar, the flecks of gold and silver in the granite seemed to emit a kind of charge, as invisible as natural radiation – and just as potent. The non-ferrous-metal banisters and the silk-black wooden rail above them glowed with a dark and unearthly energy that took up the floor's diminished sheen and multiplied its dark intensity. (133)

The passage pays close attention to detail, color, texture, and light, and to the significance of meaning emanating from surfaces. The protagonist is not motivated by simple voyeurism: it is the very tactility and physicality of these performances that mesmerize him. The staircase, the banisters, the floor, are turned into a work of art by the altered perception of the protagonist, which depends on the detachment of the re-enacted scenes from any direct context that would determine their role and significance. Like an *objet trouvé* the house is turned into a piece of art by the perception of the observer. Matter is distilled into aesthetic form.

This particular experience is aesthetic in the original sense of the word as well, in that it is based on a multi-sensual perception. Smells, sounds, and touch all play an important role in the creation of the re-enactments. Furthermore, it is an entirely disinterested perception (pace Kant) in the sense that its single *raison d'être* is to create this sensual experience, which is, repeatedly, described as ›beautiful‹ by the protagonist. The perception of disinterested pleasure is presented as the ultimate authentic experience. One finds this suspicion confirmed in a provocative »Statement on Inauthenticity« by Tom McCarthy and Simon Critchley, in which they laconically declare that

art attempts to extinguish matter and achieve authenticity as a hypnotic, monotonous, endless recurrence of repetition. This produces the trance-like stasis and intense psychic tingling that we sometimes think of as aesthetic pleasure. At times it almost feels real. Then again, so can masturbation. (International Necronautical Society 181)

Like masturbation, this aesthetic experience that constitutes the authentic is an entirely private, essentially egoistic enterprise. It extinguishes the grit of reality, the materiality of matter in a moment of hypnotic ecstasy. Just as, in masturbation, the (pro)creative act is turned into self-absorbed pleasure, the protagonist's ›art‹ abandons the status as a traditional aesthetic object with an emphatic disregard of performance conventions. It no longer displays itself to a larger audience and thus loses all social function. If this is art, it is purely monadic, exclusively created for and appreciated by an audience of one.

The aesthetic authenticity developed here differs from the conventional meaning of ›authentic‹ when referring to objects of art. Generally, authenticity of art implies that it can be traced back to an unambiguous creator or a certain historical period, obviating forgery. For Walter Benjamin, this latter understanding of authenticity is what substitutes for religious significance (*Kultwert*) in secularized art (cf.

144n8).[4] It is the authenticity of the piece of art, according to Benjamin, that brings forth the »aura« of the artwork, a quality he describes as »a unique appearance of distance, close as it may be« (»einmalige Erscheinung einer Ferne, so nah sie sein mag« 142; our translation). The aura separates the artwork from its surroundings, it evokes awe and respect by endowing the object with a special quality that is irreducible to its physical and material reality and makes the authentic work of art more valuable, even though a perfect forgery would meet the same artistic standards.[5] However, defined as such, aura is, ultimately, a category of *experience*; it is *felt* by the beholder as authentic awe and heightened awareness for the object of art. Benjamin further suggests that, in the age of technological reproducibility, the aura of an artwork withers (cf. 141). Since the aim of mass reproduction is to make the work of art available and consumable for the masses, it effectively destroys the auratic distance that is based on singularity. The artwork that can be multiplied and possessed by each, is familiarized, literally brought home to be displayed and consumed in private. The auratic cult value of the work of art is thus, as Benjamin suggests, destroyed by reproduction, since authenticity (*Echtheit*) is *not* reproducible (cf. 139-40).

But this is precisely what the protagonist of McCarthy's novel aims for: he produces, and reproduces the auratic *effect* of authenticity. Instead of dissolving in repetition, it is precisely the artificiality of

---

4   While Benjamin is mainly concerned with the effect of mass reproduction on aura and therefore does not elaborate on this shift, Nagel and Wood offer a useful distinction between two contradicting myths of art that underlie this process in their study *Anachronic Renaissance*. They argue that the value of art is either based on a performative mode, which links the object to a specific point in time as the moment of its creation, or on a substitutional mode that conceives of the object as outside of time, as achronic. In this latter case the work of art is a »structural object« whose identity »is sustained across time by the stability of its name and by the tacit substitution of its parts« (8). While authenticity is the essential measure of value in the performative system, to the substitutional mode authenticity is a meaningless concept, as value lies not in the object itself, but in its symbolic meaning.

5   Susanne Knaller offers a striking illustration of this point in her contribution to this publication (cf. 28-29).

repetition that creates the auratic moment. While Benjamin argues that reproducibility and repetition destroy the distancing quality of aura, and the disinterested contemplation it effects, in *Remainder* the endless loops of repetition detach the scenes from their context. Repetition empties them of immediate representative significance, and thus endows them with a quasi-religious numinous quality. (Post-)Auratic authenticity is thus created by the annihilation of the original in endless repetition. Here, reproducibility serves not as a means to secularize and democratize the work of art, as Benjamin implies when arguing that the disintegration of the cult value of art situates it firmly within the realm of the political (cf. 145) and that disinterested contemplation is no longer an adequate mode of reception for such art (cf. 148). Instead, repetition itself becomes the basis for a *reinstatement* of a cult value based on ritual. However, the ritualistic repetition no longer revolves around a singular, numinous idol that is its center and sole justification. The aura created by the ritual is not ascribed to a divine object, but, as an authentic (divine?) experience, is an end in itself. While authenticity is extraneous to the cult value of art and bound to the object as a guarantee of value in secularized art, it becomes, in *Remainder*, the object and aim of aesthetic production itself. Where there is no longer an original, authenticity is self-sustained and self-determined by a perpetual mirroring, in which every copy exactly reproduces the other, to the point where sign and referent merge in »the radical negation of the sign as value,« and the sign becomes »the reversion and death sentence of every reference« (Baudrillard 6). In face of such an absence of reference, disinterested contemplation and visceral affect become the only possible modes of reception. Therefore, repetition, emptied of reference and ultimately of meaning, *creates* the numinous distance, the intangible excess that is the uniqueness of aura. In *Remainder*, Benjamin's argument is thus, effectively, turned on its head: authenticity does not create aura any longer, but aura creates authenticity.

AUTHENTICITY OF EXPERIENCE

We suggest that the ideal of authenticity that emerges in *Remainder* cannot be adequately grasped within already received notions about the concept of authenticity. In her study of the theory and history of authenticity *Ein Wort aus der Fremde*, Susanne Knaller distinguishes three intersecting areas of applicability: referential authenticity (*Referenzauthentizität*), authenticity of art (*Kunstauthentizität*), and authenticity of the subject (*Subjektauthentizität*) (cf. 21-24). All of these enact the paradoxical tension between autonomy and heteronomy, since the criteria of authenticity are at the same time dictated from outside and supposed to emerge from some inner essential source or quality.[6]

As we have seen, in *Remainder* the obsession of the narrator cannot be understood as authenticity of the subject, that is, the search for a true self. Neither is it entirely based on authenticity of art, or aesthetic experience in the conventional sense, since it is not primarily directed at a material object or stable point of reference. Nor does referential authenticity capture the conceptual basis behind the narrator's drive, although referential accuracy and perfect reproduction undoubtedly play a subsidiary role. We therefore propose that the visceral quality of authenticity pursued in *Remainder* can be better understood by adding a fourth form of authenticity to the ones already outlined by Knaller, a category that intersects with all the others: *authenticity of experience*. As a quality of experience, authenticity ceases to be a stable attribute, something that can be contested and falsified. While all the other forms of authenticity suggest a transcendent ›true‹ form, an original they refer to and which authenticates them, authenticity of experience is a subjective quality that needs to be actively and constantly produced. As such, this fourth form of authenticity has acquired increasing relevance in contemporary culture (very strikingly in such enterprises based on the marketing of experiences as tourism, gastronomy, and adventure sports), mingling with, and even perhaps replacing, the previously dominant discourse of authenticity of the self.[7]

---

6   Cf. also the introduction and Susanne Knaller's contribution to this volume.

7   It is not surprising then that while this aspect of authenticity has, so far, seldom been central to discussions of literature and art, it has received much more attention in the field of tourism research. An early article in that field that is especially interesting in this context for its association of authenticity in tourism and religious experience is Dean MacCannell's »Staged Authenticity.« Cf. Cohen; Wang (we would like to thank Wolfgang Funk for bringing this to our attention).

While authenticity of experience is located within the self on a subjective level, it is evoked by the Other, by some external stimulation. It is both self-determined and externally constructed. Authentic experience thus links the other forms of authenticity in that it can be understood to be their ultimate aim. Authenticity of subject, of art, and of representation are only truly realized if they result in an authentic experience. What *Remainder* does then, is to distil authentic experience from its basis in the other forms of authenticity and to radicalize its cult value. Authenticity is no longer determinable in terms of either/or (in the sense of something being *either* authentic *or* fake); it becomes a transcendent ideal, no longer concerned with content, but emerging as pure form.

In the novel, this becomes increasingly apparent in the progression of the different re-enactments the protagonist stages. For the second re-enactment, he insists that a twenty-minute scene at a tire shop be endlessly repeated, without intermissions. While there is an original to this scene (the protagonist restages a ›real‹ experience he has had), mimetic equivalence is not his central concern. Instead, he »just wanted the motions and the words, all deadpan, neutral – wanted the actors to act out the motions without acting and to speak the words without feeling, in disinterested voices« (164). It is this artificiality that serves to create the visceral experience of tingling and gliding that the protagonist is looking for, paradoxically at its strongest when one of the actors, in an entirely monotonous voice says »*I – am – real*« (165), which, of course, he is not. This suggests that the aim is by no means a recovery of the real moment, but rather an *enactment* of the (real or imaginary) experience. Thus, for the protagonist to feel authentic means neither to avoid the artificial nor to recover a natural connection to a pristine real, whatever that might be. Rather, he wants to perceive the episode in isolation, to detach it from its surroundings and to endow it with a deeper meaning that borders on mystic revelation:

One minute I'd be really concentrating on an aspect of the sequence and the next I'd let the movements mesmerize me, like a bird charmed by a snake [...]. Occasionally [the episode's] sounds seemed to become voices, speaking words and phrases I never quite managed to make out. (167-68)

The promise of a deeper, authentic meaning therefore does not lie in a utopian establishment of a direct bond between sign and referent, but in the dissolution of signification and, eventually, in a process of de-materialization.

NIHILISTIC PASSION

From an initial obsession with connections and interrelations, the protagonist rapidly proceeds to a fascination with radical detachment, an »implosion, Fury of *Verschwindens*« (Baudrillard 162; emphasis in the original) which Baudrillard calls the »nihilistic passion par excellence« (160).[8] This shift starts during his original experience at the tire shop, when two liters of liquid, which the staff have poured into the windscreen reservoir, seem to disappear without a trace: »I'd just witnessed a miracle: matter – these two liters of liquid – becoming un-matter – not surplus matter, mess or clutter, but pure, bodiless blueness. Transubstantiated« (159-60). This transcendence of reality and the merging of the self with its surroundings to the point of dissolution, are understood by the protagonist to be true authenticity. As he puts it, his only goal is that there remains »nothing separating me from the experience that I was having: no understanding, no learning first and emulating second-hand, no self-reflection, nothing: no detour« (222). In those cases in which this works particularly well the protagonist falls into a state of unconsciousness:

I wouldn't move for long stretches of time, or register any stimuli around me – sound, light, anything – and yet I'd be fully conscious: my eyes would be wide open and I'd seem to be engrossed in something. I'd remain in this state for several hours on end. (203)

The intense experience of aesthetic authenticity thus leads to a muting of all senses, to the radical passivity of trance. Since the eternal detour the character wants to excise is, essentially, conscious awareness itself, the ›truly‹ authentic, truly immediate access to the real is only

---

8   Initially the protagonist counters his feelings of detachment by concentrating on connections, e.g. during a ride on the tube where he »kept [uneasiness] at bay by thinking that the rails were linked to wires that linked to boxes and to other wires above the ground that ran along the streets, connecting us to them and [his] flat to the airport« (16).

achievable in a loss of consciousness. The ultimate authentic experience therefore must be, paradoxically, the end of all experience. The desperate desire for authenticity is, so it seems, in its last consequence a deep longing for death.

Here, the novel is most insistently Freudian, linking trauma, repetition, and death. As McCarthy himself puts it in an interview with James McGirk, the protagonist »is living out the death-drive.« Only in death can the detour eventually be entirely dissolved. It is all but inevitable, then, that the next re-enactment the protagonist stages is a shooting, with himself taking the place of the victim who dies on the street. In death, the subject merges entirely with the moment, thereby being obliterated: »There was that widening-out of the space around me, and of the moment too: the suspension, the becoming passive, endless – then losing the motorbike, the trees, the pavement as I drifted further in, towards the core that left no imprint« (213). Annihilation and dissolution are, eventually, the aim, but at the same time this is experienced as the acme of intense feeling. By implicitly imagining this double process as an instance of repetition compulsion – the protagonist's compulsive attempt to relive the original traumatic accident – the novel clearly refers back to trauma theory. The simultaneity of intensity and numbing is one of the central paradoxes of trauma, as Cathy Caruth has argued: »in trauma the greatest confrontation with reality may also occur as an absolute numbing to it« (6). Indeed, as this quote suggests, some of the appeal of trauma as a cultural paradigm seems to stem from its disruptive force, by which the closed circuit of simulacra and illusions is violently and traumatically ruptured by the intrusion of the real. Arguably, some of the fascination with trauma is thus due, in effect, to its alleged authenticity. The real, being lost in simulation, returns as a traumatic event, or, as Geoffrey Hartman has it, drawing strongly on Lacanian theory: »The question of the real [...] cannot be answered in terms of the real, only in terms of a traumatizing *realissimum*, for which a more common name is ›the Other‹« (539-40). Thus experiencing trauma is understood to be the ultimate, and perhaps only, authentic experience.[9]

Remainder obviously endorses this fascination with trauma and its implicit connection to the desire for the authentic, but only to empha-

---

9   Discourses about the return of the real in the trauma of 9/11 are a case in
     point.

size its implicit morbidity and nihilistic force. Since for the protagonist
the ultimate traumatic encounter, the ultimate Other that guarantees
authentic experience, is death, death is glorified as a state of perfection. It is the great merger and brings about the immediacy and wholeness the protagonist lacks:

[T]his man had become a symbol of perfection. [...] in dying beside the bol-
lard on the tarmac he'd done what I wanted to do: merged with the space
around him, sunk and flowed into it until there was no distance between it and
him – and merged, too, with his actions, merged to the extent of having no
more consciousness of them. He'd stopped being separate, removed, imperfect.
(184-85)

In short: the dead man has become authentic.

As the quasi-religious, numinous moment of authenticity is increasingly associated with death, it further alludes to the idea of re-
demption. The protagonist even stylizes himself as a redeeming Christ
figure. Describing his re-enactment of the victim's death, he rhapso-
dizes:

It was sacred ground, blessed ground – and anyone who occupied it in the way
he'd occupied it would become blessed too. And so I had to re-enact his death:
for myself, certainly, but for the world in general as well. No one who understands this could accuse me of not being generous. (185)

The evocation of »sacred ground« turns authenticity into an object of
pseudo-religious worship, enacted through ritual that is imbued with
heightened, mystic meaning and that constitutes itself as numinous by
endless self-referential repetition. However, for the protagonist re-
demption is no transcendent promise, but lies in the very moment of
authentic experience. Cult ritual no longer serves to convey a revelatory truth, but is turned into an end in itself. Furthermore, since authentic experience is performatively produced as a transient quality of
experience that consumes itself in its enactment, the desire for authenticity becomes an addiction that can never be completely satisfied:
»The realness I was after wasn't something you could just ›do‹ once
and then have ›got‹: it was a state, a mode – one that I needed to return
to again and again and again« (223). The moment of death needs to be

experienced again and again, just like the death and resurrection of Christ has to be re-enacted by the faithful.

A twofold paradox evolves: not only does the search for sensual experience eventually end all experience as pointed out above, but also, even though the apparent aim is to merge with the surroundings, the experience of authenticity does not result in a closer relation between the self and the world. Quite on the contrary, the novel traces an escalating detachment of the protagonist on all levels – mental, social, and moral. While this detachment may find its final realization in death, the protagonist proceeds towards it sequentially: he is detached from his body and his memory by the accident, with the financial independence the settlement offers he stops working, he breaks off any contact with his friends, and he markedly loses himself in the artificially created, strictly confined chronotopes of his re-enactments. Since these re-enactments allow him virtually unlimited manipulative power, he soon sees himself as something more than human: not only a savior, but also a god. Human beings are purely instrumental in his designs and none of the actors is given a name; they are entirely functionalized and referred to by numbers (cf. 236-37). He himself remains nameless like God while only his closest collaborators (his angelic agents?) are provided with personal names. Maintaining absolute control over his staff, manipulating them as easily as he moves figurines on the paper models of his re-enactment scenes, the protagonist's grand design remains as inaccessible to his paper figurines as to the real people which they represent: »They were too small to make it out, of course, or even know that it was there. No: it was legible only from above, a landing field for elevated, more enlightened beings« (186). His attempt at reconnection consequently turns out to be an engagement which is forestalled by the very means that are used to bring it about.

MORAL DETACHMENT

By emphasizing the detachment concomitant with the quest for authenticity, the novel effectively contravenes Charles Taylor's tentative optimism about the possibly positive ethical thrust of authenticity as a modern ideal. In his monograph on *The Ethics of Authenticity*, Taylor argues that, although authenticity seems to encourage an ever-increasing individualism, the inherent requirements of authenticity as an ideal have the potential to counteract its most self-centered manifestations. Taylor makes his point by stressing the dialogic character of identity, which is always formed in relation to another person (cf. 32-35): »If some of the things I value most are accessible to me only in relation to the person I love, then she becomes internal to my identity« (34). On the basis of this intersubjectivity of the authentic self, Taylor argues for a communal ethics of authenticity:

If authenticity is being true to ourselves, is recovering our own ›sentiment de l'existence,‹ then perhaps we can only achieve it integrally if we recognize that this sentiment connects us to a wider whole. [...] Perhaps the loss of a sense of belonging through a publicly defined order needs to be compensated by a stronger, more inner sense of linkage. (91)

In the fictional world of *Remainder*, Taylor's hope that such an inner sense of linkage could turn into a source for ethical engagement seems vain. As an apparent exception to this rule but pertinent to our discussion of *Remainder*, Taylor names the solitary artist as mostly independent from relational considerations, but still bound by a dialogic relation to the audience to which his or her work of art is addressed. In the novel, however, the narrator as solitary artist no longer addresses himself to anyone but himself. If one understands identity as necessarily dialogic, then the protagonist's authentic ideal can, ultimately, only lead to an erasure of identity. In *Remainder*, authenticity of experience no longer needs to justify itself before an Other or strive to realize a potentiality inherent in the self. Rather, it emerges fleetingly from a momentary impression without a point of reference, not even an internal one like the ›true self.‹ Being entirely monadic and socially irresponsible, authenticity in McCarthy's story has lost its moral impetus. Following its logic of detachment, the quest for authenticity that the novel traces, progresses towards a radical severance of social, legal, ethical, and even spatiotemporal ties.

Nowhere does this become more obvious than in the final re-enactment recounted in the novel. Having sought authenticity on the other side of society in the mode of living of the homeless, in the past, and in death, the protagonist finally attempts to find it on the other side of the law and decides to stage a bank heist. Although this re-enactment begins like the others, the protagonist eventually decides to raise the stakes: no longer *re*-enacting, he *enacts*, making the fiction real without telling the hired actors. By doing so, he not only deceives them and puts their life ruthlessly at risk; he also plans to eliminate, or »vaporise« his entire staff after the bank heist to cover his tracks (254). The protagonist's reaction to his right hand and facilitator Naz's suggestion that they blow up the team in planes is characteristic: »I [...] saw in my mind's eye a plane bursting open and transforming itself into cloud. ›Wow!‹ I said. ›That's beautiful‹« (254-55). All moral concerns and all human compassion have evaporated in face of his fanatic, monomaniacal quest.

THE REMAINDER

While all previous re-enactments had been, or pretended to be, grounded in reality, the bank heist is fictional, although based on a systemic model of real crimes. Instead of merely repeating events, the protagonist now stages the transcendent, platonic *eidos* of the crime, its pure form:

In one sense the actions we decided to perform had all happened already. They'd happened countless times: in our rehearsals [...] and in the thousands, tens of thousands, maybe even millions of robberies that had taken place ever since mankind first started circulating currency. They'd never stopped happening, intermittently, everywhere, and our repetition of them [...] was no more than an echo – an echo of an echo of an echo. (259)

Thus the protagonist puts into practice what Baudrillard envisioned when he argued for the essential indeterminacy of the difference between simulation and the real: »Simulate a robbery in a large store: how to persuade security that it is a simulated robbery? There is no ›objective‹ difference: the gestures, the signs are the same as for a real robbery [...]. To the established order they are always of the order of the real« (20). The simulacrum of the bank heist turns out to be not only indistinguishable from the real. It is, in a manner of speaking, realer than real; it is the Platonic ideal on which the real is based.

What makes the experience real, or, more precisely »true« for the protagonist, is the very fact that it is such a perfect copy of their rehearsals (263). This is what Baudrillard has called the logic of the remainder: »the real disappearing to make room for an image, more real than the real, and conversely – the remainder disappearing from the assigned location to resurface inside out, in what it was the remainder of« (144). »All of the real,« Baudrillard further argues, »is residual, and everything that is residual is destined to repeat itself indefinitely in phantasms« (146). Even the novel's title seems to refer to this (re)production of the real out of the logic of the remainder. According to this logic, reality is turned into an endless loop, an infinite repetition. Only on this premise, the novel seems to suggest, can authenticity be actively produced.

Having said that, the role and meaning of the remainder in the novel decidedly differs from Baudrillard's understanding: it is, precisely, what remains irreducible in this correspondence of copy and reproduction. It is the excess of matter in its very physicality that repeatedly frustrates the protagonist's obsessive control compulsion (the sun, for example, which exasperates him by failing to reproduce the same angle of light throughout the whole year; cf. 211-12) and is at the same time the main cause for his aesthetic pleasure. By »slotting [the bank heist] back into the world,« the real events and objects exceed the copies in the very perfection of their reproduction because of their singular materiality (244). The van in which the robber re-enactors arrive is not only a perfect likeness of the one used in the rehearsals, but »was more, more even than the sum of all its likenesses. [...] it seemed bigger, its sides more faded, its tyres more bulging, its edges more turning, its steps more pebbled [...]. There was something excessive about its sheer presence« (262). Matter is thus the sole reason the bank heist results in both »a fuck-up« and »a very happy day« (260). It is when matter literally trips up the re-enactment that the protagonist feels he has achieved his authentic moment. Not because it jolts him back into an awareness of reality, but because he has detached himself from his surroundings to such a degree that even this interruption of materiality is assimilated into form and becomes a source of aesthetic enjoyment. The consequent death of one of the re-enactors and his blood seeping into the floor do not touch the protagonist beyond their formal beauty.

From this moment onward the protagonist has entirely lost his grip on reality. He »had a cylinder around [him], an airlock« (272). He fails to respond directly to the others around him and has locked himself entirely in his own delusion, in which he himself even kills another of the re-enactors, just to reproduce the events of the failed bank heist once again, to feel the tingling of authentic experience and to marvel at the texture of flesh, blood, and wound (cf. 276).

The fascination with death as the only authentic moment culminates in a deeply nihilistic paradox, which takes up and radicalizes a tendency in contemporary art that Hal Foster has described some ten years prior to the novel's publication, in 1996:

some artists appear to be driven by an ambition, on the one hand, to inhabit a place of total affect and, on the other, to be drained of affect altogether; on the one hand, to possess the obscene vitality of the wound and, on the other, to occupy the radical nihility of the corpse. [...] *It Hurts, I Can't Feel Anything.* (121-22; emphasis in the original)

McCarthy's novel can therefore not only be read as a critique of the idealization of authenticity, but also questions the role of art and the attitude of artists who, in an attempt to recover the ›real,‹ indulge in a fascination with trauma and death which is deeply nihilistic. This nihilism finds its radical expression in the very last scene of the novel, in which we leave the protagonist, suspended between heaven and earth in an airplane which he has hijacked and forces to perform an endlessly looping figure of eight, producing a »feeling of weightlessness, suspension« (283). In infinity, so the ending suggests, one arrives at authenticity and at the same time suspends it forever: a self-perpetuating paradox. The only end to such an infinite loop would be the end of time and space, the ultimate realization of an all-encompassing death-drive. Only in the annihilation of all matter can even the last remainder be extinguished:

I looked out of the window again. I felt really happy. [...] Eventually the sun would set for ever – burn out, *pop*, extinguish – and the universe would run down like a Fisher Price toy whose spring has unwound to its very end. Then there'd be no more music, no more loops. Or maybe, before that, we'd just run out of fuel. For now, though, the clouds tilted and the weightlessness set in once more as we banked, turning, heading back, again. (284; emphasis in the original)

WORKS CITED

Baudrillard, Jean. *Simulacra and Simulation*. Trans. Sheila Faria Glaser. Ann Arbor, MI: U of Michigan P, 1994.

Benjamin, Walter. »Das Kunstwerk im Zeitalter seiner Technischen Reproduzierbarkeit.« *Illuminationen: Ausgewählte Schriften*. Vol. 1. Ed. Siegfried Unseld. Frankfurt am Main: Suhrkamp, 1977. 136-69.

Caruth, Cathy. »Introduction.« *Trauma: Explorations in Memory*. Ed. Cathy Caruth. Baltimore, MD: Johns Hopkins UP, 1995. 3-12.

Cohen, Erik. »Authenticity and Commoditization in Tourism.« *Annals of Tourism Research* 15.1 (1988): 164-82.

Foster, Hal. »Obscene, Abject, Traumatic.« *October* 78 (Autumn 1996): 106-24.

Hartman, Geoffrey H. »On Traumatic Knowledge and Literary Studies.« *New Literary History* 26.3 (Summer 1995): 537-63.

International Necronautical Society. »Tate Declaration of Inauthenticity.« *Altermodern*. Ed. Nicolas Bourriaud. London: Tate Publishing, 2009. 171-81.

Kaufman, Charlie, dir. *Synecdoche, New York*. Sidney Kimmel Entertainment, 2008.

Knaller, Susanne. *Ein Wort aus der Fremde: Theorie und Geschichte des Begriffs Authentizität*. Heidelberg: Winter, 2007.

Lethem, Jonathan. *The Vintage Book of Amnesia: An Anthology*. New York, NY: Vintage Books, 2000.

MacCannell, Dean. »Staged Authenticity: Arrangements of Social Space in Tourist Settings.« *American Journal of Sociology* 79.3 (Nov. 1973): 589-603.

McCarthy, Tom. Interview by James McGirk. »The Q&A: Tom McCarthy, Author.« *The Economist: Intelligent Life*. n.d. Web. 5 Mar. 2011. http://moreintelligentlife.com/blog/james-mcgirk/qa-tom-mccarthy-author/

——. *Remainder*. London: Alma, 2007.

Nagel, Alexander, and Christopher S. Wood. *Anachronic Renaissance*. New York, NY: Zone Books, 2010.

Taylor, Charles. *The Ethics of Authenticity*. Cambridge, MA: Harvard UP, 1991.

Wang, Ning. »Rethinking Authenticity in Tourism Experience.« *Annals of Tourism Research* 26.2 (1999): 349-70.

Contributors

David Bousquet currently researches and teaches at the University of Strasbourg. He was awarded a Ph.D. in November 2010 for his thesis about dub poetry, a form of poetic expression linked to the musical practices of reggae DJs and sound systems. His research focuses on the works of Anglo-Jamaican poets, particularly Linton Kwesi Johnson and Benjamin Zephaniah, and emphasizes problems linked to the relationships between orality and writing in Creole cultures.

Melanie Eis received her M. A. in English and American Studies, Cultural Studies, and Philosophy from Bremen University. She wrote her thesis on the representation of whiteness and masculinity in Hemingway's novels and short stories as well as in the critical discourse on Hemingway's texts. She taught at Bremen University for a semester and has been a doctoral candidate at the Graduate School of North American Studies at Free University Berlin since October 2011. She currently works on a Ph.D. thesis on the Beat Generation and the role categories of difference such as race and gender play in the Beats' mythologization as representatives of rebellion in the American 1950s.

Wolfgang Funk studied German and English Language and Literature, History, and Transnational Competence at the University of Regensburg earning his degree with a thesis on the dramatist Bryony Lavery. Currently, he is working as a research assistant at Leibniz University Hanover, where he is working on a Ph.D. thesis with the working title »Discourses of Authenticity in Contemporary Metafiction.« He has published articles on contemporary British and American drama and fiction, among others on Jasper Fforde (2010), Martin McDonagh (2010), Dave Eggers (2011), and Jez Butterworth (2011).

He is the co-editor of *Fiktionen von Wirklichkeit: Authentizität zwischen Materialität und Konstruktion* (2011).

Florian Groß studied English, American Studies, and Political Science at Leibniz University Hanover earning his degree in 2006 with the thesis »»Just another appliance, a toaster with pictures«: Postmodern Literary Engagements with TV in Don DeLillo and David Foster Wallace.« Currently, he is working as a research assistant and lecturer in Hanover's American Studies division. His main research interests include postmodern literature and culture, self-conscious irony, U.S. popular culture (especially television series and comics/graphic novels), and the most recent developments in U.S. fiction. He is currently working on his Ph.D. thesis with the working title »Technology. Economy. Creativity. Post-Network Television Series.«

Irmtraud Huber studied Comparative Literature, English Literature, and Theatre Studies at the University of Munich earning her degree in 2008 with a thesis on myth in 20th-century women writings, taking a comparative approach to novels by Virginia Woolf, Angela Carter, Marina Warner, and Christa Wolf. Since 2008 she has been working as a lecturer of English Literature at the University of Berne. She is currently doing research on her Ph.D. thesis on metadiegetic uses of fantastic stories in contemporary literature, for which she has spend six months as a visiting scholar at Columbia University, New York, in 2011/12 on a scholarship from the Swiss National Science Foundation. She is a member of the Graduate School of the Institute of Advanced Studies in the Humanities of the University of Berne and of the Swiss National Academic Foundation (Schweizerische Studienstiftung).

Seth Hulse holds an M.A. (Literature, Culture, and Media Studies) from the University of Siegen and two B.A.s from the University of Houston (Communication – Media Production and German). Currently, he is a Ph.D. candidate in literature and cultural studies and a lecturer in American Studies at the University of Siegen. His Ph.D. project is entitled »The Ethics of Representation: Faking and Hoaxing« and his primary research interests include constructivist psychology, media and journalism ethics, media economies, media history, hermeneutics, reception theory, and all things fake. He has a forthcoming publication on media economies.

Susanne Knaller is Professor of Romance Philology and Comparative Literature at the University of Graz, Austria. Her main research interests include aesthetic theories (18th to 20th century), theories of allegory, history and definition of the notion of authenticity, conceptions of reality in modernity. Recent publications are: *Zeitgenössische Allegorien: Literatur, Kunst, Theorie* (2003); *Authentizität: Diskussion eines ästhetischen Begriffs* (2006), ed. together with Harro Müller; *Ein Wort aus der Fremde: Geschichte und Theorie des Begriffs Authentizität* (2007); *Realitätskonstruktionen in der zeitgenössischen Kultur: Beiträge zu Literatur, Kunst, Fotografie, Film und zum Alltagsleben* (2008), Ed.; *Realitätskonzepte in der Moderne: Beiträge zu Literatur, Kunst, Philosophie und Wissenschaft* (2011), ed. together with Harro Müller.

Melanie Mettler received her degree in 2008, and has since been working and teaching at the English Department at the University of Berne. She is currently working on her doctoral thesis on »The Brit-Asian Family, Belonging and Cosmopolitan Reconciliation« and is now on a scholarship of the Swiss National Science Foundation. She is a member of the graduate school Gender: Prescripts and Transcripts at the Interdisciplinary Centre for Gender Studies. Melanie visited the Institute of Colonial and Postcolonial Studies at the University of Leeds, and the Research Institute for Cosmopolitan Cultures at nearby University of Manchester in 2008, 2010, and 2011. She has co-organized an international workshop on Cosmopolitanism and Fictions of Mobility, a panel at an international conference on Negotiating Gender in a Transnational Space and a workshop on Postcolonial Cosmopolitanism.

Francesca Nadja Palitzsch studied English, German Studies, and Political Science at the University of Regensburg and Royal Holloway University, London. She took her M.A. in British Studies in October 2008 and received the Katharina-Sailer-Prize for an outstanding final thesis (title: »Strategies of Telling Postmodern Romance Stories? – Postmodern Theory, History, and the Romance in Angela Carter's *Nights at the Circus*, Jeanette Winterson's *The Passion*, A. S. Byatt's *Possession: A Romance* and Graham Swift's *Ever After*«). Since October 2008 she has been working as a research assistant at the English

Department at Regensburg University. She is currently studying towards a Ph.D. in English Literature; her doctoral thesis will explore the topic of wilderness in contemporary Anglophone literature. Her research interests are contemporary English literature and drama, postmodernism, the romance, ecocriticism, spatial and gender theories.

Sven Schmalfuß studied English and Political Science at the University of Regensburg and at the National University of Ireland in Galway. He finished his studies with a thesis on the gender roles in the Alice novels, the Walt Disney Alice film and a game based on the books. He has also published an article on gender roles in the game series *God of War*. He is currently working as a lecturer for Gender Studies at the University of Regensburg and is one of the founding members of the digital game studies workgroup there. He is currently working on his Ph.D. thesis on European game cultures.

Sophie Seita studied English Literature, Spanish Philology, and Musicology at Mainz and Cambridge. She is currently enrolled for the MPhil in Criticism and Culture at the University of Cambridge, working on the avant-garde memoir in the writings of Kathy Acker and Christine Brooke-Rose. She is a published poet, founded and edited the Cambridge poetry magazine *Veer* and now edits a new arts magazine and press, which is intentionally left without title. She is a scholar of the *Studienstiftung des deutschen Volkes*.

Antonius Weixler studied German Literature, Media and Arts Studies, and Political Science at the University of Constance and at University College Cork. Since 2009 he has been junior lecturer at the Bergische University of Wuppertal and a member of the board of the Center for Narrative Research (CNR). He is currently working on his Ph.D. thesis on the »Transvisual Poetics« of avant-garde writer and critic Carl Einstein. Within the CNR, he organized the 2010 and 2011 annual graduate conferences. The 2010 conference was on »Erzählte Authentizität – Authentizität des Erzählens« (»Narrated Authenticity – Authentic Narration«) and he is currently editing the proceedings in the volume »Authentisches Erzählen. Produktion, Narration und Rezeption eines Zuschreibungsphänomens« (»Authentic/ity Narration. Production, Narration and Reception of an Ascribed Phenomenon«).